REFLECTIONS
ON ROMANS

A DAILY
DEVOTIONAL JOURNEY
VIA THREE-MINUTE
MEDITATIONS

DR. RANDY L. JAMES

authorHOUSE®

AuthorHouse™
1663 Liberty Drive
Bloomington, IN 47403
www.authorhouse.com
Phone: 833-262-8899

Published by AuthorHouse   11/10/2021

ISBN: 978-1-6655-4411-5 (sc)
ISBN: 978-1-6655-4410-8 (e)

Library of Congress Control Number: 2021923175

Print information available on the last page.

Any people depicted in stock imagery provided by Getty Images are models, and such images are being used for illustrative purposes only. Certain stock imagery © Getty Images.

This book is printed on acid-free paper.

This book is dedicated to all the Christian heroes throughout the world, who through their selfless and tireless efforts in the midst of a global medical pandemic, provided hope, care, and comfort through some very challenging times. It is my sincere prayer that the many pastors, musicians, teachers, counselors, and other ministers of the Gospel of Jesus Christ, will be rewarded for their labors in this world, as well as in the next. I give you my personal thanks and honor you as the faithful servants of our God Most High that you have proven to be.

ACKNOWLEDGEMENTS

My thanks go once again to my partner in life, Mary Jane James, who painstakingly proofread this manuscript and offered guidance for its' format. Her continual influence and encouragement provided me with the desire to see this work completed and published. She is my best friend, my inspiration, and the love of my life, and I owe her more than I can ever repay.

Scripture quotations are taken from the *Holy Bible, New International Version* (NIV). Copyright 1973, 1978, 1984 by International Bible Society.

FOREWORD

It was during the early days of the Covid-19 Pandemic when the idea for this book came about. Like so many people, who during those days of total lockdown, desired to still have a way to minister to others who were in a similar situation, I decided to do a daily audible Bible devotional focus for people over the internet. By working through the means of my newsletter mailing list, I was able to email friends around the world on a daily basis with an audible message attachment, so that spiritual encouragement and enlightenment could be received wherever they might be. This audible ministry continues, but this written account of those devotional messages is the basis this work in the year 2020.

Having earlier published a devotional book, *Prayers from the Psalms*, in 2019, which was well received, the desire to produce an additional devotional aid stayed with me. Like the previous book, this one is written to be used on a daily basis, providing a spiritual focus in a brief, but hopefully meaningful and thoughtful way.

It is my prayer that my labors, done in private and in the midst of very strange times, will give understanding and inspiration for others as they also experience their daily private time with God.

All the glory belongs to Jesus, the King of kings, who inspired the words of the Apostle Paul as he wrote his letter to the church at Rome during the first century A.D. Throughout the many years since, his words have been the source of transformation for countless lives. If my labors can shed even a tiny light on his magnificent work, then this book will have been a success.

DAY 1

Romans 1:1 *Paul, a servant of Christ Jesus, called to be an apostle and set apart for the gospel of God—*

There is so much that is packed into this small portion of a sentence. No doubt it has been focused upon by scholars and preachers down through the centuries, but it's so refreshing and comforting to know it still means something for me today also.

To begin with, Paul identifies himself by name, but the description he uses to categorize himself is so unassuming, that would seem strange if I would try to use the same terms for my own life. He is a *servant*, not a boss, a superman, a bigwig, or a person of importance in the eyes of most. He sees himself as the low man on the tenured list and is ready to accept all the ramifications of that title. In his time and culture, one could hardly think about life without servants, because the wealthy and important people of the world had many slaves who performed the unpleasant tasks of life, so that the "important" folks wouldn't have to. His very name, *Paul*, literally translated from the Greek language means "small" or "humble." We don't think of him in this light normally.

There is another concept given here concerning the word *servant*, that Paul would draw from his Hebrew upbringing. A servant, or slave, could be bought from someone else, but according to the Hebrew Law, no Jew could be the property of another Jew for more than a period of six years, for in the seventh year he was to go free—unless he chose voluntarily to stay in the employ of his master. If this choice was made, it was a permanent decision, and the "slave" would then be marked physically to let everyone know that of his own volition he was the property of another person—forever!

That's exactly what Paul is saying here. Small man that he is, he has given himself fully and freely to another—forever. Jesus Christ had captivated his heart and he was in a sold-out love-slave relationship in which he would stay until his death and throughout eternity.

I think this is what Jesus expects from all His followers. I think Paul's words here are not coincidental, for I believe Jesus also wants me to be His servant and for me to give up all my rights to Him in exchange for a love relationship with Him that will last forever. What do you think?

Day 2

Romans 1:1 *Paul, a servant of Christ Jesus, called to be an apostle and set apart for the gospel of God—*

It might appear to some that Paul didn't have much of a choice in his task of being a servant, but that isn't true. All of us have options and any one of us can choose what we will answer when the Holy Spirit of God calls us into service.

The fact of the matter though, is that Paul *was* called, and he answered that call in such a way that no one can honestly say that he didn't respond and follow with all his heart. What's interesting is the vocation to which Paul was called. He was called to be an apostle; not a job that can be assumed on one's own.

An apostle is much like an ambassador. One who is tasked with this vocation is one who is sent, and the one who is sent is a representative of the one who sent him or her. The task of the apostle or ambassador is to deliver the message of the one who did the sending and live in such a way as to bring honor to the sending agent. In other words, Paul was called to the job of representing Jesus to people wherever he went, and he was to do so in a way that would bring glory to God the Father in the name of Jesus.

It may seem like this is the job of every Christian, and to some small extent, it is. However, the big difference for Paul is in the calling, for when God calls us to something, He has big plans for us in that calling. Paul could have refused, but he would never have kept the relationship with Christ that became the driving force in his ministry.

Calling is everything for the Christian. We have all been called, but to different things. We can refuse to respond to our assignment, and our relationship with Christ will never be what it could have been, or we can obey and answer the call, and see God's plan for our lives fulfilled in ways we could never have dreamed.

Every Christian needs to ask, "What have I been called to do?" There are no unimportant tasks in the Kingdom of God, and no one task is "holier" than another, for every part of God's plan is vital. The question is, when we find our calling, will we obey and fulfill it? Everything depends on how we answer.

DAY 3

Romans 1:1 *Paul, a servant of Christ Jesus, called to be an apostle and set apart for the gospel of God—*

This is about as basic as the gospel gets. Though it's true that we are saved by grace and not because of our own goodness, or anything we can do, when we come to faith we do so as servants. When we become servants, then we receive a calling from God to "be" something for His glory in the work of building His kingdom. That's the easy part. Where Paul takes us now is to the requirement upon the servant who has received the calling, namely, he or she is *set apart* for God's purpose.

What does that mean? It means that once we belong to God, we have choices before us that need to be made. Being a servant means we have to put aside all our preferences so that the preferences of God can be fulfilled. My time becomes an offering to the Lord. My money is not mine but is a possession of the Lord's. When it comes to the choice of whether to attend a secular event on the Lord's Day or be in God's house to worship, we see that we are no longer to be our own, but to be His.

Human nature dictates that we want our own way. Having to set aside what we want for the sake of what God wants sometimes rubs us the wrong way. We say, "I have my rights..." when in reality we don't, not if we a servant of someone else. Belonging to God through a relationship with Jesus Christ means that we don't call the shots anymore. He does.

The difference between the modern "cheap grace" Christian and one who has given over his or her rights to God, is the difference between those who are *set apart* and those who are not. Being set apart means Christ comes first, before family, before health, before safety, before ambition, before our dreams, and before everything else. This isn't easy; in fact, it's one of the hardest things we can ever do, but it's the way Paul chose, and I believe the way of the sanctified life.

So, here is the deal. If we choose to be a servant of Christ, we do it voluntarily. If we really are a servant, we will receive a calling from God that He expects us to fulfill. To fulfill that calling we must set aside everything in our life that would hinder us from accomplishing what God has called us to do or be. That's the path of a disciple of Christ. There is no shortcut.

DAY 4

Romans 1:2 *–the gospel he promised beforehand
through his prophets in the Holy Scriptures*

This thing called "the gospel" is an interesting and very important matter. It's what Paul was called to and what he was set apart for. It's the "Good News" that we proclaim around the world, sparing no expense or effort to get the word out to everyone, everywhere. But just so there is no confusion, we need to break it down and ask, "What is the gospel?"

The gospel is a love story. It is about how God the Father cared so much for this world and the people on this planet, that He sent His only Son into our midst to point us back to Him after mankind had gotten misdirected and lost. From the time of mankind's disobedience in the Garden of Eden and the first sin against God was committed, our Creator has been working to bring His creation back into fellowship and oneness with Him.

To accomplish this reunion, God chose a man, Abram, whose offspring would be given the task of reflecting the Father to the rest of the world, so that all would know His love and relationship. He gave this people His Law through Moses to show mankind a lifestyle that would put them into fellowship with Him, but because sin's power was so strong and mankind was so bound by it, man couldn't faithfully obey that Law.

God sent the prophets who faithfully called mankind back to the Law and to the will of the Father, but again, the power of sin was too strong for man's freedom from its grasp to be achieved. The Father then revealed to the prophets a new hope, a Messiah/Deliverer who was to come and break sin's hold on mankind once for all, and the Law would be lived out in His power.

The word of the prophets was fulfilled in the person of Jesus of Nazareth. Though born into a human home, He was and is God's Son. His life, His teaching, His death, and His resurrection from the dead broke the power of sin and gave all mankind the means for freedom and relationship with the Father once again. The "Good News" is that because Jesus died and was raised to life, never to die again, that we who put our faith and trust in Him, will also be raised to eternal life. As He died and was raised, when we die, we too will be raised to life and spend eternity with God in rich fellowship. That indeed, is "Good News!" And it comes by placing our trust in Jesus.

DAY 5

Romans 1:3 ... *regarding his Son, who as to his human nature was a descendant of David,*

At the core of the gospel message is the person of Jesus. Since He is the one and only way to the Father, it's only appropriate that He would get all the attention concerning our salvation. Jesus has always been fully-God and while he was walking among us on earth He was also fully-man. He is the one and only Godman. He remains both God and man, but now He is the first of mankind to be resurrected, to die no more, and possesses a different status as a result.

There are people, however, who can never get past the fact that Jesus was more than just a man while He was with us in the flesh. There have been rumors that He was not born of a virgin, or even of Joseph, but that Mary had an affair with someone else, and Jesus was the result of her pregnancy. There isn't a trace of evidence for such a claim, but haters are going to hate, and those who choose not to believe in Him are free to do so.

What Paul is saying here though, is that even the humanity of Jesus shows that He is someone special. Joseph's lineage comes directly from King David, and an heir of David was promised to be the Messiah who would deliver his people. Paul is saying that Jesus fills the roll of the Messiah both from the heavenly perspective as well as the historical Jewish perspective. Even though Joseph wasn't the father of Jesus, he raised Him as his son and provided the Jewish requirement for the promise.

All this may not mean too much to the average person today, except for this: It shows that God always keeps His promises. He promised Abraham and all the generations since then, that He would have a people that would bring His glory to the world, and that promise culminated in the person of the Christ. The prophets proclaimed that God would raise up someone from David's line that would be the Shepherd for His people and would provide the way back to a relationship between the Creator and the created. Jesus fulfills this promise in every way for every person in the world.

Isn't it time that we give our full allegiance and devotion to Jesus, the King of kings? Isn't it time that we share our faith in Him and the "Good News" of salvation that is offered to every person? Paul certainly thought so.

DAY 6

Romans 1:4 ... *and who through the Spirit of holiness was declared with power by his resurrection from the dead: Jesus Christ our Lord.*

We live in an age where people don't believe in spirits like they used to. Once upon a time the populations of the world were consumed with appeasing the spirits, whether it be of ancestors who had died, spirits of animals, spirits of sicknesses, evil spirits, or any number of many other superstitions. Now though, since we are such an enlightened people, we tend to scoff at such things and believe only in what our five senses can confirm for us through science, technology, or reason.

The main problem with this kind of thinking, however, is that we have thrown out the baby with the bathwater. The Bible clearly speaks of various kinds of spirits and certainly emphasizes the power of God through His Holy Spirit in our world. Other spirits will always be up for debate and there will be believers and unbelievers, but none of us should doubt that God's Spirit is real and unlike any other.

It was the Spirit of God that hovered over the watery wasteland in the first chapter of Genesis. It was the Spirit of God that inspired the prophets to write as they did about the Messiah who was to come. It was the Spirit of God that impregnated Mary and caused life to be where there was none before, and it was the Spirit of God that raised Jesus from the dead and made Him the firstborn of the resurrection that awaits all who put their trust in Him.

Most importantly of all, Paul puts his focus on the Spirit of holiness. This is the power of God that enters the life of a believer in Jesus and empowers him or her to live a born-again existence. It's that same Spirit that cleanses the heart and life of the faithful and provides opportunities for spiritual renewal and growth. This Spirit of holiness sanctifies the desires of sin-weary people and changes our "want to" into a love for the things of God rather than the things that pass.

The Spirit of holiness is very much alive, very much God, and very much intended to live in us, guide us, protect us, produce growth in us, and prepare us for eternity with the Father. Do you have this Spirit within you? If you do, then you are in Christ. If you do not, then you are not. It's that simple.

DAY 7

Romans 1:4 ... *and who through the Spirit of holiness was declared with power by his resurrection from the dead: Jesus Christ our Lord.*

Our whole world seems unusually preoccupied with power these days. Too many countries have nuclear weapons, and even where they don't, governments and local entities often vie for position to be the best of whatever they deem valuable, because with more money, fame, influence, etc., comes power.

Paul sees power on a completely different plane. He speaks of the power that comes only from God, and a power that cannot be matched by anything this world could even dream about. Our Father has the power of life and death, and the power to bring people back from the dead as well. It was this power that raised Jesus from a lifeless corpse to an eternal, immortal, living Lord, and that goes beyond anything we can comprehend.

This power is not about show, however. This resurrection power was demonstrated to prove to any who would be sceptics, who really is in charge. As Jesus was raised from the dead by the Father, even so, we who trust in Him for our salvation will be raised in a manner just as He was. Our bodies will not just rot in the ground or blow in the wind after some cremation ceremony. We who are in Christ will be fully resurrected, bodily, and live in the presence of the Almighty throughout eternity. What happened to Jesus will happen to us as well, in the days to come.

It is the Spirit of holiness that makes this possible. The Father is always working on us, His children, to make us more like Him. Throughout our life He is carving, whittling, melting, and molding us through the circumstances of our existence to make us more into His image. It is His Spirit that is doing this. He is making us holy as He is holy. We aren't there yet and will never be perfect in our actions in this life no matter how hard we try, but we can be made perfect in our desire for God, and it is that desire that He uses as fuel for the shaping furnace that is working on our souls.

How wonderful to submit to such power! God gives us power for life, power for change, power to face all life has to throw at us, and power to deliver us from the grave when our lives here are over. And in the midst of it all He is making us holy. We should bow before such power in gratitude!

DAY 8

Romans 1:4 ... *and who through the Spirit of holiness was declared with power by his resurrection from the dead: Jesus Christ our Lord.*

Lordship is not readily understood these days. When we do hear of it, it usually has to do with some kind of title for royalty or as a reference to an era long since passed.

Paul has a different idea about Lordship, however. When in reference to Jesus it signifies a relationship that is unlike any other, for it involves the giving of total allegiance of one's life to Him as Lord. We may have other things about us to which we dedicate ourselves, whether it be family, country, or personal freedom, but even these things fall under the jurisdiction of the absolute Lord, Jesus Christ.

Jesus said it so well in Matthew 6:24, "No one can serve two masters. Either you will hate the one and love the other, or you will be devoted to the one and despise the other. You cannot serve both God and money." There is only room for one thing in first place, and if we are truly Christian then Jesus is the person that occupies that spot and is our Lord.

It was the power that raised Jesus from the dead that gave Him the right to obtain the title and position of Lord. It was God's Spirit of holiness that exalted Him to the right hand of the Father and made Him ruler over all creation, and because He has been so highly exalted it is right that He should be the King of our lives.

Having Jesus as our Lord is so much more than lip service. It's more than going to church regularly, paying our tithe, and doing good to those who are around us. Those things are no doubt a part of the picture, but Jesus is to be Lord of our dreams, our plans, our schedules, our hopes, and how we live in our society. It means that as His disciples and servants, we are at His beck and call for any task that He would choose to assign to us. It means that there is no negotiation over the calling and no shirking from it.

Making Jesus Lord of our lives means making Him the boss, period. He calls the shots and we follow in all areas of our existence as obedient soldiers of the cross.

So, is He your Lord? Or is He just a lord. The difference is huge.

DAY 9

Romans 1:5 *Through him and for his name's sake, we received grace and apostleship to call people from among all the Gentiles to the obedience that comes from faith.*

I don't think we can ever overstate just how magnificent the concept of grace really is. Too many times grace is understood as God's cover-up and blind eye over our actions and sin, that is poured on our lives like a sticky syrup that covers pancakes. Some have called it the love that covers all our sins, but therein lies truth that can be grossly misunderstood.

Grace, as Paul understood it, is not something provided by God to give Carte Blanc to whatever path His creation would walk. Grace is demanding, transforming, and life-altering. Grace is the love of God that held us up when we didn't know how to stand on our own. We call this *prevenient* grace. Grace is also the power of God that convicts us in our sin and points us to a solution for the guilt and pain we feel because of our sin. Grace is the blessing of forgiveness for confessed sin from a penitent heart, that has bowed before the presence of the Almighty King of kings, and brings new life where once only deadness abided. But grace is also so much more.

God doesn't forgive us to just leave us where we are. That wouldn't be grace; that would be cruel. Grace continues to teach us how to match up our actions with God's law, His guidelines for how we are to live our lives as shown to us in the Bible. Grace shows us where we are wrong, points us in the direction of change, and provides power for us to make the needed changes. The old hymn may say correctly that God receives us, "Just as I am," but He doesn't leave us that way. Grace forgives us and makes us a new creation to live for God and show the world just how wonderful and freeing life in Christ can be.

Grace changes us and destroys the nature of selfish ambition and pride. It then fills us with the love of the Father and provides us with opportunities to walk in newness of life. After grace takes effect in our life, we can can't live like we did before God rescued us. Such a way of life would deny the power of God, but through grace we are set free to live as Jesus did—to the glory of the Father! Grace, amazing grace, is the power that raised Christ from the dead, and can raise us to new life too.

DAY 10

We don't use the concept of apostleship in present times as much as previous generations did. The temptation is to skip over the word as some kind of administrative ranking like, "Rev.", "Dr.", or "CEO." But there are a couple of things we need to understand about this term.

First, we need to note that it's something Paul claims we *received*. It is not a title that we presume to claim for ourselves. It is a *gift* and a *job* laid on us by our heavenly Father. It literally means, *one who is sent*, and in this case, it is the task of one who has been sent by God.

There have been many historical biblical characters who have initially shrunk from the calling that God placed before them. God called forth Moses, Saul, Jonah, Jeremiah, Peter, and many others who protested being sent on a divine mission. At face value, anything that God would ask of us is too much for any of us, because we are not worthy to even be in connection or communication with God Most High. But when He chooses us for a task we are immediately under a load of conviction if we do anything but accept. God's servants do not originate their ministries. They are sent and like the word, *apostle*, used here, their orders come from the highest source possible.

Second, the one who is an apostle, or one who is sent, is commissioned with a task that he or she cannot set aside. Just as no one calls or sends themselves on the mission for the King, no one can quit it either, unless the King releases that person from the call. Paul didn't see these gifts of grace and apostleship as steppingstone jobs that they could carry out until something better, easier, or more appealing came along. Moses would have given up on the Israelites, and Jonah would have rather seen the Ninevites fry than have to preach repentance to them, but God's plan was for each to be faithful until the task they had been sent to do was complete.

We today, are in the same situation. Why are you here? What has God called you to do? If He is truly calling, then you will never find peace until you obey. If He has not called, you had better stay put until He does.

DAY 11

Romans 1:6 *And you also are among those who are called to belong to Jesus Christ.*

Do you understand what Paul is saying here? Yes, he was specifically writing to the church in Rome, but what he was saying to them he was also saying to all believers. We are all called, every person ever born, to belong to Jesus. It's an offer to be included in the Divine Royal Family of God, and there is no honor higher that anyone can ever attain.

What continues to baffle all reason, is why so many people either don't understand that they are called, or refuse to answer the call that has been offered to them.

Again, scripture itself offers examples like Simon, who when confronted with a call from Jesus, told Him that he was too much of a sinful man to be included in the call. The Apostle Paul himself, thought little of such a call until he was struck down on the road to Damascus, and the call was made a bit more emphatic and personal.

All around us today we will pass people throughout our society that have chosen a different path than the royal road of Jesus. Money, fame, vanity, lust, power, and a myriad of other distractions entice multitudes to follow more base desires than their divine calling. Parents raise their children in total ignorance of Christ's loving invitations and later wonder why so many issues of life have ended up going the wrong way.

It all boils down to whom it is that we belong. Do we belong to things that will rust with age and pass away with time, or do we belong to the King of kings who will never turn us away and provides for us an eternity of purpose, happiness, and deep fulfillment? It really doesn't seem like a hard choice, but there are so many who choose so badly that it can't be coincidence.

Personally, I am so thankful to be included in the call to be a part of God's family, a brother to Jesus Himself. Belonging to Him will always be the most important thing of my life and telling others about their opportunity will be the next important duty on my list of priorities.

You too, are called. You are called to belong to Jesus. You are not your own, for you have been bought with the price of a rugged cross.

DAY 12

Romans 1:7 *To all in Rome who are loved by God and called to be saints: Grace and peace to you from God our Father and from the Lord Jesus Christ.*

One thing that appears very quickly as we read through this book is the fact that it was written to a people who are very far away from us in time and space. Rome was the center of life in Paul's day and only time would tell what an impact it would have on the Christian faith and the world. Of course, this was originally written nearly 2000 years ago, but there are some truths here that transcend all time and space barriers.

First, we can rejoice in the fact that like the church in Rome, we too are loved by God. We, the wretched creatures who mess up so mightily at times, should take great comfort in the fact that the Almighty God cares about us and what happens to us.

Second, we are called by this Almighty God to be saints, or to be holy. The call to belong to Christ (vs. 6) means that we are expected to live holy lives in His presence. This is not something that we can do in our own power, any more than it was possible for the Romans of Paul's day to do it. Paul will get into the details of how holy living is possible as we go further in this book, but for now we need to understand that holiness is not optional for the Christian. It is the very nature of who God expects us to be. That above everything else is our calling.

Finally, to help us get along in the journey of holy living, Paul reminds us of the peace and joy that we have in the Savior. This, like our calling, is a gift from God. To know the peace that passes all understanding in the midst of the varied circumstances of life, and to experience the joy of living in the presence of the Divine Trinity should provide us with confidence as we tackle our daily challenges.

Remember, we are loved by God. We are called to be holy as He is holy. We are blessed with the fruit of the Spirit (peace and joy) to aid us in our journey in life. This is more than just an introduction to a letter or some kind of ritualistic formality. This is the Gospel of Jesus Christ—love, holiness, peace, joy—these things make Christian living possible. They are gifts of God for His people and they are treasures we should claim as our own.

DAY 13

Romans 1:8 *First, I thank my God through Jesus Christ for all of you, because your faith is being reported all over the world.*

One of the wonderful things about the church at Rome was the fact that even though Paul had never been there yet at the time of his writing, he was getting good reports from others about what Jesus was doing there. Apparently, what he was hearing was praiseworthy because it caused him to speak of his gratitude to God for the church's reputation.

Of course, he may be exaggerating when he says that their faith was being talked about all over the whole world because he didn't have connections all over the world. But most likely he meant that wherever in the world he did travel he did hear about what God was doing through His church in Rome.

That's a tremendous challenge for the churches of our generation. Perhaps it's not so much that we should strive to be known all over the world, but we should try hard to make sure that what people hear about us and what they say about us glorifies the Father and causes thanksgiving to be given in His name. Too often the church is only noticed by society when something bad happens. It makes headlines when a pastor commits adultery or gets caught embezzling money from the sacred coffers of the church's treasury. When people can give the church a black eye it eases their own conscience a bit because they can declare that Christians are not different than anyone else. In fact, they might even have a case that Christians are worse because when they sin, they cover it up and play the hypocrite until the truth eventually comes out.

Paul does us a wonderful service here as he reminds us as to how the church is to be viewed and talked about. Whether our congregation is large or small, it exists to give glory to God, to bless its neighbors, and to speak justice to a world that has often forgotten it. Any church that can do that will find a thankful community who will spread their story—just like the church at Rome was spoken about abroad.

So there is our challenge for today. How can we help our local church to be the kind of entity that will cause people to give thanks to God for our existence? If we can do that, then we have truly done our job.

DAY 14

Romans 1:9–10 *God, whom I serve with my whole heart in preaching the gospel of his Son, is my witness how constantly I remember you in my prayers at all times; and I pray that now at last by God's will the way may be opened for me to come to you.*

There is no way to truly serve the Lord unless one does it with his or her whole heart. For the Apostle, that commitment meant preaching the Gospel of Jesus Christ. Anyone who has ever truly received such a call has what sometimes has been called, "The Preacher's Itch." There is a drive to preach that nothing but doing it will fulfill. Paul certainly had that.

It follows that the God Paul served was also the one that he took his constant petitions before. Though he had never met the Romans, he prayed for them. No doubt, he was anticipating the Father's blessing on them and their ministry in the empire's capital city, and there was also little doubt that they would need such a blessing if their mission for Christ was to be successful. A person who prays for those he has never met, is a person that has a task to do that is far bigger than what he or she can accomplish alone. Paul was the missionary to the Gentiles, and since that group included the majority of the world, it would take a growing church to realize the Kingdom of God fully.

The strangeness that Paul had with the Romans, however, was hopefully about to change. He anticipated a collaborative effort in the coming days, and as he writes this letter one can sense the hope that they would be loyal yokefellows together. He wants to join their number, and later will speak of how they could possibly aid him in his evangelistic task, a task which falls to all who take the Great Commission of Jesus seriously.

In any case, Paul prays for such a thing. He prays because he knows that prayer is the key to success and the route to victory in his mission. He knows that communication with the Father is not optional for believers but is as essential as one's next breath or next meal. Prayer is the fuel that propelled Paul to do what he did.

The same is for us today. We are to be people of prayer, for communion with our Creator is the life force that makes service possible. No matter how long we serve or what task we have, prayer must be our daily bread.

DAY 15

Romans 1:11–12 *I long to see you so that I may impart to you some spiritual gift to make you strong—that is, that you and I may be mutually encouraged by each other's faith.*

It has been said by many, that absence makes the heart grow fonder. While that is not always the case, it seems that Paul's separation from those to whom he longs to minister is intense. It's as if he has a secret that he is just busting to tell, because he knows that if he can just share what he has to share, everyone will be better for it.

This is not a feeling that Paul feels alone. I have watched parents waiting in anticipation, to give a special gift to their children, and have almost as much excitement as the receiver that gets the gift. Teachers at all levels of education know what it is like to have knowledge that they want to pass on to their students, knowing that it will be beneficial for them in the days to come, and they longingly hope that the lessons will not be forgotten.

Paul knows, though he has never met these Romans, that his experience with the Lord, his training in the scriptures, and his sacrifice to carry out the mission Jesus assigned him, will be good for the Christians to hear about. Every new Christian needs to be trained up in the faith, and every seasoned Christian needs to be challenged to go deeper in that faith. Paul, as the elder statesman of the church, has an obligation to pass on what the Lord has implanted in his life.

Perhaps this is where the Church is lacking in many places these days. The sense of urgency, the sense of burden, the sense of anticipation to see the hand of God at work among His followers in this world is sometimes hard to find. We do church the way we have always done church, and though there is much to be said for tradition and ritual, it must have life and must change lives or it is of limited value.

It may be that our daily prayer should go along this line: "Lord, fill me with the anticipation that I need to share You with someone in some way. Help me to remember that I am my brother's keeper, and that I need to pass along what You have passed along to me. Help me to not give up while doing good and not to quit until You call me home. In Jesus name, amen."

DAY 16

Romans 1:13 *I do not want you to be unaware, brothers, that I planned many times to come to you (but have been prevented from doing so until now) in order that I might have a harvest among you, just as I have had among the other Gentiles.*

The main message that Paul brings out loud and clear here, is the fact that he hopes for a harvest among the church at Rome. Apparently, he has been wanting this for a long time, but circumstances of life have hindered his efforts. In the meantime, he kept on working among the places God led him, but he never lost hope on his mission to the Romans.

There are so many applications that can be connected to this passage of scripture, the main one being the importance of expecting a harvest. Churches don't die because they run out of money, or even run out of people. Churches die when they stop reaping a harvest for the Kingdom of God. When week after week, month and month, and year after year, things just continue on the same path of doing what we do, without anyone's life being changed by Christ, then we have failed in our mission. Even if we are only discipling children, teaching senior citizens, or corralling unruly teenagers, we must remember that Kingdom work always has a harvest. We can't use the same scales of measurement that the world does, but we can expect God to be doing something in the lives of men and women, and boys and girls as we minister. Again, churches don't die from lack of numbers and money, they die because they are not bringing in a harvest. We had better check on what we are planting and how we are cultivating, because someday the Master is going to demand an accounting of our efforts.

A second thing to note here is that even when Paul couldn't get to Rome like he wanted, he kept on ministering where he was. He worked "among the other Gentiles," until God's timing allowed him to go on to Rome and have a ministry there.

Many times, we set our eyes on a high prize and lose sight of everything else that is not our ideal. There is great value in being Christ's ambassador wherever we are. We are soldiers in the army of the Lord, and whether that makes us a private or a general, or whether we command legions or wash dishes, God uses us where we are. May we never forget that fact.

DAY 17

Romans 1:14 *I am obligated both to Greeks and non-Greeks, both to the wise and the foolish.*

I wonder how often we stop and think about how many people have influenced our lives over the years. Of course, we begin with our parents as we see the impact that they had on us from the time of our birth and onward. It doesn't matter whether they were good parents or bad parents, or even parents that were not present in our lives. What they did or didn't do impacted us in ways that will stay with us forever.

How about our teachers and our school classmates? We all have our favorites and not-so-favorites in both categories, but do we recognize that everyone from the class bully to the cafeteria worker impacted us in one way or another?

The list could go on and on, including bus drivers, employers, employees, pastors, coaches, etc. The important thing here is to remember that none of us got to where we are today without being influenced by every person that touched our lives.

The Apostle Paul recognized this and was grateful to those who were wise and those who were foolish. He recognized that learning takes place when people succeed and when people fail alike, and we don't have to try everything to find out what works and what doesn't. We learn so much by watching what others have done and are doing and witnessing the result.

This is true for all walks of life, but especially in the realm of spiritual things. We learn to pray by watching and listening to those who pray. We learn from those who have fought spiritual battles and testify to God's amazing grace that brought them through. We see the pain that comes to those who willfully flaunt God's will for their lives and the destruction of the home that comes from personal sin.

In a world that needs guidance and consistent examples, we have the opportunity today to be an ambassador for Christ. Learn from everyone and be grateful for everyone, but always remember that just as others have had an impact on us, we are impacting others in like manner.

DAY 18

Romans 1:15 *That is why I am so eager to preach the gospel also to you who are at Rome.*

I have always wondered about preachers who really don't like to preach. Strangely enough, I have met many of them over the years. They testify to having a call from God to enter the ministry and may even serve as the pastor of a church, but really do only what the job requires, and their heart is not really into preaching.

When I was young and just beginning my days of ministry, I used to hear about people who had the "preacher's itch." The term was used to describe those who had been called by God to preach the Gospel of Jesus Christ, and just couldn't wait for the opportunity to do so.

I have had that "itch" since a December night in 1972, when I said the final "yes" to Jesus and determined that He would have me, lock, stock, and barrel. Rarely do I go into a church service not prepared to preach if called upon because I am always eager to, as Simon Peter said, "give a reason for the hope" (I Peter 3:15) that lies in me.

Paul echoes that sentiment because his expression of eagerness to preach about Jesus fills all his letters and actions. He had been delivered from his days of blindness, both physically and spiritually (see Acts 9) and he traveled continually throughout his known world to tell people about what God had done for him through Christ. It wasn't an option for him, for he says clearly, "woe is me if I preach not the gospel" (I Corinthians 9:16 (KJV).

So now I have to ask, "What about you?" You may say, "Well, I'm not a preacher." That may or may not be the case, but if you are a Christian there ought to be something within your spirit that desires to share with others what God has done in you. If may be to a neighbor, to a co-worker, a schoolmate, or even to our own children and family, but we have an obligation to share Christ and His amazing grace.

Today provides a new opportunity to tell our story of Christ's delivering power to someone. Why not ask the Lord right now to open a door for you today to do just that? You don't have to be a seminary trained pastor. Just tell someone what Christ has done in you. That's the gospel at work.

DAY 19

Romans 1:16 *I am not ashamed of the gospel, because it is the power of God for the salvation of everyone who believes: first for the Jew, then for the Gentile.*

This verse has launched many a sermon since the Apostle Paul first penned the words. It not only declares the depths of his faith, but also contains some very sound theology. It speaks of God's power to make a real change in the life of all mankind. His gift of salvation for all who put their trust in Him is the hope of Christians around the world and down through the ages. No wonder he wasn't ashamed to proclaim it.

There is a condition attached to this salvation though. It's for everyone who believes. I guess the important question to ask here is, "Believe in what?" Though Paul doesn't explicitly say, we can assume he is referring to everyone's belief that God's power really is able to bring about salvation. Salvation is about being saved, but again we have to ask, "Saved from what?"

Since it was first for the Jews and then for the Gentile, we need to look at what God did first for the Jews. From the time of Abraham, God called his lineage to follow Him unconditionally, and through that life of faith the rest of the world would be blessed (Genesis 22:18). Salvation was being given the opportunity to belong to God Most High, and as a result to obtain His favor on the believer's life.

It was more than that though. The calling from God for salvation was to spread throughout the world. Being saved is not just about being able to go to heaven after we die, for it is a commission to service while we are here. God didn't choose the Jews for a position, but for an occupation. The relationship that they would have with God would be the example that everyone, everywhere would witness, and could come to the same kind of oneness.

The Jews had a hard time understanding this, so God grafted the Gentiles into His spiritual tree. Jesus was a Jew, but He didn't just come to save the Jews, He came for all mankind. He called all people to be saved from a life of selfish indulgence in order to be life givers to the rest of society. Like Paul, we are not ashamed of our job. We have Good News to share.

DAY 20

Romans 1:17 *For in the gospel a righteousness from God is revealed, a righteousness that is by faith from first to last, just as it is written: "The righteous will live by faith."*

When I was working on my first Master's degree, I remember taking a class on the book of Romans with Dr. William Greathouse. He used a word, that he probably made up, when he said Paul was talking about God's "righteousification" of mankind. What he meant was, that the gospel reveals how righteous God is, and how He wants to make His creation righteous as well. It's a unique term, but it helped the concept to stay in my mind.

It seems like a huge leap for man to go from the state in which he was born to the point that he is considered righteous before God. In fact, it's an impossible journey for any man to traverse alone. The only way for man to be made righteous is for God to do the work of cleansing in him, and that was made possible by the death, burial, and resurrection of Jesus from the dead. Bill Gaither once penned, "Because He lives, I can face tomorrow," in his beautiful song, but it is even more accurate to say, "Because He is righteous, I can be righteous too."

This transformation is brought about by faith. It's not just any faith, but a confirmed belief that God can do the work, and that cleansing from sin is truly possible. When God works in us to forgive, fill, and transform us, it is not just so we can be ready to die and go to heaven. That's just the icing on the cake, so to speak. What He does, is fill us with His righteousness so that we will "live" by faith. The work of God is not just for a life to come, but for the life we have now. He will give us all that He promised when this life is over, but He is primarily in the business of creating living witnesses who will be a part of His plan to redeem *this world*, rather than just get us ready to go to another one.

Faith is the key. Faith takes us to the source of all power. Faith is the link that connects the earthly and the divine. Faith comes from God alone and we remain totally dependent on His mercy to provide it. This is not the time to give up; this is the time for the saints of God to rise up as we are made righteous by the power of God, from the first to the last of His creation. God's promise is true and He will bring it to pass as we live for Him in faith.

DAY 21

Romans 1:18–19 *The wrath of God is being revealed from heaven against all the godlessness and wickedness of men who suppress the truth by their wickedness, since what may be known about God is plain to them because God has made it plain to them.*

We don't like to think about the wrath of God. It's too frightening to even contemplate. However, the Bible is full, from the Garden of Eden to the end of John's Revelation, with terms and stories that describe that side of His divine nature. To think of it being poured out on His creation sounds horrible, but then, since it is His creation, He can do as He pleases with it.

It is in this wrath, though, that we see the justice of God. Paul makes it clear that His wrath is not arbitrary but is measured out in perfect accordance with His instructions. He has shown mankind what is expected of him, and He has warned repeatedly of the consequences that rebellion will bring. He does this because He loves His creation and knows that what He tells us is for our own good.

Someone has said that God's justice is for Him to allow man to pray instead of "Thy will be done," he would pray, "My will be done." He allows man to test just how much power he has within himself and gives him freedom to do whatever he pleases. The result is the penalty for his actions. Rebellion against God is sin, and sin always leads to destruction and death. There are no exceptions to that rule.

The offense here is the wickedness of suppressing the truth. Even though he knows better, the wicked man hides what is good and glorifies what is evil. If he didn't know any better, that would be one thing. But because he knows right from wrong, he has no excuse for his actions. Wickedness rules when God's rule is denied, and the penalty for such an attitude is that God allows the wicked to get what he wants.

When Paul later writes, "the wages of sin is death" (Romans 3:23), it is this very thing to which he is referring. Sin, in the form of rebellion, separates man from God, and without God man is left to fend for himself, and that never turns out well. Paul is about to explain more clearly in the following verses, and we would all do well to read them carefully and heed his warning.

DAY 22

Romans 1:20 *For since the creation of the world God's invisible qualities—his eternal power and divine nature—have been clearly seen, being understood from what has been made so that men are without excuse.*

There are two ways that mankind can know God. We can know Him through personal revelation as His Spirit speaks truth to our hearts and minds, and we can know Him through general revelation, as in the natural world and universe around us. King David, of the Old Testament, could look up to the skies at night and see the wonder of the heavens and ask, "What is man, that you are mindful of him?" (Psalm 8:4). We too have wondered as we view all creation.

All one has to do to understand how amazingly He has created us is to examine the human body. To think that such an amazing thing could just happen by accident, or by chance, goes beyond our ability to grasp. One could more easily surmise that an automobile just evolved from a collection of steel, plastic, rubber, glass, and foam. Though there are some diehard sceptics concerning God as Creator, I just don't have enough faith in man's wisdom to be one of them.

The case Paul is making here piggybacks on the previous verse. Because mankind has been given plenty of examples that exhibit God's divine creative power in our world and universe, he cannot say that God has been silent and that we have an excuse to rebel against Him. It is precisely because we know God exists and has direction for our lives that we are found guilty when we violate His commands.

Paul calls them, "God's invisible qualities," but really, they are very plain to see. It's the same case that Jesus made when He said, "If you were blind, then you would be without sin" (John 9:41). But because we can see, we sin when we rebel against God and His plans for our lives.

This is a serious matter for every person ever born. We can't brush away truth and say we didn't know because we do know. We can't hide and think that God will not see us or overlook us when we make our will our own god instead of heeding the Master. What we sow we will reap, and when we do, we will have no one to blame, but ourselves.

DAY 23

Romans 1:21–23 *For although they knew God, they neither glorified him as God nor gave thanks to him, but their thinking became futile and their foolish hearts were darkened. Although they claimed to be wise, they became fools and exchanged the glory of the immortal God for images made to look like mortal man and birds and animals and reptiles.*

Over the course of Jesus's ministry, He made one thing very clear to His disciples. Those who walk in the light will receive more light, but those who refuse the light will only go deeper into darkness. God gives every person ever born the free will to choose whether or not they will acknowledge Him as God and Lord of their life, but He never forces anyone. Our freedom of choice is His free gift to us.

However, every choice we make comes with its own set of consequences. Here, Paul speaks about those who refused to acknowledge God's claim on their lives or even His existence, and as a result they went deeper into darkness. No matter their level of education, their knowledge of many things, or their philosophy of life, without a connection to the divine, they became fools.

Foolishness is not the same as silliness, for foolishness in this respect leads people away from truth and causes them to make up their own rules. It's much like a person who doesn't believe in the law of gravity. That is his or her privilege, but they will face a hard time when they try to fly. Man has to have a god. Either he will submit to the real one or he will make up one on his own. If he doesn't make an idol of stone, or wood, or some other material, he will make himself god and think the universe centers around his desires.

Our world history is filled with examples of the futility of man's efforts to be divine, to gain immortality, or to be the master of his own destiny. However, one hundred percent of the time, he fails. As surely as men are born, they will just as surely die, and then all their prideful foolishness shows up for what it is.

Who is Lord of our life? Who has control of the big and little things of our present age as well as the age to come? Are we wise, or foolish?

DAY 24

Romans 1:24–25 *Therefore God gave them over in their sinful desires of their hearts to sexual impurity for the degrading of their bodies with one another. They exchanged the truth of God for a lie, and worshiped and served created things rather than the Creator—who is forever praised. Amen.*

Here is where the rubber meets the road. Mankind has been given freedom of choice, but when he abuses that freedom, God has a penalty waiting for them. He gives them what they want. He allows them to plunge into sexual depravity, whether that be publicly or privately. He allows them to think of themselves as the end of all purposes and make themselves a god.

This is the spirit of antichrist, to make up one's own rules when it comes to who truly is God. If people want to believe a lie, God allows it, but such a choice always leads to some form of idolatry, which is the essence of sin.

The Old Testament is a history of how the children of Israel struggled with the problem of worshipping idols and created things. One would think that we would learn from their example, but every generation seems to have to face that temptation anew. We may not worship idols of stone that are shaped into forms of animals like they did, but we have our own problems. Today we worship gold, silver, cash, fame, self-fulfillment, and pleasure. Even though the one true God deserves all praise and adoration, too many take the route of putting Him out of their minds and life while chasing after things that will eventually leave them empty.

These are hard lessons that the Apostle is teaching. He had never met the people in Rome to whom he was writing, but he knew human nature all too well. His idol was religion itself before he met Christ on the road to Damascus. He saw the letter of the Jewish Law as the foundation of all things until Jesus showed him a more excellent way, and his life was changed forever.

This is a warning for all generations. We can acknowledge God as king and give our lives fully to him or we can wallow in the ways of self-destruction that will surely bring pain and suffering before it is over. We are urged to be holy because being anything else is going to end up seeming like hell.

DAY 25

Romans 1:26–27 *Because of this, God gave them over to shameful lusts. Even their women exchanged natural relations for unnatural ones. In the same way the men also abandoned natural relations with women and were inflamed with lust for one another. Men committed indecent acts with other men, and received in themselves the due penalty for their perversion.*

Paul is very graphic and very clear here. These verses are the result of man's disobedience and willfully acknowledging things other than the one true God as God. Actions have consequences and here they are.

Many people can't seem to understand why true biblical Christianity stands against the sin of homosexual acts. These verses are some of several that makes God's attitude on the matter very clear. When women have sexual relations with women and men have sexual relations with men, God sees it as shameful. When homosexual lust is acted upon, God calls it indecent and perverse, and issues a penalty for such disobedience. The gay lifestyle which is often celebrated in the media and shown as brave when someone comes "out of the closet," is despicable in God's eyes. There is no way to understand these words other than they reek with God's disapproval of homosexual practices.

Is this sin worse that other sins? Of course not. Sin is sin, and all aspects of it need to be forgiven and cleansed by the Holy Spirit. I Corinthians 6:9–11 deals with the same subject, but Paul declared to the people of the Corinthian Church, "And that is what some of you were. But you were washed, you were sanctified, you were justified in the name of the Lord Jesus Christ and by the Spirit of our God." In other words, change had taken place.

Acts of homosexuality need to be forgiven so that the transgressor can be delivered. If it was possible for the Corinthians of the first century, then it is possible for people in the twenty-first century as well. Just as alcoholics, thieves, adulterers, and idolaters can be forgiven and changed, so can homosexuals.

We of the Christian faith need to make this clear. One can be a practicing homosexual or a Christian, but one cannot be both. This sin is a penalty for rebelling against and rejecting God. It can be forgiven and the sinner can be cleansed, but only the Spirit of Jesus Christ can make it happen.

DAY 26

Romans 1:28 *Furthermore, since they did not think it worthwhile to retain the knowledge of God, he gave them over to a depraved mind, to do what ought not to be done.*

Paul continues with his theme concerning the practice of homosexuality. When people put God on the back burner of their life, even when they know better than to do so, God doesn't just ignore it, He penalizes it. He gives them what they have chosen and allows them to see just how needy they are.

Did you hear the words clearly? God gave them over to "a depraved mind," which allows them to continue in their sinful ways. In other words, when people reject God and leave Him out of their lives, they become mentally ill. In the context of this passage of scripture, God is telling us that those who commit homosexual acts are mentally ill. They need healing and redemption, not a celebration for "coming out."

I know these are hard words and this is difficult for even Christians to grasp sometimes, but love sometimes has to be tough. Paul didn't hate homosexuals and no Christian ever should. Our attitude should be the same that we have for anyone who is lost in sin and outside the safety of God's forgiving grace. If we are not people of love toward sinful offenders then we are no better off in God's eyes than they are. However, we can never tolerate the message that everyone just has their own way to God and that one path is a good as another. The way of Christ is always the way of the cross and it is not the way of self-indulgence.

Our attitude toward people who are wrestling with this must always be bathed in love and compassion. God doesn't hate homosexuality any more than He hates gossiping and lying. All sin is rebellion against God and His plan for our lives, and all sin must be forgiven and cleansed for that person to find the fruit of the Spirit Paul writes about in Galatians 5:22-23, "But the fruit of the Spirit is love, joy, peace, patience, kindness, goodness, faithfulness, gentleness and self-control. Against such things there is no law."

May God burden us to pray for the lost, regardless of what has led them in that direction, and may we always love everyone as Christ has loved us.

DAY 27

Romans 1:29–31 *They have become filled with every kind of wickedness, evil, greed and depravity. They are full of envy, murder, strife, deceit and malice. They are gossips, slanderers, God-haters, insolent, arrogant and boastful; they invent ways of doing evil; they disobey their parents; they are senseless, faithless, heartless, ruthless.*

The problem with godlessness is that it never stays static; it always progresses. Here we see the outplay of people who sets things above the Lord in their lives. They start off with ignoring the general revelation of God, they refuse to glorify Him and they refuse to thank Him, which results in their thinking going dark and foolish. At that point God gives them over to the desires of their dark and foolish hearts and sexual impurity comes about as a result.

If that were all that happens, that would be bad enough, but it is not. Once a person has given in to their basest desires, they become filled "with every kind of wickedness, evil, greed and depravity." They are unable to see the wrong they are doing anymore, and their downhill slide goes from bad to worse as the whole world has to revolve around them to keep them happy— and of course that never happens.

How much wiser it is to avoid all this pain and sorrow by giving our Savior His rightful place as King of kings and Lord of lords. God's prevenient grace is available to keep us from going down this path of destruction and allow us a life that is more abundant in the good things He has to offer.

Make no mistake about this though, God will not be mocked. He knows our hearts and what things take the top shelf in the priorities of our lives, and He knows what our desires are. He will give us just that. If we long to serve Him and experience His great love, He will make that possible. If we long to love and serve ourselves and ignore His offer of life to us, He will make that happen too. We get to choose, but we do not get to choose the consequences of our choices.

Today is the day for us to call upon His name. Today is the day to decide that we will not go down the dark path of sin any longer. His love is great whenever we decide to come home. Our Father will be waiting with His arms open wide.

DAY 28

Romans 1:32 *Although they know God's righteous decree that those who do such things deserve death, they not only continue to do these very things but also approve of those who practice them.*

Here is a warning for those who know God's way and turn a blind eye to the sin of idolatry, that is so pervasive. Before long we may find ourselves saying, "Well, I don't live that way, and after all, everybody gets to choose their own path, so it's okay with me." The penalty from God is not only on those who choose other gods over Him, but also on anyone who would sanction what they would do.

Society has ramped up its efforts to stamp homosexuality as normal and even wholesome. The church has been guilty of two great sins concerning this for too long. The first sin is that we have ignored it or hidden ourselves from it because we are afraid that some of the tarnish might rub off on us. However, when we stop and think about it, we could never see Jesus doing that. He loved sinners and He came to seek and save that which was lost—and that should still be the job of the church. The second sin of the church is to allow such behavior to be accepted, perhaps under the well-meaning guise of love, and not call the transgressor to repentance. If we take the last line of this verse to heart, we will realize that God's family does not have the right to approve what He has called sin. For us to do so would just be wrong. God calls us all by His grace just as we are, but He never leaves us in that state. His mission is to transform all creation for His glory; to have His will done on earth as it is in heaven. We must be part of the solution and not part of the problem.

Ministry in this context will always call for the people of God to be much in serious prayer and contemplation. As children of God, we are to be His hands, feet, tongues, and arms of love. We are not to look down on anyone, but to love everyone regardless of their desire to serve the Lord or not, but we must never, out of our compassion for the sinner, excuse and accept the sin. Two wrongs will never make a right.

Would you pray this prayer with me? "Father, Lord of all, give us wisdom and love to deal with everyone we will meet today as You would. May we be firm, but compassionate for Jesus' sake, amen."

DAY 29

Romans 2:1 *You, therefore, have no excuse, you who pass judgment on someone else, for at whatever point you judge the other, you are condemning yourself.*

This chapter is a wonderful follow-up to what Paul has just been talking about. In the midst of calling out any sin in our neighbor, are we guilty of sin also? It's so easy to see the faults of others because our eyes are on them and not on ourselves. However, when we stand before a mirror and begin to ask the tough questions about our own relationship to God, where do we stand?

Again, the message is clear. We have no excuse. Unless we can be the one without sin, it is not our right to cast the first stone, for if we do, we are condemning ourselves in the process.

Is the answer then to ignore the wrongs of the world? Should we just stay away from those who break God's laws and let Him take care of their situation? As Paul would say later in this book, "God forbid!" We are our brothers' and sisters' keeper and we have a responsibility to provide them with the truth. We do not have the right to pronounce judgment on them though, for that belongs to the Father alone. Our job is to make His Gospel known to them as accurately as possible, and to live blameless in our own conduct so that others have an example to follow.

We must always remember that the Gospel is not "do as I say, not as I do," but whatever we expect from others, we need to model in front of them. How do children learn to walk and talk? They learn by watching us move about and hearing the words that we say. They try, with painful difficulty at first, to imitate what we do until they can successfully navigate the world of movement and speech on their own.

This is our task before all the world as well. We are to be the salt and light that makes a difference in our society. We should live our lives in such a way that people ask, "Why?" "Why do you do what you do?" or "Why don't you do what I do?" Then we can tell them that Jesus has transformed us from what we were into what we are, and we now put Him as our higher level of authority. No other means will change the world. No other means ever has. We are to be His witnesses. That is a main priority in life.

DAY 30

One thing we can count on is the fact that God's judgment over all of man's actions is always perfect and fair. The reason why it is so wrong for us to judge our fellow man is that we don't always have all the information. There are many aspects of every life that we don't know, or don't understand. This is not the case with God. He knows about every action, every motive, and even every thought of our life. That's why He alone is qualified to judge us honestly.

When we try to give God a hand, and preside over the affairs of others in judgment, we put ourselves at risk because our motives may be skewed. Our judgments may come out of a desire to settle scores, balance the books, or maybe even to make the wrongdoer pay for their sins. God's judgment always is full of love and has the individual's best interest in mind. He is looking to redeem everyone. Remember those words from the Gospel of John, "For God did not send his Son into the world to condemn the world, but to save the world through him" (John 3:17).

What a wonderful thing to understand! Not only does God judge others with such grace at work, but He does the same thing concerning us. All of us have messed up from time to time and perhaps feel like the Father would be more than fair if He would cast us aside and redeem some more worthy for His purposes. Thankfully, He is kind, tolerant, and patient for our sakes as well as the rest of mankind. He wants to redeem you and use you for His divine purposes just as much as He wants to save the rest of His creation.

This would be a good place to stop, bow our heads, and offer up to Him our sincere gratitude for such love. Even the Apostle Paul felt at times like he was the chief of all sinners, and no doubt we also know that feeling. But thanks be to God, we are loved and cherished by a Savior who wants only our best. Thanks be to God forever and ever, amen.

DAY 31

Romans 2:5 *But because of your stubbornness and your unrepentant heart, you are storing up wrath against yourself for the day of God's wrath, when his righteous judgment will be revealed.*

My, we are by nature, a stubborn people! None of us like to be told we're wrong, and few of us enjoy having to make amends for the things we did wrong. As a result of this disposition, we would rather hide away the things that we want to forget than own up to them, and many times we get away with doing so. Or so we think. People around us may not know the truth, but our heavenly Father knows all—and He is not going to just let things slide.

Paul knows about being stubborn and unrepentant. Before his encounter with Jesus on the road to Damascus (Acts 9), he was as bull-headed as they came. He knew that he was doing the right thing when he persecuted the church, and no one was going to convince him otherwise, that is, no one but Jesus. Meeting Him changed everything and set his course for the rest of his life.

The result of being stubborn and unrepentant when the Holy Spirit confronts us with our sin, is that we are just building a case against ourselves for when the final day of reckoning comes. There will be a day of God's wrath, a day when all the secrets will be known and all our objections, rebellions, and fits of selfishness will be brought on to the judgment stage. At that point we will have to give an account for our actions and attitudes toward God's direction in our lives and we will have no one to plead our cause. The God of love, who gives us every opportunity to make things right in the here and now, will have the final say, and we will deal with the consequences for the rest of eternity.

The Father will not be mean or unfair in His judgments on that day. He will simply give us what we have earned and what we have told Him by our lives, that we want. If we choose to not involve Him in our daily walk, then He will give us just that. But, if we choose to make Him Lord of our life and give Him the glory He deserves now, then He will make that happen for eternity as well. There is no escaping God's final evaluation of our life. Personally, I will choose Jesus now!

DAY 32

Romans 2:6–7 *God "will give to each person according to what he has done." To those who by persistence in doing good seek glory, honor and immortality, he will give eternal life.*

S ometimes Christians are unsure of what the Bible really has to say about rewards and punishments. Some believe that we will all receive the same reward, kind of like the parable that Jesus gave in Matthew 20, where the landowner gave all the workers the same pay, regardless of when they started working. Others think that there will be differing rewards, like in Matthew 25, where servants were awarded five talents, two talents, and one talent—and was rewarded according to what he did with what he was given.

Jesus was not giving out two different opinions in the parables, for both are depictions of life after death. When we seek first the kingdom of God and His righteousness in this life, there will be a place of rest and renewal in the presence of God for all. This is what we commonly refer to as heaven, or paradise. In fact, Revelation chapters 4–5 give us a good glimpse of what is going on there right now, not in the future, but in the present. We take great joy in knowing that our loved ones that have gone on before us, are entering into that great "praise party" with all the saints of God.

However, the Bible also makes it clear that heaven is not the end. Revelation 20–21 show clearly that there is a time coming when the prayer Jesus taught us to pray will be fully answered, "your will be done on earth as it is in heaven." Revelation 20:10 says, "And he carried me away in the Spirit to a mountain great and high, and showed me the Holy City, Jerusalem, coming down out of heaven from God." There will be a time when heaven and earth will be one, after this age is over, and then Christ will rule supremely. He promised the disciples that they will rule over the kingdoms of the earth. Luke 22:29–30 says, "And I confer on you a kingdom, just as my Father conferred one on me, so that you may eat and drink at my table in my kingdom and sit on thrones, judging the twelve tribes of Israel."

In the new kingdom, rewards will be given out in accordance with what we have done. I don't have all the answers, but I know that a better day is coming. We are laying up treasures as we serve the Lord here on earth right now, and we will reap them in time to come.

DAY 33

Romans 2:8 *But for those who are self-seeking and who reject the truth and follow evil, there will be wrath and anger.*

Just as God will always be faithful to reward His followers with the joys of eternal life, He will be just as faithful to punish those who reject His authority and decide to go their own way. In all honesty, the Bible doesn't say nearly as much as we would like to know about this, and I wrestle with the concept of eternal punishment as much as anything else in the Bible. I can't come to grips with a loving God that would torture people for eternity without any hope of relief.

But on the other hand, the Bible does tell us some things. The last three verses of Isaiah speak of the new heaven and the new earth and say specifically, "And they will go out and look upon the dead bodies of those who rebelled against me; their worm will not die, nor will their fire be quenched, and they will be loathsome to all mankind." John tells us in Revelation 20:14–15, "Then death and Hades were thrown into the lake of fire. The lake of fire is the second death. If anyone's name was not found written in the book of life, he was thrown into the lake of fire."

When Jesus was speaking of hell in Matthew 25:41, He said "Depart from me, you who are cursed, into the eternal fire prepared for the devil and his angels." And in verse 46, "Then they will go away to eternal punishment, but the righteous to eternal life."

I admit, the final judgment of God is a troubling thing to me. While I cannot be sure of exactly what God has in mind, for I do believe He is always a God of love and mercy, I can be sure that He will balance the scales with righteousness, and whatever He decides about any of us will be fair and completely full of wisdom and integrity.

As for me, I don't want to even think about having to face God's wrath and anger, and there is no reason that anyone should have to. We have been given this day to put our trust in Him and build our lives upon the firm foundation of Jesus Christ. There will be a day of wrath, but we need to be doing all we can to help as many as possible to change their ways and get right with God while they can. The end is nearer than it has ever been and the time to get ready for it is now.

DAY 34

Romans 2:9-11 *There will be trouble and distress for every human being who does evil: first for the Jew, then for the Gentile; but glory, honor and peace for everyone who does good: first for the Jew, then for the Gentile. For God does not show favoritism.*

This old world of ours is a bigoted one. People favor the beautiful, the talented, and the successful. Democrats favor Democrats and Republicans favor Republicans, Liberals favor Liberals, and Conservatives favor Conservatives. We may not always like it, especially if we are the ones not being favored, but that's just the way it is with mankind.

We don't have to worry about God being that way though. He is never biased or prejudiced in any way. He loves every living being regardless of color, language, political bent, talent, wealth, or looks. We are His children, His creation, and He loves us all the same.

Now, that's a good thing when it comes to doing what's right. Even when we mess things up and have to retrace our steps to get where we are going, God doesn't care. He still loves us and is willing to help us to do things like we are supposed to do them.

It's also true, however, that He judges us all equally. When our hearts are not in the right place and our trust is not in Him, He knows that and knows how to deal with us accordingly. That doesn't mean that He is waiting and looking for us to mess up so He can get us. It just means that regardless of our station in life, He will not favor one person over another. If we need blessing, He will bless us and if we need a spanking, well, He will give that to us also.

When we are parents ourselves, we say that we love all our children the same, but our judgments are sometimes flawed because we don't always know what our children are doing, or their motives behind their actions. That's not a problem for God because He knows everything about everyone. We can count on Him being fair, whether we like it or not.

Sometimes our actions bring about their own penalties or rewards. We know that the Highway of Holiness is safe and the wages of sin is a mess. If we are wise, we will travel the way that pleases the One who made us.

DAY 35

Romans 2:12 *All who sin apart from the law will also perish apart from the law, and all who sin under the law will be judged by the law.*

Sometimes people ask the question, "How can people who have never heard about Jesus be held responsible for not following Him?" After all, we read in Acts 4:12, "Salvation is found in no one else, for there is no other name under heaven given to men by which we must be saved." If Jesus is the only way to get into heaven, and some have never heard of Him, is it fair for everyone to be judged by that standard?

We must remember that our heavenly Father is always fair. Paul makes note of that fact here and lets us know that those who are without knowledge of God's plan for their lives will be judged by the general revelation He has given them. After all, we only have to look around and see the majesty of the Father's handiwork to understand that someone, somewhere made it all happen. For people who really don't know, they will be judged according to the light, or knowledge, they have received.

But for those who have been given the information of eternal life and have refused to listen, or refused to acknowledge the Lordship of Christ, they will be judged on what they know as well. God will hold each person accountable for what they know and understand, not for what they do not know.

Certainly, that is good news for us. There are so many things about life, eternal life, heaven, and eternity that I can't begin to understand, or even to count. But the one thing I do know, is that following Jesus and doing my best to live in the center of His will for my life is sure way to achieve the best things that I can in this world, and in the life to come.

We are to act on what God has revealed to us and strive to learn more in every way we can. But we don't have to worry about falling short of what God expects of us when we have done our best. God is fair, and God is faithful. We know that His compassion for His creation is endless.

Today would be a good day to renew our connection to Him. In our quiet times of prayer, or in the middle of a busy lane of traffic, He hears our voice and knows the desires of our heart. We can only know what we know and we can only do what we can do, and that's just fine with Jesus.

DAY 36

Romans 2:13 *For it is not those who hear the law who are righteous in God's sight, but it is those who obey the law who will be declared righteous.*

There are a lot of Bible experts in our world. In fact, it's hard for most biblical scholars to get a job teaching because there are about a hundred applicants for every opening at a college or university. Added to this number are all the church people who have their own opinion about how best to interpret scripture, and then there are many who have no church experience at all but are sure they know what God expects of us.

But the issue really isn't about how much or how little knowledge a person has when it comes to pleasing God. What matters is what we do with what we know. Those who know more will be held accountable for all they know and those who have less understanding will be judged likewise.

Paul makes it so simple that a child should be able to understand. It's not what you hear or what you know, what matters is whether we obey what God has commanded us to obey.

Being considered righteous by God is a pretty big deal. None of us want to come to the end of our life here and have to stand before the Lord and hear that He considers us unrighteous. We may be too embarrassed to say we are righteous people right now because our modesty may be offended by our words. But it's not what we say anyway, it's what God thinks about us that matters.

It's a bit like driving a car. We may know the rules of the road because we have passed a driver's test and perhaps have many years of experience driving. However, if we are caught by a policeman traveling twenty miles per hour over the speed limit, he really won't care how well we know the law. In fact, because we do know the law, we become more of a violator of the law when we break it.

That's how God sees us. We may be able to quote scripture and have a high level of ethical understanding, but if we are disobedient to the Father's will for our life, then we are guilty before Him. If we want Him to declare us righteous then we had better do what He says. After all, since we hope to spend a long time with Him, we'd better start doing what He wants now.

DAY 37

Romans 2:14–15 *(Indeed, when Gentles, who do not have
the law, do by nature things required by the law, they are a
law for themselves, even though they do not have the law,
since they show that the requirements of the law are written
on their heart, their consciences also bearing witness, and
their thoughts now accusing, now even defending them.)*

What is that little voice in our heads? What strange event of nature causes us to sense that some things are wrong and some things are right? Is it because of our upbringing, something due to our social environment? What caused ancient groups of people like the Babylonians, the people of Mesopotamia, the Egyptians, and even the Hebrews to come up with the idea that murder was wrong?

As much as we would like to think so, our environment is not the end-all of our personal knowledge and ethical approach to life. Some people would argue that we have a conscience that tells us what to do and what not to do. But some, in our post-modern world, say there is no absolute right or wrong. For them, it all depends on ones' circumstances, and each situation calls for each person to find his or her own way.

These verses point us in a different direction. They acknowledge that our heavenly Father has a say in how we determine justice and righteousness in our world. The law that we have for ourselves, as Paul says, is the Holy Spirit of God at work in our lives.

You may ask, "Well, how can someone who is not a Christian be influenced by the Holy Spirit?" John Wesley would call it, "prevenient grace." It's the love of God that is poured out on us before we ever knew that He existed. God has a way of providing every person ever born with a sense of natural and general revelation, and even if it is just a spark, it is a spark that has been put there by a divine touch.

If God didn't speak to sinners, no one would ever get saved. If God didn't care for everyone, no one would come to Him in repentance. But because our Father cares so much, He gives some light to all, and even greater light to those who will receive it and embrace it. Not everyone will walk in the revelation of God, but those who will, have the blessing of His continued presence always, for He helps us to meet the requirements He has for us.

DAY 38

Romans 2:16 *This will take place on the day when God will judge men's secrets through Jesus Christ, as my gospel declares.*

Judgment day. Those words bring a multitude of reactions—and most of them are negative. There is something about judgment that has a tendency to put fear in the hearts of most people because there is always the possibility that they will be found wanting.

All the world is used to the idea of judgment, for we judge livestock at the county fair, musicians in band competitions, and beauty pageants where there can only be one winner. It may sound nice to hear that an Olympian won a bronze medal in some athletic competition, but we know as soon as the place was announced that two other medals (gold and silver) finished before the bronze. Yes, there is something about judgment that speaks of the danger of not being the best.

What a difference there is though for the Christian. We can live without fear of judgment because perfect love casts out fear (I John 4:8). When we stand before God someday, we will not be judged against our neighbor and hear that someone finished first, second, or third. We only need to hear that our sins have been washed in the blood of the Lamb to have the thought of judgment change from dread into a glorious celebration.

It's true that those who have not chosen the Highway of Holiness, have much to fear from judgment, for every sin will be on display before the Father and He will announce the proper verdict accordingly. But there is no reason that anyone should have to be afraid when the penalty price for our sins has already been paid by Jesus on the cross.

For the child of God, judgment day is promotion day, celebration day, a day of victory. We can hold our heads high and glory in the cross of Christ and know that our destiny is secure for time and eternity. There is a great day coming by and by, and all the redeemed will be saying, "Hallelujah!"

I hope that you have put your trust in Christ as your Savior. If you have not, you can. You can ask Him to forgive you and allow Him to direct your path from this day forward. He is willing to do so, and you can have peace here and hereafter. It's true. He is still the answer, even in judgment.

DAY 39

Romans 2:17–21 *Now you, if you call yourself a Jew; if you rely on the law and brag about your relationship to God; if you know his will and approve of what is superior because you are instructed by the law; if you are convinced that you are a guide for the blind, a light for those who are in the dark, an instructor of the foolish, a teacher of infants, because you have in the law the embodiment of knowledge and truth—you, then, who teach others, do you not teach yourself? You who preach against stealing, do you steal?*

Paul is the master of the run-on sentence, and he gives us a little sample here. The essence of what he has to say can be summed up very simply though, "Do you practice what you preach?" Even though it is particularly addressed to Jews, the question applies to us all, because all of us will eventually stand before God and give an account as to whether we were as consistent with our actions as we were with our words.

Sometimes it's put like this: "Do as I say, not as I do." That may be a clever bit of dialog, but all of us know that such an example won't hold much water when it comes to convincing others about how to live. People look for and expect honesty, or at least they should from one who claims to be a follower of Christ.

The examples about this subject are endless. Do we say we are faithful, but refuse to love our neighbor? Do we say we love our church, but don't support it with our attendance and our finances? Do we say we want to win the world for Christ, but show little interest in any kind of missionary involvement? The list of scenarios could go on and on.

What Paul is getting at here, he could easily proclaim by saying, "Put up, or shut up!" If you can't walk the walk, then don't talk the talk. It's not a hard concept to grasp, but apparently for some folks in Rome in his day, and perhaps for some folks in our day, it's easier said than done.

Perhaps we should begin by asking for help. It could go something like this: "Lord Jesus, I realize that it is so much easier for me to talk the talk of a Christian than to actually live up to the name. Forgive me where I fail, and help me to act in such a way that would please you, and bring glory to the Father. I know I can't do it on my own, so I plead for You to empower me to be real in all circumstances. Thank You in advance for Your help, amen."

DAY 40

Romans 2:22 *You who say that people should not commit adultery, do you commit adultery? You who abhor idols, do you rob temples?*

The history of the Old Testament shows us that the ancient Hebrews had a terrible time when it came to following God's law. The Bible is full of men and women who had adulterous relationships, and there is an abundance of evidence to show that until the Babylonian exile they had a continual battle with idol worship. It seems like those seventy years of captivity did help them in that area, but they still had plenty of other issues that caused a fracture in their relationship with God.

Why are people like this? It's not just history, and it's not just the Jews I am talking about. The issue of adultery is so prevalent in Western society that it isn't even noticed in most circles anymore. Our more enlightened American society may look down its' nose at the African men who take three or four wives, because polygamy isn't considered the norm where we are. However, the African can point his finger right back at the American for their many spouses also. We just do it one at a time. Marriages aren't as solid in our society as they once were, and many have decided to just skip the ceremony and live together.

The same thing can be said about idol worship. We don't have a practice of bowing down to statues of gold, silver, or wood, unless they are in the form of money, jewelry, or possessions. Worldliness is as rampant today as it ever was.

What Paul is asking here though, is "Christian, are you like that? When the world is adulterous, are you also? When the world worships the created rather than the Creator, do you also fall into that mold? Do we who preach a holy message act differently from sinners in our daily actions?

Christians are called to a higher standard. We are called to be holy for no other reason than the fact that God is holy, and He commands us to be like Him. But the holiness God expects from us is not just to please Him. Our lifestyle is to be the example of how mankind ought to live and how we ought to interact with each other. The world is hurting from its own sin, and we have been given the solution to its problem in the person of Jesus Christ.

DAY 41

Romans 2:23 *You who brag about the law, do you dishonor God by breaking the law?*

Every once in a while, while I am driving down a highway, I see a policeman in his car fly by me at a speed that is well over the speed limit. When he has his emergency lights and siren going, I know well enough to get out of his way, because he is certainly on duty. But there are times the patrol cars pass me at a high speed, when the lights and siren are not on, and it makes me wonder. Is he really on duty and just chooses not to make a scene as he scoots along, or is he just wanting to get somewhere fast and knows that no one is going to stop him if he drives too fast?

Paul continues to hammer the point he has been making home. As he particularly addresses the Christian Jews, he wants to know if they are living up to the standard that God designed for them, or they just putting on a show and not living the life required of them.

I don't know what was going on in the church at Rome when Paul wrote this letter, and maybe Paul didn't have all the information he wanted to have either, but it sure seems that he suspects some the Hebrews Christians of hypocrisy. From verse seventeen on to this one, he has been preaching a sermon that must surely make some people in Rome feel like their toes are being stepped on. Maybe that's the way we feel too.

It can't be said enough that Christians are called to a higher standard of living than those who are not in Christ. We are to set an example for others to emulate, not because we think we are superior, but because we know Jesus is. Christ is in the process of building His church and we have been enlisted to help in that effort with all the strength, wisdom, and resources we have. We can't allow ourselves the luxury of failure because there are souls that hang in the balance. There are people who are watching us, listening to us, and wondering if there really is a better way. We cannot be hypocrites when so much is at stake.

Today, let's put all manner of hypocrisy aside, and live as children of light. Let no one on the day of judgment give us as their reason for their failure to follow Christ. Instead, be the reason someone says, "Yes" to Jesus.

DAY 42

Romans 2:24 *As it written: "God's name is blasphemed among the Gentiles because of you."*

When I was much younger, I was a runner. It kind of came to me as a surprise, when after finishing last in all my races as an eighth grader, that in my ninth-grade year I started winning races. I would enjoy pretty good success throughout the rest of my high school days, and even set a few records. That was a pretty important part of my life back then.

One race that I was never very good at though, was the hurdles. I always wanted to run them, but when I would try in practice, inevitably I would trip over one and fall. I just couldn't seem to combine speed and leaping into a smooth enough motion to clear the obstacle, and eventually just gave up the idea of being a hurdler altogether.

I have thought of how it would be a terrible thing to be a tripping point to someone else spiritually. It would be sad to have people running their life's race in good fashion, and then for me to be the cause of their tripping and falling, and perhaps not finishing the race at all. The thought of being or creating that kind of a spiritual obstacle to someone is a horrible nightmare.

Paul sees the Christian who is a hypocrite doing just that. As he has been proclaiming the necessity of holy living before God and man, he scolds the Romans who would dare say one thing and do another. He knows that Jesus warned us about the danger of making another brother or sister fall, and he wants to make sure that the Christians in Rome don't go down that trail.

One of the biggest complaints of people outside the church, about people who are a part of a church, is that they are hypocrites. Where would they get such an idea? They get it because too many times they have watched their neighbors go into a building to learn about heaven on Sunday and then watch them live like hell throughout the week. Such actions caused Paul to say, "God's name is blasphemed... because of you."

Oh, my friends, be real with your faith. Don't be inconsistent in your walk with Jesus because too many people are watching your life that might be spiritually hindered or tripped if they see you live differently from your testimony. Be Christlike at home and live for Him publicly for all to see.

DAY 43

Romans 2:25–26 *Circumcision has value if you observe the law, but if you break the law, you have become as though you had not been circumcised. If those who are not circumcised keep the law's requirement, will they not be regarded as though they were circumcised?*

Perhaps a better way to understand what Paul is trying to get across with these verses, is to put it into a modern scenario. Let's say that you are a stickler for the laws of the land. You give an honest day's work for a day's pay, you don't cheat on your taxes, you hold corrupt people accountable, you attend church regularly, and even pay your tithe faithfully. You are an outstanding citizen that is an example to all your community. However, there is one area of your life in which you have a problem with the law. You love to drive fast. When you get in your car, you just love to rev it up and see what it will do on the open road. After all, you are an experienced driver, and no one is hurt by your brief little imitation of an Indy car driver.

Paul's point is that if you offend at one point of the law, you are a lawbreaker, and it's just as if you had no regard for the rest of society's rules. You play God a little bit, by choosing which laws you will obey and which ones you won't. You may live by most of society's game plan but opt for a special privilege when it comes to your special preference.

This goes back to Paul's argument against Christians living as hypocrites. A first century male Jew was one who was circumcised on the eighth day after his birth, and if that part of the law hadn't been kept, he wasn't considered a Jew at all. It doesn't matter how many times he went to synagogue, or how many sacrifices he would make. If he wasn't circumcised in deference to the example of Abraham, and according the Law of Moses, he was not a Jew in the eyes of his people.

On the other hand, Paul makes the case that if someone who is not born a Jew, but follows all the Jewish laws except for circumcision, then he is considered more righteous than the Jew who wouldn't be circumcised because he didn't know any better.

For us, it again is a matter of being honest before God and man. We are to be real; to be what Christ has made us to be. If we are not walking on the highway of holiness, we are drifting on the path of sin.

DAY 44

Romans 2:27 *The one who is not circumcised physically and yet obeys the law will condemn you who, even though you have the written code and circumcision, are a lawbreaker.*

Have you ever known people who were not Christians, but were nicer, kinder, more generous, and loving than some other folks who claimed to be Christian? I think most of us have some images of faces that would come to mind if we really consider the question. That being said, it's a pretty sad commentary on what Christians should be like.

The attitude of many people without faith that I have met over the years is, "Well, I'm as good as so and so. They go to church every Sunday, but if heaven is going to be full of people like them, I don't think I really want to go there anyway."

It must have greatly frustrated Paul to have to say what he did to the people in the church at Rome. Remember, that in this section of scripture, he was addressing the Jews specifically. For them to consider that people who were not Jews would possibly be more like God than the people God had called, would have been a concept that would be hard for them to swallow. After all, the Jews were the ones to whom God had directly given His law. The Jews were the ones with the ancient holy rituals. The Jews were the ones God had specifically called to be His people, out of all the people on the face of the earth. Is it possible that others could be closer to God than they were?

But just as it is not fair nor right for people of faith to judge those who are not in the faith, it is also not fair nor right for people outside the faith to judge those who are in the faith. That doesn't stop people from doing it though. If we talk the talk, we had better walk the walk, or someone is going to point out our deficiency to us.

Today, we have been given a brand-new opportunity to live our lives in such a way that people will notice the Spirit of God who lives within us. We may have messed up in the past, but today provides a fresh, new chance to honor the Lord with our word and with our deeds. We need to do this because we don't want to shame the Master who has saved us and called us, and we don't want to give unbelievers an opportunity to miss seeing what Christ can do, and is doing in our lives, do we? Well, do we?

DAY 45

Romans 2:28–29 *A man is not a Jew if he is only one outwardly, nor is circumcision merely outward and physical. No, a man is a Jew if he is one inwardly; and circumcision is circumcision of the heart, by the Spirit, not by the written code. Such a man's praise is not from men, but from God.*

Just who are God's chosen people? Throughout my years of growing up in the church, I always heard that Hebrews, the Jews, the direct descendants of Abraham, were the people God favored above all others. As I have come to understand the Bible better, and especially the writings of the Apostle Paul, my opinion has changed drastically.

I have come to understand that God has no national borders, nor does He favor one group of people over another. God is interested in people, all people, and He wants them to have their hearts cleansed completely by the power of His Holy Spirit. It is at that point, the point of allowing God the freedom to do in us whatever He desires, that we truly become "Jews," or children of God.

You see, when God chose Abraham and his descendants, they were not chosen for a position—like being the most favored, or the best—they were chosen to do a job. They were chosen to bring God's light to the dark world and to help others, all people, everywhere, to understand the love, the majesty, and the grace of their heavenly Father. As the Lord said to Abraham in Genesis 22:18 (NIV), "and through your offspring all nations on earth will be blessed, because you have obeyed me." It was because of an action that Abraham did, that such a blessing was pronounced. Again, it wasn't because of who he was; it was because of what he did.

In this passage of scripture, Paul is telling the church at Rome and the world that all people can be "true Jews." The title doesn't come by birthright, but by faith, and such faith is demonstrated by carrying the message of the Almighty to the world. One who is a Jew physically only, had no more claim on God than did a Roman or a Greek in Paul's day, but when one enters into a relationship with the Son of God, Jesus the Christ, then that person becomes a new creation and a true child of our heavenly Father.

A change of the heart is needed, not a pedigree certificate. Thanks be to God! That change is possible for anyone, anywhere today because of Jesus!

DAY 46

Romans 3:1–2 *What advantage, then is there in being a Jew, or what value is there in circumcision? Much in every way! First of all, they have been entrusted with the very words of God.*

Since Paul has built his case in the previous verses that all people in Christ are considered by God to be His children, with the same rights and privileges as did any child of Abraham, what advantage is there to being a Jew by birth? It's a good question and it deserves a clear answer. The answer is very simple; they were first. Though all of us can claim the title, "Child of God," only those who are Hebrews through their natural bloodline can claim that God spoke to them before He spoke to anyone else.

Now, this fact is a good thing and also a bad thing to consider. It's always a wonderful feeling to know you are first at something. Students strive to be first in their class, runners glory in being first in a race, and reporters love to scoop everyone else by being the first one to report a new story. Everyone who has ever had a romantic relationship remembers their first love, their first date, and their first kiss. For generations, being born first in the family line meant receiving the bulk of the family inheritance, the birthright, or even the throne—if you were royalty. Who wouldn't rather be first than last?

But being first also carries liabilities with it. Jesus made this clear when He told the parable of the master who gave varying gifts for investment to his servants. When he returned, the first thing he wanted to know is, "What did you do with what I gave you?" Rewards and consequences quickly followed.

It's the same way with being a Jew. Our heavenly Father certainly approached Abraham with the covenant of grace before He did anyone else, and that covenant was passed along for millennia to his offspring. However, even though they were first to receive the blessing, it was hoarded and not passed along, so another means of grace had to be given, in the person of Jesus, to demonstrate that with great blessing also comes a great responsibility.

You may be the first in your family to know Christ. You may be the first of your tribe to go to college, to answer a call to ministry, to be a blessing to others today. The question is, "What are you doing with what you have received?" Being first carries a huge assignment for each recipient.

DAY 47

Romans 3:3–4 *What if some did not have faith? Will their lack of faith nullify God's faithfulness? Not at all! Let God be true, and every man a liar. As it is written: "So that you may be proved right when you speak and prevail when you judge."*

It's a very true fact that not everyone believes in God. Though I really don't believe that atheists are as plentiful as some would want us to think, it is reality to understand that there are people without faith. That very fact creates a whole new conversation on another level, but it really doesn't alter the truth of another fact—God is, whether we believe in Him or not.

It's like a blind person saying, "I don't believe there is a moon that revolves around our planet." But we know that just because one doesn't see something, that in itself can't be the reason we deny that something's existence. There are many people who have very little understanding of the world of bacteria, viruses, and microbes, but their impact on our world proves their existence—whether we think so, or not.

Make no mistake about it. What was true for the people of Paul's day and for our time is the same when it comes to the reality of the divine. I personally have met people on various occasions, who tell me, "I don't believe in God." My response is usually one of two statements. First, I might say, "Well, of course you don't believe in Him, you don't know Him." But I also like to follow up with, "That's okay, He believes in you." All the world may doubt, but the reality of God goes on.

When society becomes more secular in the various parts of our globe, or when it has never been enlightened with the truth about the resurrection of Christ, it becomes the task of the Christian to be more of an example of the power of grace than ever. Jesus told us that we are to be His witnesses to everyone, everywhere, and we have not fulfilled that task yet.

This is why we need to be filled with the Spirit of God, so that our lives lived for Christ is not something we put on, but something we exude because of His power and love living in us. Doubters may doubt, and haters may hate, but Christians just keep on loving and sharing because, well, that is who we are, and that is what we do. God is, whether folks believe it or not, and we have a job to represent that love to everyone we meet.

DAY 48

Romans 3:5–6 *But if our unrighteousness brings out God's righteousness more clearly, what shall we say? That God is unjust in bringing his wrath on us? (I am using a human argument.) Certainly not! If that were so, how could God judge the world?*

People often blame God for all kinds of things. If a child dies, God gets the blame. If storms destroy crops, God gets the blame. If disease strikes, God gets the blame. And if someone loses their job unfairly, you guessed it, God is held responsible for it.

What is not always considered, is whether our own choices or actions had anything to do with the bad things that happen in our lives. I saw a posting online one time that said, "Most of life's problems are made by our own choices, and sometimes because our choices are just stupid." It's easy to blame God when things don't go the way that we would like them to go, but our own responsibility also has to be reconciled with the end results we face.

God is not in the business of allowing good things to come to good people and causing bad things to happen to people who are not so good. Our heavenly Father does pour out His blessings daily, but like the rain that falls, it falls on the just and the unjust. He cares so much for us all that He is not out to get anyone; He just wants us to avoid pain as much as possible.

Think about this scenario. You buy a nice, new guitar for which you have been saving up to buy for years, but when you come home from work one day, your four-year-old has decided that it would make a great baseball bat and has been hitting rocks with it. The guitar is severely damaged, and you are naturally upset. Is it unjust of you to punish the child? Of course not. But this is a great teaching moment and you don't beat the child with the guitar to make your point. As angry as you might be, a good parent doesn't take out his anger on an immature mind with vengeful actions.

Are we better than God? Aren't we all God's children? Doesn't He love everyone in such a way that He teaches us, but is not out to get us in wrath? He is a faithful Judge and we never have to worry about Him being unfair. After all, He can do what He wants, but what He really wants, is us. As others have said, "God loves people more than anything!"

Day 49

Romans 3:7 *Someone might argue, "If my falsehood enhances God's truthfulness and so increases his glory, why am I still condemned as a sinner?"*

The argument that Paul is making here creates a straw man scenario as he purposes a way to "help God." He seems to say, "If my wickedness makes God look better, then why is that not a good thing?" But the illustration doesn't hold water in reality. It's a bit like saying, "If my gluttonous eating and calorie abandonment makes my best friend look skinny, then I am doing a good thing."

Of course, the problem with all this is that the argument misses the point. It is true that God is always the source of truth and deserves to be glorified, but the fact is, our providing a contrast for Him is not needed. It's not like God's goodness cannot be seen when compared to ours, for after all, if we lived out our moral existence to the very best of our ability, our heavenly Father would outshine us like the sun to the moon. Like Isaiah said, "All of us have become like one who is unclean, and all our righteous acts are like filthy rags;" (Isaiah 64:6).

What is at issue here is what is good for us. Our righteousness is not in competition with God's for He is always good, and any goodness we have is only a pale reflection of His. Our falsehoods in life, however, destroy us and such actions become offensive to God because of what it does to us.

Because God so loved the world that He sent His only Son to redeem us and provide for us the hope of eternal life, He doesn't want us to walk in darkness and live a lie. Sin does not only show a contrast when compared to God's goodness, but it destroys the sinner. Sin and falsehood tear down all that the Father is trying to do to build us up.

That's why we need to continually strive to be imitators of Christ. We don't glorify God by having our actions show a contrast to His, but by living in such a way that we remind people of Him. God is good, and His mercies endure forever; His love extends to all generations. We show that love by providing those around us an opportunity to see a life transformed by Him in action. Like Paul, we should do all we can to make God look good by being ambassadors of Christ to everyone we meet.

DAY 50

Romans 3:8–9 *Why not say—as we are being slanderously reported as saying and as some claim that we say— "Let us do evil that good may result"? Their condemnation is deserved. What shall we conclude then? Are we any better? Not at all! We have already made the charge that Jews and Gentiles alike are all under sin.*

One problem that makes Paul's time contemporary with ours is in the fact that sometimes people misquote us or lie about what we say. This is represented in the daily news on a regular basis as political operatives find ways to spin any type of information to such a degree that it meets a predetermined agenda, regardless of what the original intent was.

Perhaps the reason this is so, is because throughout all generations, people are selfish. We are born with a nature that says, "Me first!" Therefore, anything that can be used to further our own situation, or make facts appear in my favor is fair game. At least that's the way natural man looks at it.

Paul brings to light three specific ideas here. First, he shows human nature for what it is and relates the slanderous things that are going on. Therefore, it is wise for people of all generations to take the advice of another biblical writer, when he says, "Everyone should be quick to listen, slow to speak, and slow to become angry" (James 1:19). We need to check our sources before buying in to any so-called "truth" that may be presented to us.

Second, condemnation is a reality. Though it is not our place to judge, there is a Judge who is taking note of every word and deed, and He will have the last word on the balancing of the scales of justice.

Finally, when condemnation does fall on the perpetrator of evil, it will be a righteous judgment. Our heavenly Father knows the hearts and minds of His creation and His verdict will be fair. There is plenty of scriptural evidence that testifies of righteous actions and deeds of God, so we can rest assured that all will be as it should be when He is finished.

Paul actually asked a question here, "Why not say..." The answer is implied but needs to be stated. Why not say what is wrong? Because it's wrong, and wrongness is never the way of the holy walk. God calls us to be like Him and our utmost for His glory should always be our path in life.

DAY 51

Romans 3:10–12 *As it is written: "There is no one righteous, not even one; there is no one who understands, no one who seeks God. All have turned away, they have together become worthless; there is no one who does good, not even one."*

Here the Apostle calls on his memory of Old Testament references as he pulls verses from Ecclesiastes 7:20, Psalm 14:3, and Psalm 53:3, and mixes them together to make his point. The Old Testament was the only scripture he had and over the next several verses he refers to it liberally.

We don't know exactly what circumstances Paul faced as he penned this passage, but it's doubtful that he had access to the many scrolls that made up the Hebrew Bible. He most likely had to depend on his recollection of previous days of learning to be able to quote the sacred text as he does.

Can we do this? Do we have the ability to reach back into our memory banks and pull-out verses to help us in our daily walk? If not, why not? Surely, we have much more access to the Word that Paul did. Almost anyone can memorize portions of the Bible if they set their mind to doing it.

Perhaps part of the reason we don't as we should, is in what Paul is saying here. We are not righteous in our own regard, so it is not a natural part of us that drives us to learn what God has to say to us. Even after we have been delivered from the power of darkness through the greater power of Christ, there may be tendencies to laziness and a reluctance to learn still with us.

Any verse chosen and quoted at random can easily be misconstrued and misinterpreted by those who choose to twist its meaning. That's why it is so important that the people of God get really familiar with their Bibles. If we can't use it as the sword of the Lord, then those who misuse it will have the upper hand.

This would be a good day to begin a project of Bible memorization. Begin with a Psalm, a promise, or some favorite portion that means something special to you. Study it, pray over it, and ask God to help you to fully understand it and remember it. Remember, God's Word will not return void. He will take what we use for His glory and make it a blessing to us and to others with whom we may share it. What better thing could we do today?

DAY 52

Romans 3:13 *"Their throats are open graves; their tongues practice deceit."*

Paul continues here with his litany of verses from the Old Testament. This one comes from Psalm 5:9 and in its original setting the psalmist is describing his enemies. In that same passage he is referring to those who are wicked, arrogant, untrustworthy, and are an open grave. Even though this account doesn't directly correspond with Paul's situation, he sees this in common; when people distort the truth, they are part of a bad company.

When I was young, I was advised not to hang out with the wrong crowd. Of course, "wrong" was always defined by the person who was giving the advice. It's a pretty good rule to consider though, because we are often judged by the company we keep.

Many times, the church is accused of being too harsh and too judgmental when it comes to the ills of society—and maybe that is true in some situations, but there is something more to consider here. Paul is saying that we are all in this boat together. When he is referencing the enemies of God from the past, he isn't pointing his finger at someone else. He puts himself right in the mix. Look again at verse 9 of this chapter: "What shall we conclude then? Are we any better? Not at all! We have already made the charge that Jews and Gentiles alike are under sin."

It has been said that everyone is equal at the foot of the cross of Christ. There's a lot of truth in that, and I think it's exactly what the apostle is trying to get across. The Jews are not more righteous because they first received the Law, and the Gentiles are not more righteous because they were sometimes quick to respond to the gospel message. All are equally broken before God and need a Redeemer.

We do not have the privilege today of looking at someone else when it comes to casting stones at sin. All of us have sinned, and all of us will have to give an account as to what we did about it. Thankfully, we have an Advocate with the Father, Jesus Christ the righteous one, who intercedes on our behalf. His gift given to us through His resurrection from the dead, opens the portal of forgiveness and life everlasting. As Paul will say a little further on, "While we were still sinners, Christ died for us" (Romans 5:8). Glory be to the Father, who has made renewal for His creation a possibility.

DAY 53

Romans 3:13 *"The poison of vipers is on their lips."*

This time the apostle quotes from Psalm 140:3 as he compares the present unrighteous of his day to the psalmist plea for deliverance from his enemies. As these comparisons are made, it's not hard for us to fall into the same practice, namely, to equate some evildoer or evil deed with some example from the past.

Have we ever used the phrase, "You are just like your mother!" Or how about, "The bad behavior of your friends is rubbing off on you!" Of course, in the political world, we have all heard the utmost of denigrating remarks when someone is compared to Hitler or the Nazis. That always seems to be the fallback comparison when politicians can't think of anything original, and they want to slam their opponent.

What catches my attention here is the focus on one's lips. In the book of James, the writer phrases a similar remark when he writes, "If anyone considers himself religious and yet does not keep a tight rein on his tongue, he deceives himself and his religion is worthless" (James 1:26). Or consider the same writer a little further on, where he spends a good deal more space describing the tongue. "The tongue also is a fire, a world of evil among the parts of the body. It corrupts the whole person, sets the whole course of his life on fire, and is itself set on fire by hell" (James 3:6).

That's pretty strong stuff. Paul realized, as did the psalmist and James, that our mouths have a lot of power. With a few words of praise, we can bring a huge smile to the faces of many, or with a few words of condemnation, we can bring people from an emotional high to a point of pitiful despair. No wonder much is written about it.

Today we will choose whether our tongue will be used for building up or tearing down. We will make someone happy to see us or make us wish we had never stopped by. Our powers can be influential for good or for evil and we get to decide which it will be.

I've never been bitten by a snake, but I know that some venom can be deadly. I have been attacked verbally and have experienced great sadness as a result. Why not rather decide to be a blessing with our words instead?

DAY 54

Romans 3:14 *"Their mouths are full of cursing and bitterness."*

As the Apostle Paul continues his series of quotations from the Old Testament, this verse is a reference to Psalm 10:7, where the psalmist describes, "the wicked man." In this psalm there is a litany of the evils of this man, and apparently the writer feels God needs to be informed about them.

We need to remember here, that this verse and the series of quotations Paul is making in this section of scripture, points back to verse nine, where he is claiming that all people, Jews, and Gentiles alike, are under the penalty of sin. He isn't just pointing the finger at someone else because he is including himself in this list.

At first blush, this accusation seems very unfair. After all, Paul is writing to the church. Aren't these people supposed to be the ones who live their lives differently than the wicked man that the psalmist is writing about? Do Christians curse? Are Christians bitter?

At one time in my life, I would have given a resounding, "No!" However, I have spent several decades of my life in the pastorate and have encountered a number of people who profess to be Christian, who do indeed curse, and are indeed, very bitter. It ought not to be, and it doesn't have to be, but the fact remains, it is a reality.

What we need to remember is that every action has a reaction, and every time we utter some vulgarity, or do something out of bitterness, we are showing people the wrong picture of true Christianity. If bitterness is where we are in our present experience and if cursing is common to our lips, then we need to go back to the Christ who delivered us, ask His forgiveness, and pray for His Spirit to clean up our hearts and lives.

It may be true that we all start out the same way and we all tend to live in rebellion against authority and against God, but that's not the norm for the person who has been transformed by Jesus. We are Kingdom people, and our lives need to reflect that fact by our conduct, attitude, and words. Wickedness is where we begin, but that is not where we should stay. We have been redeemed through the sacrifice of God's own precious Son on the cross. Let's act like it, so that the world may know, Jesus saves!

DAY 55

Romans 3:15-17 *"Their feet are swift to shed blood; ruin and misery mark their ways, and the way of peace they do not know."*

As always, it is important to go to the source that the writer, in this case, the Apostle Paul, is quoting. Here he pulls from Isaiah 59:7-8. When we look it up, it may not look exactly like the verses we have in our Bible, but we must remember that when the ancient writers penned their words, they didn't use any chapter or verse divisions.

Isaiah's setting was in a time when the nation of Judah had been invaded and destroyed by Babylon, and he is calling upon the nation remnants to turn from their evil practices and seek the Lord for restoration and healing. It's because of Judah's sins that calamity had come upon them, and Paul is using this reference to prove his point that Jews and Gentiles alike are under the influence of sin.

Though our current situation may be completely different from the ills of society that both Isaiah and Paul faced, the results of sin on our world is the same. There is enough evidence of the ruination and misery caused by man's disobedience to God to overflow many huge libraries. All of mankind throughout the ages bear witness that sin brings about destruction. Whenever we place anything or anyone on the throne of our lives except the King of all kings, Jesus Christ, the natural ramification of destruction will soon follow. In Isaiah's time, rebellion and idolatry led to the collapse of the kingdom and caused captivity in a foreign land. For Paul, the Jewish society had become subservient to the Roman empire and the rebellion of previous generations men and women would turn to their selfish ways, not realizing the consequences. To this day, the nature of mankind has not changed.

This is why the coming of Jesus in history made such a difference. Through His death on a cross and His resurrection from the grave, the power of sin had been broken and a new age of hope has begun like never before. We today, don't have to live under sin's oppression and consequences, because in Christ the new kingdom of God has arrived. Jesus announced the age of the Spirit of the Lord, who would empower God's people to new hope, new power, and a path to eternal life in Him. The contrast is clear; sin destroys and new life in Christ restores. Our choice should be easy.

DAY 56

Romans 3:18 *"There is no fear of God before their eyes."*

Paul quotes from the Old Testament one more time before he changes his focus and presentation. This verse is first found in Psalm 36:1and it speaks about the sinfulness of the wicked. The person described here has chosen the way of foolishness and evil.

It is a sad thing when people either do not know about or choose to ignore the Lord God as the King of their lives. In days gone by, it was quite common for almost every child, at least in our Western culture, to be exposed to Christianity on some level. Whether through Sunday School, Vacation Bible School, church services, community events, or even occasionally on television. Sadly, that isn't the case today. More and more I come across people who have had no religious instruction of any kind, and the only times they have ever been in a church is for a wedding or a funeral. The church has much to do to rectify this problem.

Even more disturbing though, are the numbers of society who have some knowledge of God Most High, but choose willfully to disregard His instructions, and even scoff and laugh at those who choose a righteous path. It seems to be this crowd to whom Paul is referring. These are people who know better but choose to be their own gods and ignore the forgiveness, grace, and abundant life that has been offered to them. Certainly, they will eventually reap what they have sown.

Living in the fear of God is not living in fear of judgment from Him, for when we are in Christ, that kind of fear has been replaced with love. Living in the fear of God is showing Him the respect, honor, and reverence that He deserves. He is the King; we are the servants. He is the Creator; we are the creation. He is Lord of all; we are lords of nothing, but our own vanity and pride.

This is why it is so important for us to put Jesus first in our lives. We must keep Him before our eyes, listen to His words in our ears, and draw near to Him in daily prayer and communion. He loves us and longs for us to be close. Doing otherwise shows arrogance and presumes that we can handle whatever life throws at us. We can't do it, but He can, and will do so if we let Him.

DAY 57

Romans 3:19-20 *Now we know that whatever the law says, it says to those who are under the law, so that every mouth may be silenced and the whole world held accountable to God. Therefore no one will be declared righteous in his sight by observing the law; rather, through the law we become conscious of sin.*

Are you under the law? Do you even know what that means? Jesus said, and I quote, "Do not think that I have come to abolish the Law or the Prophets; I have not come to abolish them but to fulfill them. I tell you the truth, until heaven and earth disappear, not the smallest letter, not the least stroke of a pen, will by any means disappear from the Law until everything is accomplished" (Matthew 5:17-18).

In this modern, or post-modern age, we often hear that we are not under the Law any longer but are now under grace. Sometimes it is said that the Law was just for the Jews until the time of Jesus, but now we are freed from the Law and its impact on our lives. Really? Is that what Jesus said?

No, I think we need to understand that we need the Law that was given to Moses from God as much now as we ever did. The Law is our measuring stick to see how we are doing in our relationship with the Father. He didn't give it with an expiration date, or a go out of effect clause, because without it we would be in a world of hurt.

The Ten Commandments are for us today, just as they were for the followers of the Almighty in Old Testament times because the Bible is meant to be understood in its entirety, not in two separate editions. The Law is to be held up for us to see just how powerless we are without Christ. Do we steal? Do we commit adultery? Do we take the name of the Lord in vain? These and other aspects of the Law are roadmaps for our lives. However, as it was with Jews of old, we can't live according to them on our own. We need power from above to help us in keeping them. Jesus makes it possible, for His victory over death, hell, and the grave, gives us access to the Father, and His Spirit provides the grace needed to live up to His divine standards.

We have scales to measure our weight. We have rulers to measure our height. We have the Law to show us where we need to live and how badly we fail at it without Jesus. God still holds us accountable.

DAY 58

Romans 3:21 *But now a righteousness from God, apart from the law, has been made known, to which the Law and the Prophets testify.*

There is no doubt that things changed when Jesus showed up. Not only is time itself divided into segments of B.C. and A.D., but lives changed, and have continued to change down through the centuries, even to the present day. Because of the victory of Jesus on the cross, our connection to the Father has been made possible continually, and the outcome of the world has been sealed.

What Paul refers to particularly in this verse, is that not only did Jesus fulfill the points of the Law but established a way for us to be made righteous in the sight of God—when previously mankind failed miserably at it.

Another way of looking at it is to compare our life in the Lord to automobile racing. There was a time when people were astounded that a car could reach the high speed of sixty miles per hour, or a mile per minute. But now, because technology has advanced so far beyond that point, all motorists have the option of cruising much faster than that without fear of problems.

When man tried to live under the Law to please God, he found himself falling short of the mark continually, but now things are different. Because today as we are filled with the Spirit of God, we can go far beyond the minimum requirements and live abundantly in God's own power. We don't have to settle for just getting by. We can be victorious in our spiritual journey because God's righteousness has been revealed to us in the person of Jesus. In His power and in His strength, we are not bound by rules, but freed to live in the Father's pleasure.

Once we needed the written Law to show us where we needed to go and what we needed to be like, but now we do by nature what the Law required because our nature has been changed as we conform to the image of God.

All of this is a gift from our heavenly Father and is provided to all by the sending of the Spirit of Jesus into the world. There is no one who is not invited to live this way, and no hoops we have to jump through to be what we should be. We live by His Spirit, abide in the love of Jesus, and find that all that is required of us—and more—is taken care of. Thanks be to God!

DAY 59

Romans 3:22-24 *This righteousness from God comes through faith in Jesus Christ to all who believe. There is no difference, for all have sinned and fall short of the glory of God, and are justified freely by his grace through the redemption that came by Christ Jesus.*

There are those words again: "righteousness", "faith", "believe". These are the themes Paul has been writing about throughout this letter. Each one is a gift from God and each one deserves consideration and study for their own merits.

It is in these verses, however, that a very major error is made by many sincere Christians. Verse twenty-three is part of the "Roman's Road," an evangelism tool used by millions. The idea goes along the theme that since all have sinned and fallen short of God's ideal, that such a life becomes the basis for sin. There is truth here, for the essence of sin is when a person is an idolater and forgets that God's plan for us is to reflect His glory and grace to our world. However, no verse can rightfully be taken out of context, and especially words out of the midst of a sentence. Paul's emphasis is something different here.

Read through those three verses again. They are connected. It is true that everyone falls short of the glory of God, but it is also true that everyone is justified freely by His grace. This blessing is a result of the victory that Jesus won on the cross, and we are all freely given salvation because of His sacrifice.

When Jesus said from the cross, "Father, forgive them, for they do not know what they are doing" (Luke 23:34), who was He forgiving? The soldiers who were torturing Him? The mob that scorned Him? The women who wept before Him? I believe He was forgiving everyone who ever sinned against the Father, even you and me. His forgiveness was universal and complete. That means He forgave both thieves on their crosses, not just one. He forgave Pilate, Caesar, Herod, the Sanhedrin, and Simon Peter. He forgave every dastardly person who has ever lived. His forgiveness is complete.

We are justified freely by His grace and called to live a life of faith. Not everyone will do this, but we have all been called to do so. Redemption is available for all who will believe. He loves us all just that much.

DAY 60

Romans 3:22–24 *This righteousness from God comes through faith in Jesus Christ to all who believe. There is no difference, for all have sinned and fall short of the glory of God, and are justified freely by his grace through the redemption that came by Christ Jesus.*

The subject of sin is a topic that has fallen on hard times in recent years. When someone speaks of sin, it is usually used in the context that causes people to playfully wink, or sheepishly grin as though they had done something bad, but had gotten away with it.

The truth of the matter though, is that sin is not a laughing matter, and no one gets away with it. Sin is a slap in God's face, a rebellion against the Creator who loves us more than any other part of His creation, and an open flaunting of ourselves as the ruler of our own destiny. Sin causes pain not only to the people who are involved in the act, or those who are affected by the act, but also to God, who so loved the world that He sent His precious Son to die on a cross because of what sin had done to people He created.

Sin began in the Garden of Eden when Adam and Eve chose to ignore God's orders for their conduct and decided that they would do what they wanted to do anyway. Their sin was listening to the temptation of the serpent and questioning the wisdom of God's restriction to them, not understanding that God's warning was for their benefit and blessing.

It must have been a great puzzle to them as they considered they could eat from every other tree of the garden except that one. It seemed that he tree of knowledge of good and evil loomed before them as a prize that needed to be claimed for their curiosity to be satisfied.

They did gain knowledge, but their knowledge led to their downfall, and as a result of that downfall, all mankind after them have been born into a state where we also want to be our own god and make our own decisions as to what is right and what is wrong.

Thankfully, God in His mercy, provided mankind with another chance. Jesus became the way of salvation from sin for all who will believe on Him. His gracious act that led to His death also was the gracious act that led to our life. Sin still destroys, but Jesus can still save us from it.

DAY 61

Romans 3:25–26 *God presented him as a sacrifice of atonement, through faith in his blood. He did this to demonstrate his justice, because in his forbearance he had left the sins committed beforehand unpunished—he did it to demonstrate his justice at the present time, so as to be just and the one who justified those who have faith in Jesus.*

There are times when the translation of the Bible we are using does indeed make a difference in the meaning of the words we read. In the King James Version, verse twenty-five talks about Christ being the "propitiation" for our sins. Propitiation is not a word that we use very often, but the KJV gives completely the wrong idea for what Paul is trying to say. Propitiation brings about the idea that Jesus had to die to appease an angry, bloodthirsty God who was out to get us. Nothing could be farther from the truth. Christ died to "atone" for our sins, to bring us back into fellowship, not to face God's wrath if He wasn't satisfied.

Atonement is a bit of a hard concept to grasp. Perhaps the best way to really understand what is going on here is to break the word down to read, "at-one-ment." Creation was separated from its Creator and the sacrifice of Jesus brought them back into "oneness." This short devotional doesn't allow time or space to bring this idea fully into play, for volumes have been written on it, but perhaps it is sufficient to say that through the cross Jesus made oneness with God a possibility for all mankind.

In this way God proved His justice. Sin could not be left unpunished by a righteous God, so Jesus became sin on our behalf. He took on Himself the sins of the past, present, and future, so that no one would have to pay the penalty for his or her rebellion against God. We have been justified, or "made just," or "acquitted" in the sight of God, so that fellowship and oneness can be a reality between Creator and creation. The break in the relationship has been healed when we by faith trust in the work of Jesus on our behalf.

What a wonderful thing Jesus has done for us! How great the Father's love for His creation must be to bring about such a miracle of mercy and grace! Today, and every day, we should praise Him for His care for us to the point that He would stop at nothing to have fellowship with us. We matter to Him! The King of all kings wants to commune with us! Thanks be to God!

DAY 62

Romans 3:27 *Where, then, is boasting? It is excluded. On what principle? On that of observing the law? No, but on that of faith.*

It's often hard to see what God is doing in our world. When we look around at the problems that cover our planet, it is easy to ask where God is in the midst of pandemics, plagues, wars, financial crisis, civil unrest, and death. Our best efforts many times come up short, and so we ask, "Where is God?"

Life for the Christian is a faith-walk. There is no other way to journey with Jesus. We can't boast about being better than other people, because we are not. We can't get extra points with God by going to church, reading our Bibles, spending time in prayer, or doing good deeds to others. These things help us to grow and enlighten us as to the heart of God, but they in themselves don't draw us any closer to being Christian.

For Paul, everything came down to faith. His faith in Jesus as the Messiah of Israel began on the Damascus Road when he was blinded by a bright light. It grew more as he was led into the city and fasted for days as he searched for answers. His faith continued to increase as Ananias prayed with him to receive his sight and taught him about the presence of the divine. As Paul learned to share what had happened to him with others, and preach the resurrection of Jesus from the dead, his faith grew. Later on, as he went to the desert to wait upon the Lord, then joined with the church at Antioch, and went on his missionary journeys with Barnabas and later with Silas, he was growing in his knowledge of the Lord, but also growing in faith.

It wasn't lost on him when he experienced shipwrecks, hunger, thirst, prison, beatings, and stoning. He didn't find comfort in the Law during those times, but he did in the Lord. And through it all, his faith continued to grow and God continued to use him as a result.

We face life as Paul did. Our circumstances no doubt vary a great deal, but God is using the things we endure and face each day to help us grow in our faith. As children of the King of kings, we grow in our dependence on Him as adversity comes our way and we find ourselves with no other direction to turn, but to Him. Faith is a gift of God and it is what links us not only to the saints of the past, but to the very throne of the Almighty. Life itself is our teacher that brings us to faith in God.

DAY 63

Romans 3:28 *For we maintain that a man is justified by faith apart from observing the law.*

For many Christians and non-Christians alike, this idea of faith versus works causes a bit of confusion. There are many places in scripture where we are instructed to "do" things to please our Lord. Matthew 25 comes to mind, as Jesus warns us about the dangers of omission, as well as the blessings of doing for others in His name.

Adding to the confusion is the concept of rewards after this life, namely "laying up treasures," or being judged as to what we have done with the talents God has given us.

What Paul is focusing on here though, is how a man is justified before God, or how he is saved. It is his opinion that actions, though beneficial and worthy, are not what brings about salvation, but it comes by faith in the work of Jesus on the cross for our sakes. The law makes us aware of what we should be like, but it is deliverance from sin that makes such actions possible. Faith in Christ alone is the basis for our relationship with Him.

So where do works, or observing the law come in? What benefit is there for "laying up treasures?" It is in understanding the power of the resurrection that these things are made clearer. We are saved by faith in Christ to redeem us, but then our actions flow from that transformation as a witness to the world around us that Jesus has truly made a difference in our lives. These actions, Christian deeds and works, glorify God and provide us opportunities for ministry in His name.

When we come to the end of our life here, the Christian goes to a place of rest and renewal that we call heaven, or paradise. But when the final resurrection comes and heaven and earth become one, then we will be bodily raised to live out eternity as the fully redeemed people of God. That is when the prayer of Jesus will be answered fully as the Father's will is done "on earth as it is in heaven." Then and there is where the accounting for our works is considered and rewards are obtained.

We are saved by faith, but then we work to glorify God in our world, so that our light will shine for Him all throughout eternity.

DAY 64

Romans 3:29–30 *Is God the God of Jews only? Is he not the God of Gentiles too? Yes, of Gentiles too, since there is only one God, who will justify the circumcised by faith and the uncircumcised through that same faith.*

For much of my life I have heard the phrase, "The Jews are God's chosen people." Within that phrase is the idea that there is some special kind of relationship the Jews have with God that the rest of society can never attain. Paul has something to say about that.

It is true that God first chose Abram and his descendants to be His vessels for telling the world about Jehovah and His majesty. In a world filled with local gods, national gods, gods of the hills, gods of the valleys, and worldly gods of every shape and size, having a view of just one true God was a radical idea indeed. The truth was given to one man and from that one man the message spread.

However, the message eventually took on the focus that the one God was just for one people. On the cross at Calvary, Jesus settled once and for all that the good news of eternal life and freedom from sin was available to every person ever born, regardless of their ethnic or national heritage. Therefore, God is God of the Jews, but yes, He is God of the Gentiles also.

The only caveat to this blessing is in the arena of faith. If Jews place their faith in Christ as Savior and Lord, then they will be saved from sin and its ravages. If Gentiles place their faith in Christ as Savior and Lord, then they too will receive all the promises and blessings given to Abraham and his descendants. It is our faith that makes the difference, but what is good for one is good for all.

This may or may not be a radical thought to you, but it certainly was for the people of first century Rome. No doubt there were many Jews who were shocked and many Gentiles who were overjoyed. They all eventually realized that if they were in Christ, they were family. They were not only family, but they were all equally commissioned with the task first given to Abram, namely, to glorify God and spread His goodness around the globe to all generations. Today that is still our priority. Jesus makes us one and Jesus has given us a commission to work for the developing of His Kingdom in this world.

DAY 65

Romans 3:31 *Do we, then, nullify the law by this faith? Not at all! Rather, we uphold the law.*

I like to use the analogy of brushing teeth to explain what Paul means here. When our children were young, we taught them how to brush their teeth, when to brush them, and the reason why they should brush them. As time went on, they were expected to do this task on their own without us. We would check up on them from time to time and ask, "Did you brush your teeth?" They eventually picked up on the necessity of this habit by themselves and brushing their teeth became a part of their daily habit because they discovered it was good for them. Now, as they have been on their own for many years, it would be a strange thing for me to call them on the phone and ask them if they had brushed today. They do it because they should. It is a habit that has become natural to them.

This is much the way the Law affects the people of God. There was a time in our spiritual walk, when we were infants, that we needed to have the law read to us and have someone over us, like the church, to help us make sure that we did what we should do and avoid what we shouldn't do. But as time went on, we learned to obey the instructions of God because we found out it was good for us to do so, and it became a way of life for us.

Paul doesn't discredit the Law; he is thankful for it. It served a purpose in training him and guiding his steps and actions for the foundation years of his life. But once the Spirit of God settled upon him, he began to obey the Law, not out of obligation, but because it was natural for him to do so.

Today we still value the Ten Commandments, but not because we are slaves to them. We follow their guidance as a lifestyle because the same God who gave them to Moses guides our lives also. We live according to its instruction for our benefit, not for our bondage. We have freedom to follow its teaching or not, but experience has taught us that when we do things God's way, life just turns out better.

There is joy in having boundaries and guidance. We can be free yet know there is a structure that provides helps for our daily walk. Life in Christ in not a list of rules for us to obey, but a lifestyle that incorporates the love of God and the Law of God as one. His hand guides us still.

DAY 66

Romans 4:1–3 *What then shall we say that Abraham, our forefather, discovered in this matter? If, in fact, Abraham was justified by works, he had something to boast about—but not before God. What does the scripture say? "Abraham believed God, and it was credited to him as righteousness."*

There are people who spend their entire lives doing good. Some have the ability to make money, and as a result they give much of it away. Some study hard to become doctors and nurses, and as a result they often put their own lives in danger to help others with various physical needs. Some pastors don't make much money, but they feel the call of God on their lives to preach and minister to the flock of God. They may be counted foolish by others, but they answer to a higher authority.

What do all these people have in common? They try to better mankind by their works. While they should be commended and even rewarded for their many efforts here, their works of righteousness don't get them any closer to being made righteous before God in themselves. Paul gives a lengthy account of his own credentials of self-worth in the third chapter of Philippians, but even his labors do not gain him the notice by God that he seeks.

What matters primarily to God as far as our salvation is concerned, is whether or not we truly believe. Do we believe that God sent His Son into the world to bring about our redemption? Do we believe that God has a path for our lives that would be better than anything we could ever plan? Do we take God at His Word and trust Him to see us through to the end, no matter what the circumstances would be in which we find ourselves?

It's important that we understand this. Faith is the foundation of any and all relationships with God. We must believe that He is, and that He is a rewarder of those who seek Him (Hebrews 11:6). In fact, in the whole chapter of Hebrews eleven, the writer emphasizes the necessity of faith, for without it we are nothing.

One of the great dangers for the church of today is to think that good works alone will be sufficient to meet the needs of mankind. The only thing we have to offer people is God, and the only way we can offer God to them is through the avenue of faith. It was good enough for Abraham, it was good enough for the Apostle Paul, and it will be good enough for us as well.

DAY 67

Romans 4:4–5 *Now when a man works, his wages are not credited to him as a gift, but as an obligation. However, to the man who does not work but trusts God who justifies the wicked, his faith is credited as righteousness.*

I spent a good deal of my growing up years on a farm. Living on a farm means that there are chores to do every day, but the only pay would come in the form of having a home, clothes, food, and whatever else the household allowed. However, in the summer I would often hire myself out to milk cows or bale hay for the neighboring farmers, who would usually pay $1.00 per hour or one penny per bale, depending on the farmer. At the end of each day I got paid, and getting eight to ten dollars in a day was a really big deal, because there was no doubt after baling hay all day, I had earned my pay.

My daily wage back then was an obligation from the farmer that I expected. If he hadn't paid me what he promised, then I doubt if I would have showed up the next day. However, if it was supposed to be a two or three-day stint, then I would trust the farmer to pay me when the job was done. I had faith that he would do the right thing.

This is probably a crude analogy, but it does bear out what Paul is saying here. When I worked for pay, I earned it from the neighboring farmer. If I had to wait a day or two to get paid, I trusted in the goodwill we had developed that he would eventually pay me. But when I did the same work at home, the pay was different, and the expectation was different. My parents made sure that I was well fed, clothed, sheltered, and educated. That was what was expected, and I knew it.

When God bestows His gift of righteousness on us, it is for nothing we have done. We don't earn it, we don't deserve it, and there is no way that we ever can. He offers His grace and forgiveness to everyone whether or not we believe that He even exists. That's just the way God is. His nature is love and mercy. He gives rain to the just and the unjust in the same way that He provides hope and abundant life for all who simply trust Him to do the right thing.

It's doubtful Paul ever worked on a farm, but in his work for the Lord he learned about trust and grace. He was considered righteous like Abraham, and so are we, not because we deserve it, but because God is good.

DAY 68

Romans 4:6–8 *David says the same thing when he speaks of the blessedness of the man to whom God credits righteousness apart from works: "Blessed are they whose transgressions are forgiven, whose sins are covered. Blessed is the man whose sin the Lord will never count against him."*

As the Apostle Paul referred to the time of Abraham earlier in this chapter, he now connects with David, the second king of the nation of Israel. The connection between the two is not accidental, for he is building a case that God has been working out His plan in man's history down through the centuries. Just as Abraham was made righteous by faith, so also David followed in the path of forgiveness, and he too was proclaimed free from sin as a result of faith.

Throughout this chapter Paul is going to reference Abraham repeatedly, but his purpose for bringing in a quotation from David is to show that down through the ages God has been on the same path. Faith was the key to victory for Abraham, the hope of righteousness for David, and we will eventually see that even though they were before the time of Christ, it is in His sacrifice for the sins of the world that would justify mankind once and for all.

The beatitude that David names here though, is threefold. Specifically, he focuses on transgressions forgiven, sins covered, and sin negated by the heavenly Father. They all mean pretty much the same thing, but they drive home the point that no man, not Abraham, not David, nor anyone else could make themselves righteous enough for this to happen. Forgiveness of sins is because of the mercy and grace of God, and no one's work will ever be perfect enough to pay the price for such a gift.

It doesn't matter how many times or how often we attend church, how much money we contribute to the offerings, how many acts of compassion and labor we provide as to our defense of who we are in Christ. It is a matter of faith in what Christ has done on our behalf that makes us righteous before God, and that faith is what puts us in the same camp as Abraham and David. We too are debtors to God. His grace alone can set us free and that is a story worth telling to as many as we possibly can.

DAY 69

Romans 4:9-10 *Is this blessedness only for the circumcised, or also for the uncircumcised? We have been saying that Abraham's faith was credited to him as righteousness. Under what circumstances was it credited? Was it after he was circumcised, or before? It was not after, but before!*

Paul continues with his theme concerning the validity of faith as compared to work or deeds as the determining factor of our being made righteous before God.

Many times, in our world of political intrigue and investigation, people want to know what someone knew and when they knew it. It would seem to the evidential pendulum of our society that these are often the all-important questions. Paul approaches his point in the same way. When was Abraham made aware of his righteousness before God, and what were the conditions that helped him reach his conclusion? The obvious answer is that his standing before God was not reached by the actions that he took, but in his belief in what God told him before he had taken any actions.

The same is true for everyone today. We never achieve a state of "rightness" with God by doing things. Far too many have been confused at this point and so they make their religion something about the reading of holy scriptures, kneeling as they pray, going to worship, doing acts of kindness, or even sacrificing themselves for the sake of others. All of these things are noble in themselves, but none of them justifies a person before God. We are made righteous, or holy, by our faith in God, and the work of Christ that was done on our behalf on Calvary. Our state of believing is the basis for any relationship we have with our heavenly Father.

So, are all these things we do just immaterial then? No, they are valuable and needed, but again it is a matter of order and sequence. We don't do in order to be, but because we are, through faith, we do. Salvation at work bears fruit to our world, but without faith our good works are only window dressing without any real substance.

Being in Christ by faith is everything. Our knowledge may increase, and our talents may be many, but faith is the essential ingredient to be people of God. As our faith grows and our relationship with Jesus deepens, the new doors for ministry open. Jesus and us together make a great team!

DAY 70

Romans 4:11 *And he received the sign of circumcision, a seal of the righteousness he had by faith while he was still uncircumcised. So then, he is the father of all who believe but have not been circumcised, in order that righteousness might be credited to them.*

Paul reminds us that Abraham received a sign and a seal. It was a physical reminder of the fact that those who have been chosen by the Father, truly do belong to the Father. We are not our own, for we have been chosen specifically by our Creator to work for His glory.

The essence of what Paul is trying to get across through this section of scripture is that belief tops works. Both have their places, and both were initiated by God, but it was not the act that Abraham did that caused him to be declared righteous by God, it was his faith. Belief was necessary before action could be taken. Even obedience was not possible before faith kicked in. After all, how can you obey someone you don't believe in?

For the church at Rome, to whom Paul was writing this letter, there were no doubt people in both camps of Hebrews and Gentiles. Some held on stubbornly to their heritage as being necessary to please God. After all, they were children of Abraham, God's chosen ones. Others, who came along later, depended on the grace of God as discovered by faith and experienced by a personal transformation. Both ideas had their place and Paul didn't want to disavow either.

However, faith in God is foundational to everything else about our spiritual lives. We may or may not be asked to do something as radical as circumcision, but whatever God asks us to do, we will do it only if we have faith that He really has called us to obey.

Do works and faith compete for dominance in your life? Is it a reality for you that faith was kindled by your hearing the Word of God and then as spiritual transformation took place, you were enlisted with an assignment to complete? That's usually the way it seems to work in the faith walk. We must remember that we are not called for position, but for action. Action, however, is preceded and combined with faith. Both are necessary, but one comes before the other. Faith in God will lead to action every time. Obedience is the sign that our faith has taken root and is growing.

DAY 71

Romans 4:12 *And he is also the father of the circumcised who not only are circumcised but who also walk in the footsteps of the faith that our father Abraham had before he was circumcised.*

Does God favor the Jews? Sure, He does, but no more than He favors the Gentiles. Yet, there has to be a reason, which may be known only to His divine mind, as to why He chose Abram when He did. There has to be a reason for Him to institute the ritual of circumcision for the male children of Abram's family and descendants. It's actually pretty amazing that the God who created all things would take a special interest in any part of His creation over the rest of it, but apparently, He did.

The focus here again is on faith. It wasn't actually the ritual that made the big difference in Abraham's life, though the impact of that procedure affected his family to this very day. Paul sees the important thing that Abraham did was to believe. It is his belief concerning what God told him that really transformed his life in its entirety. The ritual was just a reminder of what had already happened.

This is very much the same for us. A comparison could be made to equate our baptism with the Jewish ritual of circumcision. The circumcision was a declaration that the child was part of the Hebrew family, just as our baptism is a proclamation that we have joined the family of God in Christ. The circumcision was a symbol, while faith was the substance. Our baptism is a symbol of the faith that we have declared in Christ. It is not the ritual that makes a difference in us, though it can be very emotional and meaningful. It is the faith that we have in our Redeemer to have changed us and made us new creatures that matters.

Just as God is the God of the circumcised and uncircumcised who live by faith, a similar case could be made for the baptized and unbaptized who live by faith in Christ. It's not that we shouldn't be baptized, because we were instructed by Jesus to do so, but this involves our witness, not our transformation. God favors the Jews who are circumcised or not, and God favors Christians who are baptized or not—if their faith is in their Creator and not in the ritual.

It's a lot to take in, but then, He is a great big, wonderful God!

DAY 72

Romans 4:13 *It was not through law that Abraham and his offspring received the promise that he would be heir of the world, but through the righteousness that comes by faith.*

It is helpful to understand that the emphasis Paul is making here concerns the covenant which God made with Abram back in Genesis 15. It also might be helpful if one would go back and read that section of scripture in order to put these ideas of law and faith into a proper perspective.

The time between Abraham and Moses is about 650 years. That means Moses wasn't even a twinkle in Abraham's eye when God made the covenant of blessing established by faith. Moses didn't receive the law from God until the Israelites had left Egypt and were on their way to the Promised Land. So, in the question of which came first, the promise preceded the law by centuries.

Why does this matter? Paul says this is the proof that the relationship God wants us to have is like the one He had with Abraham. He wants us to enter into a faith-walk and enjoy the closeness of relationship that we can have with our Creator. The law was important so that the people of God who had come out of many years of slavery could understand what it was that God expected of them. He gave them the pattern, but His desire was that they would come to live by His rules naturally rather than ritually. The law wasn't given to create religious robots that had to conform or be killed, but to show the way to fullness of life between the Creator and His creation.

As far as being "heir of the world," as the apostle mentions here, this is a foreshadowing of what Jesus would relay later, when in the Sermon on the Mount He would say, "Blessed are the meek, for they shall inherit the earth" (Matthew 5:5). It would be within the relationship of man with God, that is established by faith, that the full blessings of this world and the world to come would be realized. Meekness is not weakness; it is strength in the power that made us to control the circumstances that enable our lives to be blessed. We become heirs with Christ when we are made righteous, and we are made righteous by faith. It was that way for Abraham, that way for Moses, that way for the prophets, that way for the apostles, and that way for us. Being in Christ makes the promises of God to Abraham, ours as well.

DAY 73

Romans 4:14–15 *For if those who live by law are heirs, faith has no value and the promise is worthless, because law brings wrath. And where there is no law there is no transgression.*

The Apostle Paul had once been a Pharisee. Pharisees often get a bad rap in scripture because they were many times the kind of rule-keepers that considered the rules more important than the people who had to live by the rules. Jesus was continually in conflict with them, so it's not unusual for us not to think highly of them ourselves.

However, the rule-keepers of the world are not all bad. After all, if there were no rules, and no one to enforce them, how could society ever manage to get along and survive. If no administration said that stealing was wrong and had laws to penalize thieves, then robbers would abound, and victims would have no recourse.

When Paul speaks about the necessity of faith for the follower of Jesus, he isn't saying that the law is bad. He is just saying that once faith has been received and righteousness has been bestowed upon us, then we live by the spirit of the law without having to be made to do so. We are by faith made into new creatures for whom the desire to please God, which is what the law points to, is now our new nature.

His point is to see how close we can get to God, not to see how close we can get to the edge of His grace without leaving it. Many times, over the years, I have been asked the question, "Is it sin if I _____?" or, will I be able to go to heaven if I _____?" When I hear such questions, I know that the focus is really, "What can I do, or how far can I go, and get away with it without being penalized?"

For Paul, this is all backwards. He would say that trying to live this way, under the bare letter of the law is "worthless," because it is all about the penalty or the severity of the penalty. Faith is where real Christian living is reached, not in obeying a set of rules. It's true that we are only judged according to what we know, but sin is sin and when God sees our attitude toward playing with it, He is not fooled. Flouting God's grace is playing with fire, and living by faith is a fire escape. Righteousness before God is always the goal for which every Christian should strive.

DAY 74

Romans 4:16 *Therefore, the promise comes by faith, so that it may be by grace and may be guaranteed to all Abraham's offspring—not only to those who are of the law but also to those who are of the faith of Abraham. He is the father of us all.*

Have you ever made a promise to God? Maybe it was when you were in a bad situation and you said something like this: "Lord, if you will just help me and get me out of this mess, I'll serve You as long as I live." If that is the case, you wouldn't be the first to make such a request. History is filled with people who have tried to make deals with God.

But here is another question. Has God ever made a promise to you? According to the Apostle Paul, He certainly has. In Genesis, chapter fifteen, He made a promise, or a deal if you will, with Abraham. He called it a covenant. He promised that He would have a relationship with him and that all the world would be impacted by that relationship. He said it again in Genesis, chapter twenty-two, when Abraham was promised that all people would be blessed because the patriarch was obedient to the voice of our heavenly Father.

God has promised to receive us, when we come to Him in faith, and the relationship that was promised to Abraham and his descendants has been passed on to us. It was not just for the Jew physically, but for the children of Abraham spiritually to receive the favor of God and be claimed as part of His family. God is our Father, regardless of who we are or what we have done, when we come to Him by faith.

That's awfully good news for people in a world that is continually not very kind to its citizens. For some, their home life hasn't been very pleasant, and some have wondered if anyone even cares about them at all. The good news of the gospel of Christ is that all have been forgiven from the cross, and as a result, through the avenue of faith, all can enter into a real-time connection with God.

We don't have to wonder. We don't have to wait. We can claim our inheritance from Abraham through faith in the work of Jesus Christ to bring us into the royal family and break the power of sin and death. Life abundant has been promised, and that is just what Jesus provides.

DAY 75

Romans 4:17 *As it is written, "I have made you a father of many nations." He is our father in the sight of God, in whom he believed—the God who gives life to the dead and calls things that are not as though they were.*

Abram, the man God first spoke to in Genesis 12, literally means, "Father of many." It must have been quite a point of laughter among the locals as he aged and wasn't even the father of one. When God changed his name to Abraham, He was announcing that he would now be "the Father of nations." That must have gotten a big snicker from the crowds who knew the circumstances.

It is strange then that he has become the father of three major world religions: Judaism, Islam, and Christianity. All three point back to him as the patriarch of their faith. If Abraham's friends could see what has happened in the world, they probably wouldn't laugh so much now. God always knows what He is doing, however, and His words would prove true.

What Paul focuses on here, however, is not a bloodline, but a line of faith. It was because Abraham believed God and was considered by God to be righteous as a result, that we have an example of how we are to live our lives. We can't do anything about our blood heritage because no one gets to pick the family he or she is born into. We can have a say in our faith heritage though, and when we believe God as shown to us in the Bible, then we have become part of Abraham's family, complete with all the promises made to him.

Like Abraham, we can put our trust in God—even to the point of knowing that He can and will bring life from the dead. We are all going to die, but there is also going to be a resurrection, and we have hope and faith in the promise of God that we are going to be a part of it. We aren't given a roadmap of what that journey is going to look like, but we are given signposts along the way to head us in the right direction. Jesus is the way, the truth, and the life, and that's all we really need to know.

Today is a good time to renew our faith as we look to the Lord and pledge our allegiance to Him once again. Abraham did in his day and his sons did after him. Since we are part of his family, we too can put our faith into action and claim life eternal through our God who raises the dead.

DAY 76

Romans 4:18 *Against all hope, Abraham in hope believed and so became the father of many nations, just as it had been said to him, "So shall your offspring be."*

Talk about an impossible situation. At the seemingly older age of seventy-five years, Abram left the home of his mother and father with his wife Sarai, who herself was sixty-five years of age. At this point, neither of them had been able to have children. Under the instruction of the Lord, they traveled to Canaan, where Abram built an altar to the Lord in reverence to his divine call. They went from there to Egypt because of a famine, but after their return to Canaan there was a dispute with his nephew over land. Abram went the way that Lot didn't want to go, and again built an altar to the Lord because God had again promised him a tremendous family legacy.

Many events would pass in Abram's life before in Genesis fifteen God made a covenant with him and once again promised that his offspring would be like the stars in the heavens. It was at this point that Abram believed, and it was credited to him as righteousness in the eyes of God. Something very special was happening in the relationship between God and Abram then.

What wasn't happening, however, was children. Abram and Sarai were still barren, and the years kept on rolling by. Sarai chose a custom of the area, for Abram to have a child in her name through her servant girl. So when Abram was eighty-six years old, Hagar the servant girl, finally made him a father.

However, thirteen more years would go by before God would meet with him again, institute the ritual of circumcision, change his name to Abraham, and tell ninety-nine-year-old Abraham that his heritage would be through his eighty-nine-year-old wife, Sarah, who would be called the mother of nations. And here Paul reveals this amazing truth, Abraham believed. It was against all hope, but in hope, he believed God.

It's easy to believe when the risk is small. It's easy to believe when the outcome doesn't make that much of a difference. But this old man had to have really big faith to believe God for such a promise to be fulfilled. We have to hand it to him. He was truly the father of the faithful. Would we do as well if we were in the same situation? I wonder. Something to think about.

DAY 77

Romans 4:19 *Without weakening in his faith, he faced the fact that his body was as good as dead—since he was about a hundred years old—and that Sarah's womb was also dead.*

I haven't met a lot of people who were one hundred years old, but I have met a few. Some of them I have pastored and some of them I eventually buried. It is a great accomplishment to live to be that old, but I have never heard of anyone during my lifetime who became a father at that ripe old age, and I certainly haven't heard the news of any woman becoming a mother for the first time—or anytime—at ninety. This thing with Abraham and Sarah is no doubt a very unusual story.

I was only three days shy of being twenty-three when my last child was born—and he was two months early. We thought it was a wonderful miracle that he survived, but it was nothing like the miracle that these two early Jews experienced. Now that I have entered the last half of my sixties, I can't even imagine the talk of those who know me if I would father a child at this age, and I am still thirty-three years shy of Abraham.

Yet when I read the story in Genesis, Abraham took it all in stride. It was really a simple matter. God promised that it would happen, and Abraham believed Him. Oh, he laughed when first heard the news and so did Sarah, but perhaps that's why they gave their child the name Isaac, because in Hebrew Isaac means, "He laughs."

Again, the great part of the miracle here is that Abraham did not waver in his faith that God would do what He said He would do. God said it; he believed it. And it happened as God said it would.

Here is where we draw some great insights from the story. First of all, Abraham was in such a relationship with God that they communicated. Second, he believed God no matter how outlandish the promise was. Can we say the same about our walk with God? Do we have a consistent relationship where we talk together? Do we believe and act on our belief as God directs us? Jesus came to make such a relationship possible for all people everywhere. The facts and odds may be against the norm, but if we receive guidance from God, we need to act on what He says. Only God knows what depends on our actions of faith.

DAY 78

Romans 4:20–21 *Yet he did not waver through unbelief regarding the promise of God, but was strengthened in his faith and gave glory to God, being fully persuaded that God had power to do what he had promised.*

I have been intentionally walking with the Lord since late August of 1960. Over that period of time to the present there have been many times that I have stumbled in my walk, but thankfully Jesus has been faithful to pick me up and strengthen me to go on a little farther. He has never failed me even one time, and I am convinced that He never will.

Where does such faith in God come from? Certainly, not from me. I have too many flaws and inconsistencies to account for anything noteworthy, but one thing I know, God is faithful—always. It is our heavenly Father who calls us and sets us on the journey with Him, and it is the same God who provides us with faith to keep us on the way.

For Abraham to believe God in the face of unprecedented obstacles is an amazing thing. However, "he was strengthened in his faith," by his unseen divine companion and came to know within his heart that God would come through on His promise just like He said He would.

The key thought that jumps out at me in this reading of scripture about Abraham comes from the words, "he did not waver." Because his reality of God was different from the reality of his neighbors, he was able to hold fast in his belief even though everything he knew about the natural world screamed out for him to not believe. No doubt, like us, Abraham had his ups and downs as he made his trek with God, but his faith held fast, and he kept on going.

Today we may face issues of life that challenge our faith. That challenge may come from things beyond our control, from people who are close to us, or from something that comes completely out of the blue. What we need to learn from Abraham is to hold fast. Our God has not forsaken us, and whatever He has promised to us He will bring to pass. Others may scoff at our beliefs and there may even be a price to pay in relationships, finances, or in other ways, but we must hold on. Too many people are watching us to see how deep our faith goes. Too many souls hang in the balance for us to give up. God is faithful, so give Him glory, and keep believing.

DAY 79

Romans 4:22–24 *This is why "it was credited to him as righteousness." The words "it was credited to him" were written not for him alone, but also for us, to whom God will credit righteousness—for us who believe in him who raised Jesus our Lord from the dead.*

Occasionally I go online and check my financial credit score. I often don't have any real reason to do it, except to see if everything is up to date and that no one has done anything that might hurt my credit rating.

We depend a lot on credit these days. If not in the area of finances, then it is in the areas of personal trust, reliability, and reputation. We don't want to be given a bad report or rating in anyone's eyes, because our good name and our relationships depend on how people see us.

How much more important it is to consider how God sees us. Abraham had a good credit rating with God because God found he could be trusted. It wasn't that Abraham didn't have any flaws. Anyone who reads through the chapters of Genesis and looks at some of the decisions he made would find that he had feet of clay and was human like the rest of us. However, he was faithful in the area that mattered; he believed God. God saw that faith, knew that it was genuine, and credited him to be righteous in His eyes. When the Judge of all judges gives you a triple-A rating, you know you are doing something right.

Paul reminds us here that we have the same opportunity that Abraham did. Our belief is in the fact that God raised Jesus from the dead, never to die again. In the same manner we believe that as God raised Jesus bodily from the tomb, He will do the same for us someday. There will be a day when the earthly part of our existence will be resurrected to never die again, and God will do it bodily. Jesus didn't leave his bones behind in that grave and we won't either. As wiser men have said, "We don't have a soul in our body, we are a soul that has a body."

Believing in this sounds crazy. The whole world knows that dead people don't come back to life after they die—just ask anyone! But Christians know differently because our faith is that Jesus was the first to be raised, and we will follow in the same way on that resurrection morning. Faith is hard and faith is simple, but faith is the key to having credit in the eyes of God.

DAY 80

Romans 4:25 *He was delivered over to death for our sins and was raised to life for our justification.*

I can't even begin to imagine the full impact of what this verse really means. The fact that Jesus was delivered over to death seems to be a very human thing. Thousands of Jews hung from Roman crosses in that time and being delivered up to that kind of death, though terrible, was not really that uncommon.

Being delivered for our sins is another story. To think of every bad thing that had been done in the world from Adam's rebellion until the close of the age on this planet is where I begin to lose my comprehension. I am awed, humbled, and grieved that my Lord would have to face such a death for me, and for many others like me. I know that we are not worthy of such a sacrifice, and I have no words to say except, "Thank you!" This certainly can never be enough.

The idea of resurrection, being raised to life also staggers me. No one else has ever experienced what Jesus experienced. Others may have died and been raised to life again, but no one else to this time has ever experienced resurrection. He is the only one who has died, been bodily raised in a glorified state, and will never die again. It is an amazing thought in every way, and I can only try to get my head around it all.

But to be raised to life for my justification before the Father is the topper of all concepts. Death is common now and someday resurrection will be common, but the work of Christ to provide me an audience before God the Father as clean, forgiven, and made righteous in His eyes is overwhelming. It's like being given a do-over in this world. In Christ, I have been truly made into a new creature.

What amazing grace! What a wonderful gift! It's no wonder that the history of the world swings on B.C. and A.D., for no event in the course of mankind has ever affected this planet like the life, death, burial, and resurrection of Jesus for our sakes. He snatched victory for all of us out of the jaws of defeat and changed everything forever. I am a child of the King because of Jesus. I am free to live as righteous before God all my days because of Jesus. I give myself to Him forever as my offer of thanksgiving!

DAY 81

Romans 5:1 *Therefore, since we have been justified through faith, we have peace with God through our Lord Jesus Christ,*

Some have used the analogy that justification is that because we have been reconciled with Christ, we are now "just-as-if" we had never sinned. That is partly true, but in other ways it is not. Sin always brings about a payday, whether we have repented or not.

Let me illustrate like this. Supposed your dog gets out of its pen and goes over to your neighbor's house and takes a nap under his truck. While the dog sleeps soundly, the neighbor unknowingly gets in his truck and starts to drive away, running over the dog and killing him. Alarmed at what he has done, he carries the lifeless dog back over to your house and confesses to you what has happened and how sorry he is. Because he really didn't mean to do it, and because accidents do sometimes happen, you forgive him and you *justify* him in the matter of your dog's death. Your relationship with your neighbor continues and it is just as if the incident never happened. Well, almost. Even though your neighbor has been forgiven and is justified for his actions, the dog is still dead.

That's the way sin destroys our lives. It's also the reason that it is so important for us to raise our children to know the Lord early so that they will avoid the scars of sin that so many have to bear. Our choices have consequences and some of those consequences stay with us for a lifetime. Sin always leaves a scar of some kind.

But the good thing that happens when we are justified by faith is that there is a residue that remains to help us in our journey, for "we have peace with God through our Lord Jesus Christ." If we had to bear our scars alone then we would certainly not be able to stand it, but God knows that and provides grace for each of us in the form of peace. This peace is not the absence of conflict, for some of us face that all our days, but it is the awareness that God is right in the midst of our conflict with us, and that He will never leave us.

Peace with God is a wonderful gift. It's what allows us to lie down at night and sleep. It's what provides strength and courage in us for what we have to face when we get up. God's peace is different from anything that anyone else can give. It's the peace of family, for we are heirs with Christ.

DAY 82

Romans 5:1–2 *Therefore, since we have been justified through faith, we have peace with God through our Lord Jesus Christ, through whom we have gained access by faith into this grace in which we now stand. And we rejoice in the hope of the glory of God.*

This state of justification that Paul is writing about takes us to two other words with which we have become very familiar around the church. The first is *faith* and the second is *grace*. Both are gifts of God and are made possible because of the sacrifice Jesus Christ provided for our forgiveness.

What we receive is grace, that is, undeserved love from our heavenly Father. Regardless of how bad or good we have been, how many times we have rejected Him in the past, or what excuses we may produce, when we surrender to the Lordship of Christ and are justified before God, we not only have peace, but receive God's mercy in the form of grace.

The pathway to our getting this grace is the avenue of faith. It's such an easy concept, but down through the centuries people have misunderstood it, and Paul's words here. Folks try to buy God's favor, compete for God's favor, make a deal for God's favor, and even sometimes go to war to prove we have God's favor, but all that is required is faith. We wrestle with this because our world is upside down from the way God wants it to be, and our task as the Christians in the church is to do our part to help right it again. We are believers, the redeemed, and have been set apart for God's purposes, but it is all made possible by faith in the resurrection of Jesus.

This takes Paul to the next step of his message as he proclaims that this grace, obtained by faith, produces joy to the glory of God. This ingredient of joy is what separates those who have received the Spirit of God and those who have only participated in a religion.

Justified by faith, peace with God through Jesus, and grace received through faith, equals joy and hope. That's why we serve the Lord! That's the message we proclaim! That's why we want everyone to know what having Jesus in their life can do, because what this world needs now and always is joy and hope. People try to fill the void when those things are missing, but joy and hope are only found in Christ. He is now, and always will be, the answer to what makes life in this world worth living.

DAY 83

Romans 5:3 *Not only so, but we also rejoice in our sufferings, because we know that suffering produces perseverance;*

Paul had just said that he rejoiced in the hope of the glory of God, but as he continued, he said he also rejoices in his sufferings. At first glance, for most people anyway, this sounds a little strange. We certainly understand rejoicing in hope because we all hope for something, however, the idea of being happy in suffering pushes the envelope a little.

But isn't this the same thing that James said in his book? "Consider it pure joy, my brothers, when you face trials of many kinds, because you know that the testing of your faith develops perseverance" (James 1:2-3).

There is that word again, *perseverance*. Both Paul and James tell us that if we want to persevere, we must do it through the avenue of trials and sufferings. We don't like to hear such things. We like the easy way, the smooth way, the coasting downhill way. When we have to face hardships, we grimace and usually do anything we can to find another way to travel.

What we don't always remember is that the Christian way is the way of the cross. The early church father Tertullian said, "The blood of the martyrs is the seed of the church." A former student of mine who presided over many churches in Africa told me that if there is no shedding of blood, the church doesn't grow there.

Why does this have to be? What are Paul and James, and even Jesus, talking about? It's about separating the talkers from the walkers, the sheep from the goats, and true believers from the "also-churched." It means that Christians have discovered the pearl of great price, and they are willing to give up anything and everything to keep it. Our relationship with Christ is not to be compromised for any person, fortune, or fame. We would rather face hardship and suffering in order to be like Jesus and help establish His kingdom on earth as it is in heaven.

But we must remember that we don't do this gritting our teeth and despising the experience. We do it with joy! We do it for Jesus! This is not possible on our own, but only as the Spirit of Christ fills us and empowers us for service. We are led and filled by Christ, so that we can rejoice in Him.

DAY 84

Romans 5:3–4 *Not only so, but we also rejoice in our sufferings, because we know that suffering produces perseverance; perseverance, character; and character, hope.*

You have heard no doubt, about the snowball effect. Economic guru Dave Ramsey has used it as an illustration for years when helping people to get out of their financial debt. The idea is simple. When one pushes a snowball down a hill, it will continue to grow as it accumulates more snow, until at the bottom of the hill it is much larger.

Not only is this true for snow and economics, but absolutely true for spiritual disciplines as well. When we rejoice in our sufferings, Christ works in us to produce perseverance, or staying power, and then adds to our perseverance, character, and to our character, hope. In other words, we grow in grace as we learn to be joyous in the tough places.

Anyone can moan and groan when hard times come. No one is exempt from them, so whether we are wealthy or poor, beautiful or ugly, strong or weak, young or old, we are going to go through unpleasant situations at times. We may think that we are all alone in this, or that no one else has ever experienced the valley of despair like we have, but that's just the enemy playing mind games with us. More often than not, there are people in other parts of the world in much worse situations than what we experience, but we just don't know about them.

The idea of perseverance building character is a true concept. When we learn to consistently give God praise and thanksgiving in the hard times, we become different creatures. We become examples to those around us to the glory of God, and people do notice whether we are upbeat in our pain or like to complain about it. It cannot be an act, however, for character is what we are when no one is around. We must allow Christ to build this character for real within us.

The end result of such development is hope. It is not only hope for our lives, that God will be glorified through our reaction in times of trouble, but that people around us find hope also and will begin to consider what a difference Jesus might make in them. As we are faithful, God will use all times, good and bad for His glory. In pain, we grow, and God gets the credit.

DAY 85

Romans 5:5 *And hope does not disappoint us,
because God has poured out his love into our hearts
by the Holy Spirit, whom he has given us.*

What do you hope for? What is it that you have set your heart on and really long for as your dream to come to pass? We as humans sometime have skewed desires and aspirations, and too often our hopes are just pipe dreams without any possibility of becoming reality.

Take, for example, the modern lottery system that is popular in many parts of the world, but especially in the United States. Every day people stand in line to pay their hard-earned money to buy a ticket in the hope that they are going to be the one to hit the jackpot and have riches galore for the rest of their lives. I have never purchased a ticket, but even so I have almost as much of a chance of winning the lottery as those who do. Such a hope is unfounded and unrealistic because the odds against the player are grossly immense.

Some people think that we Christians are just as foolish. They would say that we worship a God we can't see and put our faith in something that we have only heard about, without any tangible proof that what we hope for is real or possible. But that is where they are wrong.

Paul reminds us that our hope is not based on a pipe dream of what may happen. We are not looking for pie in the sky by and by, for we are confident of the reality of God's mercy right now. We have hope because God has already given us a down payment of what we can expect throughout all eternity. He has "poured out his love into our hearts by the Holy Spirit," and we have been transformed from what we were into the kind of creature that can co-exist with God forever. The deposit of God's love in us is our guarantee of what is to come. It's like the appetizer before the meal, or the meal before the dessert. It's a taste of the blessing, but the best is yet to come.

How good it is of our heavenly Father to give us a foreshadowing of eternal life! We don't know what eternity after death will be like, but we know Jesus will be there because we have already experienced Him to some degree when He placed His love in us. As God's children we have the perfume of the divine upon us, and as we wait, we are to fill the world with that fragrance.

DAY 86

Romans 5:6 *You see, at just the right time, when we were still powerless, Christ died for the ungodly.*

There are only seventeen words in that verse, but what they say speaks volumes. I've been reading them for years and I still struggle to get my head around the impact of the truth given here.

It begins with God's timing. Jesus wasn't born to Mary at just any time; He came to us at the right time. When it comes to how God calculates all of the events of the world in His day planner, your guess is as good as mine. But the one thing of which we are assured, is that He knows what He is doing. He is never too early and never too late. Everything He does is, "at just the right time."

There is much to consider about our powerlessness. We don't like to think of ourselves that way. Especially we who live in the Western World love our independence and take great pride in the fact that we don't need anybody or anything, anytime. We like the image of the lone cowboy taking on the world and coming out on top. However, we know that isn't the case. We are a needy people and there was nothing we could do about the sin problem that plagued our lives and the world. The enemy was winning, and it was impossible for us to do anything to stop him.

That's where Jesus comes in. "Christ died for the ungodly." We didn't deserve it and we didn't even ask for it. We were so far down that we didn't even know how to look up, but God knew that and sent His Son to be our Savior, Redeemer, Comforter, Guide, and Friend. We, who could never be worthy or deserving enough to provide our own salvation, were given the gift of eternal life, and a hope for today and tomorrow.

That's the way God is. He always has our best interest in mind and has gone to every extent we could ever ask of Him to provide for our needs and bring us into a right relationship and fellowship with Him. In the death, burial, and resurrection of Jesus, the dark powers of the world were defeated once and for all, and we now can live to tell the story. We have been given a new opportunity at life here and now—and in the world to come. Yes, everything is going on right as planned. God's in His heaven and all is going to be okay with our world. That's a promise we can believe it.

DAY 87

Romans 5:7–8 *Very rarely will anyone die for a righteous man, though for a good man someone might possibly dare to die. But God demonstrates his own love for us in this: While we were still sinners, Christ died for us.*

This is the stuff of which movies are made. We have seen the idea played out many times where a hero gives his life for his family, his lover, his country, or some other worthy cause. Of course, no one in his right mind really wants to do this but being noble is the bedrock of all such dramas that pull at our heart strings.

Paul is right when he claims that such actions are rare because we often see the results in the news that show the depravity of mankind. We hear of parents abusing their children, of elected officials taking bribes, workers trying to find ways out of the work for which they are being paid, and the list goes on and on. Let's face it, there is a lot of evil in our world and many people put their own needs and wants ahead of everyone else.

Still, there is good in many people. I see it in the mother who goes without food so that her children can have something to eat. I see it in the father who works two or three jobs so he can provide for his family. I see it in the pastor who prays over the sick and sits up and cries with those who grieve. There are plenty of examples to show us that even though self-sacrifice may be rare, it is around us and we should always be thankful for that fact.

What Paul is doing is obvious. He is making a comparison of the usual role of mankind with the sacrifice of Jesus on our behalf. We are people who look out for our own needs, but Christ died for us anyway. It's not that we were righteous, or noble, or deserving, for we were sinners. Jesus knew that and knew that the only way for us to ever break the bonds of sin was for Him to win the victory for us—and He did it at the price of His own blood.

This is the heart of the gospel message. We were lost, evil, and helpless in our sin, but Jesus died to provide us with a new destiny, a new normal, and a new hope. We, who were alienated to God have been made one with Him through the sacrifice of His Son on our behalf. Where we couldn't find the way to freedom, Jesus died to open the doors of our sinful prison.

It is the story of amazing love. Jesus died so that we could live. Amen.

DAY 88

Romans 5:9 *Since we have now been justified by his blood, how much more shall we be saved from God's wrath through him!*

We sometimes get the wrong idea concerning what Jesus did for us on the cross. Part of the reason for this theological error comes from a poor translation of I John 2:2 in the King James Version of the Bible, where it reads, "And he is the propitiation for our sins." The New International Version reads, "He is the atoning sacrifice for our sins," as does the New Revised Standard Version.

You may ask, "Well, what difference does it make," and "What does I John 2:2 have to do with Romans 5:9?" Actually, a lot. The word "propitiation" gives the idea that Jesus was offered up to appease an angry God, much like you may have seen in old movies where island people would sacrifice a virgin to a volcano to make the volcano god not be mad at them anymore. Nothing could be further from what Paul is saying here.

God was not mad at mankind and made His Son to be our sacrifice so that He wouldn't be angry with us anymore. That's not divine justice. That's carnality on the highest level. Christ died for our sins so that the powers of darkness that held us captive would be defeated once and for all. His blood justified us, or freed us, so that sin would no longer be the master over us. The cross was not because God was at His wits end with us, and as a last resort He killed His own Son to pay off our sin debt. God loved us so much that He gave a part of Himself, a part of the Holy Trinity to destroy the powers of darkness on our behalf and set us free.

Of course, much more needs to be said about this, but there isn't time in a three-minute devotional. Suffice it to say that we have always been God's highest priority and the cross was His answer to the sin problem that always tears us down and destroys us.

We will be saved from God's wrath on the final day of judgment by trusting in the work Christ did on our behalf and devoting ourselves to the life of forgiveness that was demonstrated for us on Calvary. Everything God does is out of love and Jesus personified that kind of love as a demonstration of how we should give our lives for others. We now are a part of the divine team through the cross of Jesus. Let's act like it for all to see!

DAY 89

Romans 5:10 *For if, when we were God's enemies, we were reconciled to him through the death of his Son, how much more, having been reconciled, shall we be saved through his life!*

I doubt if very many people ever think of themselves as being an enemy of God. After all, who in their right mind would ever want to pick a fight that they know they can't win? However, when we live in such a way that we are in opposition to what God considers righteous, we are indeed enemies of God.

The good news is that we are no longer in that situation. Because of the sacrifice of Jesus on our behalf on the cross, we were reconciled to God and forgiven for everything that would have made us an enemy of God. The chains of sin were broken for all who will believe that they have been freed through Christ, and this old world was changed forever. Our reconciliation to God makes us a new creation.

The idea of reconciliation is an interesting concept. If you have ever had a relationship that was estranged or broken, then you know how painful that can be. It is especially hard when we have to be around the person continually with whom we have had a falling out. Imagine trying to not be around God. He is everywhere, aware of our every thought, and if our relationship with Him is broken, we can never have peace.

That's why what Jesus did is so important. Where once we battled against God and made ourselves His enemy, Jesus mended the rift and made it possible for us to be changed and enter into a righteous and wholesome relationship with God. Where once we were outsiders and interlopers, now we are in the relationship of family and can come to our heavenly Father without fear of retaliation.

All of this is made possible by faith. Again, we will never be good enough to connect with God and have a restored relationship, but the transforming power of the sacrifice on Calvary's cross broke the power of sin once and for all and made it possible for anyone to be on good terms with God.

No wonder we call it "Good News!" We have been reconciled, healed, and adopted by the King of all kings. We are truly saved through His life!

DAY 90

Romans 5:11 *Not only is this so, but we also rejoice in God through our Lord Jesus Christ, through whom we have now received reconciliation.*

This is kind of an interesting phrase that Paul uses, "rejoice in God." What do you think that means? To me it speaks of focusing on the presence and person of God and considering all His attributes that make me happy or thrills my soul. Putting it another way we could ask this question, "What is it about God that makes you smile?"

So here is my list. Today, I smile because I know He is watching over me as He walks with me everywhere I go. He protects me as I sleep each night. He speaks to my heart and communes with my spirit. He puts a joy in my being that stays with me regardless of the circumstances that happen around me. He forgives my sins. He gives me a purpose in my life. He constantly is renewing me into His image and making me so much more than I could ever be myself.

Of course, this is just the starting line. One could go on to talk about how God provides our family, our shelter, our food, our clothes, our income, and our material possessions of all kinds. He causes the sun to rise on a new day and gives us darkness to help us sleep at night. He is the Reason for our songs, the Muse for our poetry, and the Captain of our team.

I haven't even spoken of what He has prepared for those who love Him after we leave this world, and the reunion He will provide for us when we link up once again with those who have gone on before us. All these things make me smile and rejoice in God, and certainly the list could go on and on by more creative thinkers.

But what makes me to rejoice in God more than anything else is the hope that He has placed within my heart. Whether a person lives in luxury or in squalid surroundings, He provides hope for what is yet to come. Whether our relationship with other people is beautiful or we are in the midst of great conflict, He gives hope for a day when peace will come at last. Whether we are young and have many years before us or are old and most of our time in this world is past, we have hope for what still lies beyond the horizon. Yes, I rejoice in God! I smile when I think about Him. Paul knew what He was talking about. I hope you do too.

DAY 91

Romans 5:12–13 *Therefore, just as sin entered the world through one man, and death through sin, and in this way death came to all men, because all sinned—for before the law was given, sin was in the world. But sin is not taken into account when there is no law.*

The concept of original sin is a tricky thing. It has been debated, talked about, preached, and scoffed at for centuries. The idea behind it is that since Adam and Eve rebelled against God's command in the Garden of Eden and ate the fruit from the forbidden tree, all mankind has been cursed with the nature of rebellion against God.

A non-religious view is the ancient Greek story of Pandora's box. Because she was too curious, she opened the forbidden box and allowed evil to escape into the world. It's a similar story to Adam's sin, but one that is given only to the world of fables.

In any case, Paul believed in the concept that Adam's sin had an impact on the whole world, because from that sin, death entered the picture for mankind. He doesn't debate it here, or even try to explain the concept, but his point is not about the sin itself, but the timing of it.

Before God gave Moses the Law, or the Ten Commandments, sin was already in the world. The Law was given to show the way to deal with the fact of sin and qualify it. It was from the time the Law was given that sin began to be shown for the evil it is and judged before God. Whether man had an excuse before the Law was given is debatable, but once God made clear what He expected, sin is judged for the evil it is.

I guess from this idea comes the claim, "what you don't know can't hurt you." In a sense, that is true. If we don't know something is wrong, we can't be judged in the eyes of God as doing wrong. We will face the natural consequences of our error, but God doesn't hold it against us. However, once we are made aware of sin by the definition of God's Word, then we are responsible for our actions.

Sin is destructive because it tears at the very fabric of human existence and leads to death. God loves us too much not to warn us that sin destroys, and His grace brings life. His way is still the smart and safe way to live.

DAY 92

Romans 5:14 *Nevertheless, death reigned from the time of Adam to the time of Moses, even over those who did not sin by breaking a command, as did Adam, who was a pattern of the one to come.*

Adam and Moses. We can't get two more biblical names, or more famous names. The stories of the lives they led and the deeds they did have traveled throughout the world through many centuries, cultures, and languages. Sermons and jokes alike have dealt with the subject of Adam's sin in the garden, and Moses has claimed the reputation of being God's friend and one who dealt with Him directly.

We don't know exactly, or even approximately how much time passed from Adam until Moses came along, because the Bible is not a history book (though it contains a lot of history), but a theology book. The focus of the book is on God's message to mankind much more than a timetable of how He did it.

What we do know from this verse is that death came along as a result of Adam's rebellion, and people died once the Garden of Eden was off-limits, and the tree of life was no longer accessible. We also know that it wasn't their breaking of the Ten Commandments that caused them to die, because God didn't give His commandments for His people until the time of Moses, which at the very least was many, many centuries after Adam. People died because sin produces death, and after Adam, everyone was born in sin and estranged from the fellowship and oneness that Adam and Eve had shared with God in the garden.

The whole story of mankind from the time of man's first sin until the present is about God bringing man back to Himself and restoring what was lost when He was disobeyed by Adam and Eve. The pattern that is found in Adam is the state he was in before the sin. That is what was represented by Jesus, and that is the state God is moving humanity back to as time progresses.

Jesus is the second Adam. He is the example of what God wants from all of us. He not only lived blamelessly before His heavenly Father, but in doing so, gave us a pattern of how we should live our lives. As He died and was resurrected, someday, as we trust in Him, we will do the same. What was started in Adam is finished in Christ, and we will benefit from that forever.

DAY 93

Romans 5:15 *But the gift is not like the trespass. For if the many died by the trespass of the one man, how much more did God's grace and the gift that came by the grace of one man, Jesus Christ, overflow to the many!*

It is a simple point that Paul makes here. The trespass and the gift are different because the trespass brought about death for all, and the gift of grace through Jesus Christ brings life for all. That's about as stark a difference as can be.

What does that mean to us? Let's look at it from a biblical example. The first three chapters of Genesis have a very basic theme, one that will be repeated over many centuries that follow. It goes like this: God puts mankind in a good place, mankind rebels against God's authority over their lives, and God removes them from the good place where He had originally placed them. Turn over to the last nine chapters of Deuteronomy. It's basically a retelling of the law and warnings to the people of Israel that though God is taking them to a good place, if they rebel and turn away from Him, He will exile them once again, just as He did to Adam and Eve back in the beginning.

These two examples are chosen from among many that tell the same story. The trespass against God brings exile and death, but the gift of God's grace through Jesus produces life in the best place we could possibly be, namely, the center of fellowship with the Father.

People often reject Christianity for many different reasons. Some see it as superstition, some see it as a fire escape for the weak, the old, and the dying. The communist Lenin called religion an opiate for the masses. What these and others never seem to realize is that the gift of grace from God through Christ produces good as opposed to all other options, which eventually produce bad. This is not always apparent in real time because God plays the long game, not the short one. He knows that we would choose ice cream for every meal if given the option, so He provides a better diet to help us grow stronger for the work He has prepared for us.

God's love, mercy, and compassion overflow from His bounty to all who will turn their hearts to Him through Jesus. He desires the best for all His creation, but He also knows how to bring about exile when a course correction is needed. He picks the best for all who leave the choice with Him.

DAY 94

Romans 5:16 *Again, the gift of God is not like the result of the one man's sin: The judgment followed one sin and brought condemnation, but the gift followed many trespasses and brought justification.*

Gift giving is a wonderful attribute of civil society. Most of us love to give and most of us love to receive. That's very true if the gift is something we want, but not so true if we are to receive something we don't want. If someone says, "I'd like to buy you a banana split," then I'm all ears and smiling. But if someone says angrily, "I'm going to punch you in the face and break your nose," then of course, we don't relish the other person's generosity.

When Paul compares the two issues of grace and sin, these also are good and bad "gifts" upon the world. Grace is something that every sane person appreciates, but sin, though it may come in the appearance of something very desirable, also comes with a heavy and painful price tag.

Just look at the words Paul uses to describe these two things. Sin involves judgment, condemnation, and trespass. God's gift produces justification or being made righteous in the eyes of our Creator. The contrast is drastic and should provide us with an easy choice as to which one we want. The tempter brought about sin, guilt, the breaking of relationship, and exile. Jesus provides mercy from God at His expense.

Sin's spread and grace's application are both very much like a pyramid structure. Sin began once and spread all throughout the world of all ages ever after. Grace was poured out at the cross of Christ and spreads all throughout the world thereafter.

Today, as I write these words, the world is being impacted with a lethal corona virus, that though unseen, is wreaking havoc on societies everywhere. It began in one place, with one person, and has spread and continues to spread its deadly effect on mankind globally. Likewise, when a vaccine is developed, it will be made available to all so that relief and rescue can be given. Sin is like the virus and its impact is deadly.

However, Christ is like the vaccine for sin and cleanses completely. He is able to do what no one else can and provide what no other antidote can. Freedom from sin is the essence of the good news we spread, and the hope we have in Christ. He truly is the answer for the ills of our world.

DAY 95

Romans 5:17 *For if, by the trespass of the one man, death reigned through that one man, how much more will those who receive God's abundant provision of grace and of the gift of righteousness reign in life through the one man, Jesus Christ.*

It is true that one man, or one woman, can indeed make a difference. It was sure true for Adam in the Garden of Eden and it was true for Jesus on a hill called Golgotha. The first man's actions brought about death. The second man's actions brought life eternal. One man can make a difference.

Because of what Jesus did on our behalf, we receive grace from God and are considered righteous in our actions as we put our trust in Christ for our salvation. There will never be another gift that we could ever receive that will mean more to us in time or eternity.

In Jesus the Jewish nation was encapsulated and He fulfilled the role perfectly that God had planned for the Hebrew nation when He first called Abraham. The Jews would be the tool God would use to bring a lost world back to their loving Creator. Abraham's descendants failed to bring about God's plan, so He sent His Son to be the embodiment of the nation and be the "true Jew" who would perfectly fulfill what God had promised and planned all along.

This is why both the Old and New Testaments are so valuable to us. The Old Testament just isn't history or genealogy or laws. It's the out-workings of God using His people to bring the rest of the world to Himself. In fact, it seems that the Old Testament may well be the eliminating of options on man's part, showing him that he would never be good or righteous enough to accomplish God plan on his own. Jesus had to come to set the record straight and show the rest of the nation and world the way to the Father.

What this means is that we are going somewhere. Time isn't just passing without purpose. God is working His plan down through the centuries of time to bring about a renewal of all He first created. There will be a time when heaven and earth will become one and the kingdoms of earth will be become the Kingdom of the Lord. Righteousness will reign through the one God sent, Jesus Christ, that perfect Lamb, slain to free us from the bondage of sin and set us on the course to a new world. Thanks be to God!

DAY 96

Romans 5:18–19 *Consequently, just as the result of one trespass was condemnation for all men, so also the result of one act of righteousness was justification that brings life for all men. For just as through the disobedience of the one man the many were made sinners, so also through the obedience of the one man the many will be made righteous.*

No one can ever accuse Paul of not repeating himself when he wanted to make a point of emphasis. He holds on to this idea of how the trespass of one man is weighed against Christ's one act of righteousness like a dog with a bone. He had found it to be so, however, so he wanted to make sure that others got the message clearly.

Being justified before God is no small thing; in fact, it is the most important thing that we could ever imagine. The frustrating thing for so many people though is that the matter of their justification is really out of their hands. On the cross Jesus forgave all of us, like it or not, and He alone made it possible for us to stand before God as new creatures. All we can do is believe on the work that was done. That belief will transform our lives by the power of the Spirit, making a change for time and eternity.

Adam got us into a lot of trouble by his rebellion against God in the Garden of Eden, and mankind has suffered under the penalty of sin produces ever since. All of that came to an end at the cross, however, because sin's hold on us was broken forever and everyone, everywhere, can be free to live a life of holiness and righteousness before God.

You may say, "Well, if that is true, and Christ has won the victory, then why are there so many examples of sin that still plague our planet?" It's a good question, and one that deserves an answer. So here it is: Yes, Adam's breaking of God's command started us on a path of destruction and that destruction carries on to this day. What Jesus did though, when He conquered the grave, was break sin's stranglehold on us. Once mankind could not be free of sin's power and the grave's hold, but a new day dawned for us all when Jesus walked out of the grave, the first to do what we too will do someday. Evil is still out there because we haven't finished telling people that they are forgiven and can be free. We have work to do. God is building His Kingdom though, and someday our work will be complete.

DAY 97

Romans 5:20–21 *The law was added so that the trespass might increase. But where sin increased, grace increased all the more, so that, just as sin reigned in death, so also grace might reign through righteousness to bring eternal life through Jesus Christ our Lord.*

These verses are too often taken out of context and used to proof-text one's own opinion. Sometimes grace is used as a "get-out-of-jail-free" card that allows people to do anything once they have been baptized and made a profession of faith in Christ. Paul never had anything like this in mind.

The law was given to us as a measuring stick so that we could understand what God desired of His Kingdom people. However, when God's grace is applied to our lives, it is given to change our hearts and free us from the kind of thinking and actions that were brought about by sin. Sin always leads to death, but grace leads to real life and a righteous standing before God.

There are some who will say that we will sin continually until we leave this world because that is the basic nature of man. It's true that sin is man's basic nature, but when grace is applied and new life begins, the nature is redeemed, and our desire for the things of God comes into bloom.

Grace is transformational. Grace pulls us in the direction of righteousness. Grace defeats death and grace produces eternal life. No matter how great the sin, God's love goes beyond what we are or did and provides us with a new option for eternal life through Jesus the Messiah.

We must always remember that this is only possible through Jesus. There is no other way for anyone to move from death to life and no other way to be changed from darkness to light. Christ is at the center of all we need and all that the law requires. Christ's grace is bigger than whatever is the matter.

Again, this is the "Good News," the gospel. When we were lost, Jesus found us. When we were trapped in sin, Jesus freed us from our bondage. When we were deserving of hell for our thoughts and actions, Jesus showed us a better way and set us on the path of holiness, producing righteousness within us as we stand before God.

This is grace, the unmerited favor and love of God. It is personified in the person of Jesus, who died for our sins to make us one with the Father.

DAY 98

Romans 6:1–2 *What shall we say, then? Shall we go on sinning so that grace may increase? By no means! We died to sin; how can we live in it any longer?*

Aformer professor of mine once told the story of when he was pastoring many years ago. He went out to the back door of his church one day and found one of his churchmen sitting on the steps smoking a cigarette. He watched in silence for a while and finally stepped outside to talk to the man. When the startled and embarrassed parishioner saw the pastor and knew that he had been caught smoking on church property, he offered this excuse, "It's okay, pastor. I'm not sanctified yet."

As I thought on that story it first made me smile, but then the truth sank in that many Christians don't know that when they begin to follow Jesus, the sin business stops. This is not to debate whether or not cigarette smoking is sinful, but to point out that apparently the parishioner in the story thought it was and needed to make an excuse for his actions.

Paul is crying out here that we who are in Christ need to quit the sin business if we are living the life Jesus called us to. In our baptism we died to the old ways of selfishness and personal privilege. We gave up all our rights just as surely as if we were going into the grave. Baptism is the public declaration that we have died to the things of the dark nature. When we are raised from the water it is symbolic of resurrection. Not only is it a statement of faith for our belief in the final resurrection to come, but a statement of faith that we are within that Kingdom of God right now. We no longer live to please ourselves and our personal preferences, but now we are alive unto God.

The practice of continual sinning after we have begun our walk with Christ is antithetical to the gospel message. We don't keep sinning and expect God to keep pouring grace over us like a holy pancake syrup to cover all our misdeeds. We are to stop the sin business, the rebellion against the will of God for our lives, when we enter into our new relationship with Him. To do otherwise would be like a new groom keeping all his old girlfriends and expecting his bride to just understand and forgive him continually.

Our walk with God in Christ is a relationship; a precious communion that we must never abuse. In Christ, we are freed from sin to live in it no more.

DAY 99

Romans 6:3 *Or don't you know that all of us who were baptized into Christ Jesus were baptized into his death?*

D o you remember your baptism? I certainly remember mine. It was in the very cold water of White River, just outside of Anderson, Indiana at Killbuck Park. On that spring day the water was so icy that I thought I really was being baptized into death before I came up.

I remember the first time that I baptized people as a pastor. This time it was in a borrowed baptistry at Anderson, Indiana Parkview Church of the Nazarene on a warm summer Sunday afternoon. However, the host church had not turned the heater to the baptistry tank on, so again the water was ice cold. My teeth chattered not only from nervousness as a young inexperienced pastor who immersed five or six people, but from the cold water that I continued to stand in until the service was over.

Though I have baptized so many people since that day that I have lost count, I am convinced more than ever that one's own baptism should be a very memorable experience. It truly is a matter of life and death, and an event so dramatic should make a profound personal impression.

Paul reminds the Romans that everything changed with their baptism. It was not that there was something special about the water or even in the ritual itself. It is that someone dies and someone is resurrected when a baptism takes place, at least symbolically. It's like Paul would tell the church in Corinth, "Therefore, if anyone is in Christ, he is a new creation; the old has gone, the new has come" (II Corinthians 5:17)!

To use a baseball analogy, it's a bit like changing teams. Once a player might have played for the New York Yankees, and played for them with all his might and ability. However, when his contract was purchased by the Los Angeles Dodgers, then his skill, efforts, and talents belonged to that west coast team.

When we are in Christ, the old person of self has died and the new person in Christ has come alive. That's the meaning of baptism for people of all generations. We might have sinned mightily at one time, but now we are to be holy unto the Lord with all our heart. Anything else is treason.

DAY 100

Romans 6:4 *We were therefore buried with him through baptism into death in order that, just as Christ was raised from the dead through the glory of the Father, we too may live a new life.*

Symbols play a big part in our lives. In these days of computers and cell phones, the little icons, or avatars, hold the place of what we wish to convey to others, who we want to connect with, or even how we see ourselves. A raised fist of an African-American can symbolize black power. Holding up two fingers in the shape of a "V" can symbolize victory, as it did for Winston Churchill during World War II. Symbols are everywhere, and if a picture truly paints a thousand words, then modern symbols are giving that value a close run for its money.

In religious life symbols are important also. Universally people wear crosses, often not even knowing what that cross stands for. We see that same symbol on the top of church steeples, on emergency services, and certainly at the front of many sanctuaries. As Christians, we truly do cherish the old rugged cross.

Baptism is a comparable symbol. We know that water is just water and whether one is immersed in it, has it poured over their head, or is sprinkled with it, the idea is the same. That person has made a decision to change their life from following their own desires to a new life of following Christ. Actually, it is even more. It's a testimony that not only is their will involved in the experience, but that the very presence of Jesus Himself has transformed them, because He has entered their life in a real and personal way.

The symbolism of dying and being brought back to life goes along with our understanding of being born again. On the last page of his wonderful book, *Mere Christianity*, C.S. Lewis stated, "Nothing will ever be resurrected which has not first died." The idea echoes Jesus, who told Nicodemus in John, chapter three, "You must be born again." We are born into this world, we die to our selfish nature when confronted with Jesus, and then we are born again to new life in the Spirit. Baptism is the symbol for all that. All this is to the glory of the Father, who is working out His plan and building His Kingdom on earth as it is in heaven. He is doing it through the church His Son founded, and we who are baptized are a part of that church in Christ.

DAY 101

Romans 6:5 *If we have been united with him like this in his death, we will certainly also be united with him in his resurrection.*

In His high priestly prayer as recorded in John 17:21, Jesus prayed that His disciples would be made one with Him and with each other, as He was with the Father. That state of being united is key to understanding the Christian life on any level. All around the world brothers and sisters of many cultures, colors, backgrounds, and languages have borne witness of the oneness that Jesus prayed for coming into reality in their lives. We praise God for the unity of purpose that His Spirit binds us together in.

Here Paul is speaking of something a bit different though. He is not talking about being united with Him in life, but in death. And he is not referencing a time after we leave this world alone, but also the death that we experience when we are baptized into the faith. The ritual of baptism is every bit as much about death as it is about life, and we forget that at our own peril.

Baptism says that we have died to the person we used to be and have been made anew in the plan and purpose that God has for us. Too many times people think of baptism as just a nice ritual that goes along with church membership, but it is so much more than that. It's about being changed from darkness to light, from emptiness to fullness, and from a lack of direction to a purpose that supersedes all others.

This radical transformation is necessary not only for us to be equipped to carry out the mission of building Christ's Kingdom here on earth, but it also has to do with our oneness with Him for eternity. Jesus has given us the example of what we can expect as a result of our transformation and baptism. As He was bodily raised from the dead, someday we too will be raised up and presented to the Father as a member of the new heaven and earth that is being prepared. He was the first to be raised, and of that we have no doubt, but we also will be raised just as He was. It's exciting to even think about.

This is why Paul wanted the Romans, and us, to be sure of how it all works together. Our baptism is our declaration of faith in the work Christ is doing in us here and in the hereafter. Oneness in Him is how it all comes together. Baptism is more than a ritual. It is a rite of passage for believers.

DAY 102

Romans 6:6–7 *For we know that our old self was crucified with him so that the body of sin might be done away with, that we should no longer be slaves to sin—because anyone who has died has been freed from sin.*

Paul uses interesting terms here as he tries to describe what happens to the believer in Christ. What he calls "our old self" is our natural state that we lived in before Jesus made a difference in our life. The idea of being crucified is often thought of as being just a metaphor, but I really don't think that's what the apostle had in mind.

When Jesus spoke of His followers taking up their crosses and following Him (Luke 9:23), this is what He was speaking about. There is a part of us that literally dies when we surrender ourselves to the call of Christ. The selfish part of us passes away and what is left is what Jesus can use for His glory in the world. Sin has to come to an end so that real life can begin, because the two are completely incompatible. Sin can't abide with holiness any more than darkness can abide with light. This is because sin always enslaves us. It is never content with anything other than our total alienation from God, and that always takes us down the dark path of our destruction.

But because of the victory of Christ over the sin and the grave, we now can be set free from sin also. We too can eventually conquer the grave by His grace and power, but that will have to wait for a later time. Our freedom is not found waiting on the "other side" though. We can have freedom from the slavery of sin right here and now because of Jesus in us. We die to our selfish desires and come alive unto God in Christ. This is what real freedom and real life is all about.

There are so many people who try to live the Christian life while still under that hindering umbrella of sin. It's like trying to run a race with an iron ball and chain attached to our leg. The race is not successful and the pain of trying is all too real. Trying to live as a child of darkness and also as a child of light is never going to be successfully accomplished.

Are you struggling in your Christian walk? Maybe it's because you have not yet died to sin and been freed from its enslaving grasp. If so, then a full surrender to Jesus is in order today, so glorious freedom can be yours. This freedom is yours for the asking, right now!

DAY 103

Romans 6:8 *Now if we died with Christ, we believe that we will also live with him.*

By this time, we have pretty well gotten the picture that Paul was trying to paint concerning dying with Christ in baptism. Perhaps it will be helpful to consider what he meant by saying that we will also live with Christ. Is he referring to something of this world, something of heaven, or is he talking about something different altogether?

The answers to those questions are, well, yes. Living with Christ is about a daily walk with Him right now. Every person who has been baptized into the faith and has turned from their sinful existence, has a one-on-one communion with the Divine on a continuing basis. After all, Jesus did promise that He would come to us (John 14:18) and that He would remain with us until the end of the age (Matthew 28:20). He is as close as our next heartbeat and is never unable to hear our quietest prayer. He truly is the friend that sticks to us closer than a brother.

It is also true that after this life is over, we will move our address to the next level of living. We call that place heaven, or paradise, the city of gold, or name it by some other celestial title. A picture of this existence in given to us in Revelation, chapters 4-5, among others, and we see an atmosphere of praise, rest, and joy continually. Heaven is the bonus we have long been waiting for so that we can recover from all the experiences that weren't so good while we lived here on earth. I like to think of it as an extended vacation place, or a heavenly spa for ultimate renewal and restoration.

However, when the age comes to an end and time is recorded no more on this planet, then there will be a unifying of heaven and earth. It is what Jesus prayed for (Luke 11:2) and what He promised in Revelation, chapters 21-22.

During this present age, Christ is building His Kingdom through His church. In the age to come, we will have resurrected bodies and inhabit the Kingdom that has fully been restored, and Christ will reign over the nations of the new earth eternally (Matthew 19:28-30).

When we die to sin, we are raised with Christ, and we will be with Him eternally; now, in heaven, and in the new earth that is coming.

DAY 104

Romans 6:9–10 *For we know that since Christ was raised from the dead, he cannot die again; death no longer has mastery over him. The death he died, he died to sin once for all, but the life he lives, he lives to God.*

Paul brings up some interesting thoughts here. Throughout biblical history there have been people who have been raised from the dead. First, there was the widow of Zarephath's son who was raised to life by Elijah (I Kings 17:17–24). Then there was the Shunamite's son who was raised by Elisha (II Kings 4:20–37). II Kings 13:21 tells of a dead man who came back to life after his corpse touched Elisha's bones in the tomb.

In the New Testament there are three accounts of Jesus bringing people back to life, such as the widow of Nain's son (Luke 7:11–16), the twelve-year-old daughter of Jairus (Mark 5:35–43), and His friend Lazarus (John 11:1–44). Simon Peter raised a seamstress named Tabitha, or Dorcus (Acts 9:36–41), and Paul raised to life a young man named Eutychus, who fell asleep during his preaching and fell out of a third story window (Acts 20:7–14). Though this certainly isn't a common occurrence in the Bible, it happened enough times that each case deserved to be considered.

However, what Paul is referencing in these two verses is the fact that Jesus Himself was raised from the dead, but unlike all the other examples given in our holy text, He will never die again. All the people who were brought back to life in both the Old and New Testaments eventually went the way of all men and women and died again. Having more than one funeral for one person would be unusual, but no doubt that is the case.

Because the return to life in Jesus followed the death He died for our sins, He was not just revived, or resuscitated, He was resurrected. He died to conquer death for all and now His resurrection is a promise that we too shall be raised as He was. Someday there will be an empty tomb where the saints of God used to be as resurrection will happen on that final day and our bodies will be made new and eternal. And like the resurrection of Jesus, we too will be raised to die no more. Our new bodies will be immortal and we will live in the glory and presence of God forever.

This is bigger than what my finite mind can grasp, but I believe the Bible. Paul was announcing something wonderful, and it's all because of Jesus.

DAY 105

Romans 6:11–12 *In the same way, count yourselves dead to sin but alive to God in Christ Jesus. Therefore do not let sin reign in your mortal body so that you obey its evil desires.*

The idea of being dead to sin is an interesting one. Of course, how we understand its meaning, depends on what we understand sin to be. There are two main thoughts on this topic.

The Greek word for sin is *hamartia*, which literally interpreted means, *missing the mark*. In the pure literal sense of this idea is that anything short of absolute perfection is sin. It's like shooting arrows at a target and anything but dead center puts us in the sin category. This is the standard Calvinistic view of sin.

The other idea, of which John Wesley was famous for defining, is that sin should be understood as *a willful transgression against the known law of God*. Paul has made it clear in this book that we are only held accountable for what we know, so how can we sin if we don't know it is wrong? It may be wrong, but if we don't know it is wrong, why should we be judged guilty for committing that sin? This is the traditional Wesleyan view of sin.

How we interpret this three-letter word will determine how we understand what Paul is saying. If every infraction, intentional or unintentional, is sin, then how can he expect us not to let sin reign in our mortal bodies? None of us are perfect in actions in this world, so it would seem that Paul is asking the Romans—and us—to do something that is impossible for us to do. However, if we are forgiven and freed from the bondage of sin, then we are free also not to obey its desires.

There are many wonderful and good brothers and sisters in Christ who will come down on each side of this argument. Naturally, since I am a Wesley-Arminian in my theology, I am going to side with John Wesley on this. I know I will never be perfect in my actions, but I can be made perfect in my intentions. I believe it is the heart God judges and not what we don't understand.

We are called to be rid and done with the sin business. Living in complete surrender to Christ we can experience the path of victory, not defeat.

DAY 106

Romans 6:13–14 *Do not offer the parts of your body to sin, as instruments of wickedness, but rather offer yourselves to God, as those who have been brought from death to life; and offer the parts of your body to him as instruments of righteousness. For sin shall not be your master, because you are not under law, but under grace.*

It's pretty clear that Paul was writing these words to the church, his fellow Christians. They had found the way of salvation already and like many others, were learning what being a follower of Jesus really meant. We have 2000 years of reflection to consider how these words hit us, but our task is always to try to understand what the first readers were intended to glean from the writer.

Living free of the law and under grace is a wonderful and powerful way to live. When we are bound to the law, we are bound to a list of rules that must be kept without any exception always. Freedom from the law gives us options, and those options mean choices, for God doesn't want us to be robots, but individuals who love and serve Him because we want to, not because we have to.

When we are presented with true options, it is necessary then for us to choose. No longer can we look to a list of rules to govern our behavior because we are now free and can make up our own minds about how best to serve the Lord.

This is why Paul admonishes the Romans not to offer their bodies as means of sin. When we are in Christ, our choice needs to always take into consideration what would be pleasing to our Master. When we were in sin, we had no choice but to sin, but now in Christ we can choose to walk in the light He provides for us, or to return to shades of darkness.

It's a bit like growing up. When we lived at home with our parents, we had to do what they told us to do, and many choices were made for us. But when we moved out on our own, we had to make our own way. We were responsible for what we ate, when we went to bed, when we got up, or whether or not we went to work. Being an adult requires making choices. Likewise, in Christ we make choices, but we are to choose His way if we want to find true freedom, not the way of self and sin. What we have in Him is liberty, so we no longer play with the ways of sin. The benefits are for the here and now, and for the hereafter.

DAY 107

Romans 6:15 *What then? Shall we sin because we are not under law but under grace? By no means!*

Because it is not rational to many, there are some people who just don't understand Christianity. Coming into a relationship with Christ is not only a union of a human with a divine being, but there is a transformation of the human when such a joining occurs. Christ remains the same, but the human is altered completely. There is a changing of desire, a changing of world view, a changing of attitude, and a changing of eternal destiny. With all this change that is going on, how is it possible that some could think that our choices and actions don't have to change as well?

Unfortunately, many people have the idea that once they have made a public confession to follow Christ, repented of their previous sins, and been baptized into the faith, that life can then go on with business as usual. The public rituals have been observed, so now all the bases are covered, and they can just live in any manner that suits them.

To this kind of thinking, Paul cries out, "Absolutely not!" The grace that covers us and brings about our salvation is not like gravy that covers a biscuit. It is transformative and regenerates what was dead into a new life. Things can't remain the same because we who are in Christ are new creatures. We are no longer the people who served self and sin, for now we are remade into the image of Jesus. Our task and mission in life is to represent Him to the world and we can't do that by living in the gutter of the old life we left.

To live otherwise, but in the power of the Spirit and as a reflection of God in Christ, is to not be changed at all. Living like the world when we are citizens of the Kingdom is like putting lipstick on a pig. It may fancy it up a little, but it's still a pig. A person in Christ has been freed and no longer bears the stain of the sinful life.

What this means for us today is that our goal in life should be to live without sin, without doing anything that would put our transformation in a bad light or our Savior in a compromising situation. Grace is free, but it is not cheap. It is the power that will eventually transform the world. This is the Kingdom that is coming through the Church Christ is building.

DAY 108

Romans 6:16 *Don't you know that when you offer yourselves to someone to obey him as slaves, you are slaves to the one whom you obey—whether slaves to sin, which leads to death, or to obedience, which leads to righteousness.*

This whole concept of slavery has taken on new dimensions of meaning in the twenty-first century. Human trafficking around the world is a scourge that has been brought to light, and in places where slavery has abounded in centuries gone by, there's a lot of rethinking about its present-day impact.

However, slavery has been around as long as there have been people. Not only have humans taken advantage of those whom they conquered in battle or through capture, but since the Garden of Eden sin has been enslaving people of all races, languages, and cultures.

It is this slavery that Paul is addressing in this verse. Most people don't think of sin as enslavement. It sure isn't portrayed that way on the movie screens and television. People who cheat on their spouses and get away with it are excused, while couples who have sex outside of marriage are considered as normal behavior. Usually, a bar scene is one of laughter and good-natured buddies hanging out together and having a great time.

The problem is that those scenes only show a small portion of the complete picture. It isn't glamorous to see how family units are destroyed, how children are separated from their parents, how drunk drivers kill and maim the innocent, how hospitals deal with lung cancer and heart disease patients who have forsaken their health for a life of "good times."

Sin always has consequences because sin is rebellion against God, the ultimate authority for our lives. The wages of sin are not only death, but a ball and chain of slavery that gives the slave no choice but to obey.

Jesus came so that we might be freed from the slavery of sin and have real choices with our lives. Righteousness is a possibility with Christ and nowhere else. Goodness, wholesomeness, and real freedom is only through the way of the cross. Obedience to the King of kings provides the answer to life's problems because the One who made us knows what we need to achieve all that is best for us. Once again, we see Jesus is the answer.

DAY 109

Romans 6:17 *But thanks be to God that, though you used to be slaves to sin, you wholeheartedly obeyed the form of teaching to which you were entrusted.*

At the source of all good things is God. It is appropriate that the Apostle Paul recognizes that fact as he proclaims deliverance for those who used to be slaves, as converts now to a life of freedom in Jesus Christ. There are three things he especially credits to our Lord.

First, it is God who caused the believers to be in a state of "used to be." The old gospel song, "Just as I am," tells the story of how anyone can come to Christ at any time. However, the gospel story doesn't leave us in the state in which we came. Jesus frees us from our slavery to sin and makes us new creatures as we are born again by His Holy Spirit. These Romans had been slaves to their dark nature but were no more.

It is also important to notice that God enabled the new believers to be able to "wholeheartedly obey." This is no small thing. God makes us new creatures for us to be able to obey new truth that we hadn't seen before. The evil powers of the world continually hammer away at mankind, trying to get them to think that darkness is light and bad is good. Through our spiritual transformation God gives us the ability to see truth for what it is and to be blinded to it no more.

Finally, this passage tells us that God has not only redeemed and enlightened those whom He transforms, but then He puts His trust in them. Do you realize this truth? God trusts us. He trusts us with the words of life and believes in us enough to allow us to be His representatives and ambassadors to the whole world. How great is the love of God for His creation and for His church!

Paul is full of thanks to God for these things and we should be too. We have received blessing upon blessing and can know the hand of the Divine on our lives as we sense His breath upon our actions. We, like the Roman believers, were once slaves, but we have been redeemed. We were once ignorant of the truth, but we have been taught by God's Spirit the right and proper way to live. We, who are unworthy, have been placed in a situation of trust by the King. Certainly, we should be thankful as well!

DAY 110

Romans 6:18 *You have been set free from sin and have become slaves to righteousness.*

The Christian life is full of paradoxes and Paul uses a big one here. After speaking about the freedom that comes from being released from sin's hold on a person's life, he turns right around and declares that slavery is what is waiting on the other side of that change. It's an interesting play on words, but the meaning should be crystal clear.

Really, he paints two pictures for us. The first one is of a person who is bound by all the habits that destroy his or her life. The picture is one of sexual immorality, greed, hate, idolatry, and continual strife. The slavery is complete, for there is no way that freedom can be found without help.

That help comes from Jesus the Messiah, who not only forgives the sins of one's past, but then regenerates life within the individual, breaks the bonds of misery, and sentences that same person to a lifetime in His care. This picture is totally different from the first, however. Where once slavery meant despair and loss, this new kind of slavery is to love, joy, peace, companionship, purpose, and hope. It is a whole new relationship that sets the prisoner free, but in exchange gives life a new meaning and direction.

Now, if being a slave to righteousness brings about that kind of bondage, well then, sign me up. Giving up all the things that were painful and bad for me to enjoy all the things that provide life and joy for me is a pretty good exchange. Who in their right mind wouldn't jump at the chance to be slave to such a wonderful life?

It is true, though, that some people choose to stay in the first form of slavery instead of choosing the second. Some prefer the pain and misery of sin instead of the freedom, joy, and purpose of righteousness. We are all free agents and can make whatever choice we decide upon. However, the choice of the first is death and the second is life. There is no other option for us to consider.

For one, I am thankful that I entered bondage in Christ long ago. There were, and are, many other choices that I could have made, but through God's grace I was able to choose the best. Jesus is the best choice always.

DAY 111

Romans 6:19 *I put this in human terms because you are weak in your natural selves. Just as you used to offer the parts of your body in slavery to impurity and to ever-increasing wickedness, so now offer them in slavery to righteousness leading to holiness.*

Paul really nailed it when he stated that we are weak in our natural selves. Not only is this true for all people in various situations, but we don't outgrow weakness as we get older. If anything, our strength fades as time takes its toll on us.

But in the context of Paul's argument, he lets the Romans, and us, know that without Christ as Lord we are slaves to our basest desires throughout our life. Self-discipline can go a long way in helping us establish and maintain a moral existence, but even then, when left on our own, we are slaves. Sin takes a hold on us when we enter this world and will not be conquered until it is confronted with a stronger power.

That power is found in the person of Jesus the Messiah. Where once we lived in sin and were on a spiral downwards to death because of the destructive nature that possessed us, in Christ we found the bonds of sin broken and a freedom to escape the terrible fate that awaited us. Not only are we freed by Christ from the downward drag, but like a rebound we can now move heavenward as we develop in righteousness and pursue the path of holiness.

Holiness is not a second dose of something we already had. Holiness is our total encounter with God. It encompasses prevenient grace, the transforming grace of being born again in initial sanctification, as well as the crisis and continuing development in righteousness by entire sanctification. Absolute perfection is out of our reach in this world, but our continual growth in grace is not only possible, but a reality as we develop into the likeness of God.

Paul shared wonderful news with the church at Rome so many years ago. Sin enslaves, but the Spirit of Christ sets us free. Once we were destined to death, but in the Master's hands we have our sights set on higher things in this world and in the world to come. Whom the Son sets free is free indeed. Thanks be to God!

DAY 112

Romans 6:20 *When you were slaves to sin, you were free from the control of righteousness.*

I remember sitting in a hospital room with my grandfather before he passed away. He was in his late seventies and decades of smoking had caused a state of emphysema that would eventually take his life. My grandfather, at that time, had slipped into a deep sleep and really didn't have much of an awareness of what was going on around him or who was in the room. But as I watched him, I saw him continually lift his fingers to his mouth as if he were smoking. The many years of a bad habit still hung on, though tobacco was nowhere to be found in the room.

Because I have spent the majority of my life in some form of ministry, I have made countless trips to hospitals when people have overdosed on drugs, had car wrecks because of alcohol, and suffered greatly when sin's chains took their toll. I have performed many dozens of funerals over the course of my life, and too many times a life was lost because the wages of sin had strangled the life from a victim.

You see, when we live in sin, we don't have a choice to do otherwise. One may think, "Well, tomorrow I'll do better." Or they may say, "I've learned my lesson and I'm never going down that path again." This is just wishful thinking, however. No one breaks from sin until Jesus sets them free. Twelve-step programs won't do it. Positive thinking won't do it. Going to a counselor or therapist won't do what surrender to the will of God can do. I'm not saying that counseling programs and the like aren't helpful, but they are only a means to an end. Freedom, true freedom, is found only in the person of Jesus Christ. He is still the only way that a person can be rid of the chains of sin and death once and for all.

I know this is not a popular stance. In our world we are plagued with problems of racism, human trafficking, war, riots, and physical abuse. Man will never solve these problems on his own, for only a complete transformation of one's mind and heart can do that, and only Jesus can make such a transformation possible.

There is a new world coming and it is closer every day, but until then, we get ready by allowing Christ to free us from what plagues us here and now.

DAY 113

Romans 6:21 *What benefit did you reap at that time from the things you are now ashamed of? Those things result in death.*

We all have a past. No doubt there is not a reasoning person alive who has not done something in their earlier days that was less than perfect and something of which they would rather not be reminded. We are all human and being a human means we have feet of clay, and are creatures born with a sinful nature.

The difference between those who are in Christ and those who are not, is in the fact that we who are in Christ know that our misdeeds displease God and cause Him grief. Because we are in such holy company, causing God to not look favorably on our actions, brings waves of remorse and sorrow to our hearts.

A person who has not given our heavenly Father the allegiance He is due, sees things differently. For that person, sin is enticing, even fun, and the more one can get away with wrongdoing seems like success. However, they don't realize they have fallen for the enemy's tricks and are ensnared in his trap of death.

It's interesting to me that Paul can say these things about the people in the church at Rome even though he has never met most of them face to face. He apparently knew human nature very well though. The things the people of the world brag about are often the very things that bring shame to a person who has seen the error of his or her sinful ways.

There is an old saying in the news media game: "If it bleeds, it leads." In other words, the worse things are to present, they are the very things that will entice society's interest more quickly and deeply. This is why we hear so much bad news over the internet via social media and through our traditional sources of information. Bad news spreads rapidly and that is what makes money for information distributors.

As children of light, we glory in the things of goodness, but blush over the times we have disappointed our Savior. The ways of the world are not glorious, but shameful. They do not profit us but bind us. Only through full surrender to a loving God can we ever hold up our heads.

DAY 114

Romans 6:22 *But now that you have been set free from sin and have become slaves to God, the benefit you reap leads to holiness, and the result is eternal life.*

There are times when some people drift through life without knowing what they are doing. This often comes because they have no goals, no plans, and no purpose for their current actions, let alone for their future. If the Apostle Paul is correct in his assessment here, then this is because life without God is a life that is bound by sin, and a sinful life cannot control its own destiny. When a person is bound by sin, they are a slave to sin, and they will do whatever sin tempts them to do.

The message of the gospel is that a life that has been freed by the power of God is now truly free to leave the actions of sin behind. There are too many people who misunderstand this truth. Freedom from the bonds of sin's slavery means we are to leave the ways of sin behind, not dabble in it whenever temptation rears its head. Christ frees us from sin so that we will not choose sin any longer.

Once a person has been freed, then a new walk along the path of righteousness is established. This path is not a way of aimless wandering, however, because God has a purpose and plan for our lives, and that plan is to make us holy as He is holy. He created us for His own good pleasure, and He wants to have fellowship with us, so He is working in our lives to perfect the new life we have received through His grace.

Holiness is not a station upon which we arrive when we begin our walk with Christ. Holiness is the journey itself, with Jesus as our tour guide, sustainer, and equipment provider. He has shown us how to live and we have His example in the Bible to lay out that pattern for us. His continual presence guides us along the journey to be reformed into His image so that we can help remake our world for good to the glory of the Father.

The end result of it all is eternal life in His presence. That eternal life as a kingdom child begins the moment we step on the highway of holiness and will never end. If we are in Christ, our eternal life has begun and will continue throughout our days in this world and all through the next. Thanks be to God forever and ever, amen!

DAY 115

Romans 6:23 *For the wages of sin is death, but the gift of God is eternal life in Christ Jesus our Lord.*

This verse reminds me of an Old Testament passage where Moses lays out the choices for the people of Israel as they journeyed from Egypt to the Promised Land (Deuteronomy 30:15–20). They were given a choice, just as we are now, between the way that leads to life and the way that leads to death. Unfortunately, then, just as it is now, there are those who are made aware of the choice and choose poorly anyway. Their destiny is on their own heads.

Our Father never intends for anyone to perish. He has done what He can do to set us on the right path and continues to work on our behalf to help us make choices wisely. He even helps us correct our course when we go astray, for He wants everyone to have eternal life through His Son.

The reality is, however, that some people have set their hearts against walking on the highway of holiness, and of course, with every choice we make in life there are consequences for that choice. It's popular these days to think otherwise, but that's just denying reality. Just as surely as this verse promises eternal life in Christ, it also promises that the way of sin leads to death. Not death sometimes, but always. There is no way to escape the judgment that falls on the one who rebels against God's offer of life. It's like Adam and Eve in the Garden of Eden. When God told them that they would die for eating of the forbidden fruit, they didn't drop over dead on the spot, but they did die, and as a result, death comes to all people eventually.

God provides the only antidote to the problem of sin. These bodies we have will eventually come to an end in this world, and our spirit will be with God. But there is coming a resurrection day when the graves will be opened and our bodies will be raised to life again, but to a life that will never end. That is what the Jewish religion teaches and what Christianity confirms. The difference between the two religions is that Christianity recognizes that the Messiah has already come in the person of Jesus and that the first of the resurrections has already taken place by Him.

It's this simple. The way of sin brings death. The way of Jesus brings life. It's not a hard choice, but one that every person must make.

DAY 116

Romans 7:1-3 *Do you not know, brothers—for I am speaking to men who know the law—that the law has authority over a man only as long as he lives? For example, by law a married woman is bound to her husband as long as he is alive, but if her husband dies, she is released from the law of marriage. So then, if she marries another man while her husband is still alive, she is called an adulteress. But if her husband dies, she is released from that law and is not an adulteress, even though she marries another man.*

The phrase, "the long arm of the law," is usually used in governmental circles and in American society refers to the extended reach of the police. When Paul speaks of the law, however, he is referencing the Jewish Law that was given to Moses by God on Mount Sinai. Of course, the Jewish scribes and lawyers had been making interpretations concerning that law for over a thousand years by the time Paul came along, but there is one truth that never changes. When you are dead, the law no longer has any effect or jurisdiction over you.

We all know of cases like the one he mentions in this passage. We know of men and women who have lost their spouse to death and have later remarried. No one is accusing them of doing something wrong, because death changes everything. Even though taxes may be due when someone dies, the dead never have to worry about paying them.

If this is true with civil law, how much more is it so with the spiritual law that reigns over our actions, thoughts, and habits. Paul isn't speaking about marriage here, per se. This is only an illustration to clarify his point. What he really is saying deals with sin and its hold on our lives. Once we have died to sin and come alive unto God, the law of sin and death no longer has any jurisdiction over our lives. We are free to live in harmony with our new love, Jesus Christ, in a new place, the Kingdom of God.

It is amazing to me that so many people who have committed their lives to Christ still don't understand this. We are not to be sinning Christians! We are to be Christians that have been freed from sin. We have died to sin and live only to the Lord. The sin that bound us has lost its charm and its hold over us, and we are free to love as the Spirit of God enables us. In baptism we had our funeral to our sinful state and now we live as new creatures.

DAY 117

Romans 7:4 *So, my brothers, you also died to the law through the body of Christ, that you might belong to another, to him who was raised from the dead, in order that we might bear fruit to God.*

The point Paul is making repeatedly has to do with ownership. To whom do you belong? Do you belong to the powers of darkness and sin, or do you belong to God through your relationship with Jesus the Messiah? Those who continue to live in a state where sin dictates the way that they act, belong to the flesh, or sin. Those who live in the freedom and joy of the Spirit, not participating in the works of rebellion and sin, belong to God. Ownership is everything in spiritual matters.

Along the same line is the matter of bearing fruit. In his letter to the Galatians Paul makes the matter of fruit bearing very clear. "The acts of the sinful nature are obvious: sexual immorality, impurity and debauchery; idolatry and witchcraft; hatred, discord, jealousy, fits of rage, selfish ambition, dissensions, factions and envy; drunkenness, orgies, and the like. I warn you, as I did before, that those who live like this will not inherit the kingdom of God" (Galatians 5:19-21).

Just as clear is the fruit of the Spirit, listed in the same chapter. "But the fruit of the Spirit is love, joy, peace, patience, kindness, goodness, faithfulness, gentleness and self-control. Against such things there is no law" (Galatians 5:22–23).

Our job is to "bear fruit to God," not be involved in acts of darkness and rebellion against Him. The difference between the two areas of fruit-bearing he lists are stark and no clear-thinking person should have any doubt about what is intended. Paul does us a great service here.

Bearing fruit to God is living in such a way that people notice our lifestyle and recognize the work of God in us by our actions and give God the credit for them. That is how we glorify God.

As has been said by many before me, we can be a part of the problems in our world, or we can be a part of the solutions. Because we have been born again by the Spirit of God and have been raised to a new level of living by our regeneration, we are to live to bring God glory. Anything else is sin.

DAY 118

Romans 7:5–6 *For when we were controlled by the sinful nature, the sinful passions aroused by the law were at work in our bodies, so that we bore the fruit for death. But now, by dying to what once bound us, we have been released from the law so that we serve in the new way of the Spirit, and not in the old way of the written code.*

Nobody likes to be controlled. No one wants to feel like they are a puppet whose movements are operated by someone else. We like to be free, and we want to feel like we are the masters of our own destinies.

The problem that Paul points out here is that freedom is not obtained by just declaring we are free. Regardless of the determination of a person or even the mind games one can play on oneself, freedom is only obtained through someone's sacrifice.

When we see the results of sinful actions that hurt innocent people and destroy what someone else has worked to build up, we can remember that those who protest and clamor for freedom can never be free without someone granting that freedom. The sinful nature is a powerful force that can control our bodies all the way from a point of understanding to the grave—and that is where sin always leads—to the grave.

Paul offers a different path, however, through Jesus the Christ. Instead of mindlessly and often unknowingly being controlled by sin's nature, we can be truly free by allowing the Spirit of God through Jesus to enter our lives, break the bonds of our nature, and give us life instead of death. Actually, there is still death involved, but when one comes to Christ we die to self and sin so that we may be free to live in such a way that leads to joy, peace, and righteousness. Instead of being part of the problems of our world, we become part of its solutions.

The law makes us aware of our sinfulness, then the Spirit cleanses us and makes us able to live without sin. We can never break the chains of the dark world on our own, but we don't have to. Jesus has already done that for us on the cross at Calvary. We just need to believe in His work done on our behalf, surrender our will to Him, and allow Him to set us free. There is no other answer for the problems of rebellion and death. Jesus is the chain-breaker who allows control back into the hands of the One who loves us.

DAY 119

Romans 7:7 What shall we say, then? Is the law sin? Certainly not! Indeed I would not have known what sin was except through the law. For I would not have known what coveting really was if the law had not said, "Do not covet."

I'm pretty much addicted to the cruise control on my car. Whether I'm in town where the speed limit is twenty-five miles per hour or on the Interstate System where the speed limit is seventy or seventy-five, I set my cruise on whatever the upper limit is. It is very rare to find me driving without using the cruise control.

Why do I do that? Because over the course of my driving days I have had five speeding tickets. But in all honesty, in every one of those incidents I was completely unaware that I was speeding until I saw the flashing lights of the police car. The long arm of the law didn't care about my ignorance in any of those situations, and I have paid hundreds of dollars in fines as a result. Therefore, these days I use my cruise control wherever possible so that such an event won't happen again.

Paul didn't drive a car, but he did understand much about the law and what it meant to those under its rule. The law as given to Moses as the means by which the children of Israel understood what God expected from them. The other nations had to stumble along and find out the hard way how their pagan beliefs led to death. Israel was let in on the secret to life. They would eventually be expected to pass that secret along, but that's a totally different issue. The point that Paul makes here is that they became aware of right and wrong only as they understood what the law was revealing to them.

Some may ask, "Well, if we are not guilty when we don't know, why don't we live in ignorance or at least let others live in ignorance? That way God won't hold their sins against them!" The problem with that way of thinking is that ignorance doesn't diminish the grief, destruction, pain, and death that sin brings about. We share because we care. We share because we have been given the secret to life and we want others to know the truth also.

If people didn't know that fire would burn them, wouldn't we want to let them know about the pain burns cause? The law informs so that we can be protected. God cares about us all just that much!

DAY 120

Romans 7:8 *But sin, seizing the opportunity afforded by the commandment produced in me every kind of covetous desire. For apart from law, sin is dead.*

It seems like the older I get, the more of a sweet tooth I have. Chocolate has a hold on me more than it used to, and if someone offers me a piece of cherry pie, my resistance to it crashes. Don't even get me started on ice cream. There's no doubt about it, I have a very active sweet tooth.

This creates a problem for me in more than a couple of areas. First, I know that if I take in more calories than I burn up, I will gain weight that I don't need. Second, excess weight not only makes my clothes shrink, but my health suffers as well. I also have to consider how my health issues affect those around me who might have to take care of me if I get sick. Oh, the travesty of a sweet tooth.

Like all analogies, this comparison to what Paul is talking about has its flaws, but I hope it does help us to see a little more clearly how theology is very practical. Where I speak of a sweet tooth, Paul is referring to sin's hold on us. Because I know the dangers of eating sweet things, it becomes a struggle to stay away from them because they taste so good. Because Paul shows the law's commandment against sin, the temptations of sin show up as a struggle because, let's face it, sin can be fun at the time of the action. If it wasn't attractive and enjoyable, people wouldn't be drawn toward it.

Paul is beginning to build a case here that he will grow in the coming verses. The commandment exposes sin, but also our attraction to it. It's like the dieter with a box a candy saying, "Well, one little piece won't hurt me." Sin was a piece of fruit in the Garden of Eden but look at where we are now.

If we didn't know that too many calories were bad for us and that sugar was bad for our teeth, we could happily enjoy another piece of cake without a thought. But because we do know the facts, we are conflicted when tempted. If we didn't know sin was forbidden, we wouldn't feel guilty when we give in to desire. It is knowledge that creates the struggle. If only there were some solution to this problem! That is Paul's cry, but in verses yet to come we will find that there is. Thanks be to God. He does provide a remedy as we trust in Him. God never leaves us to face sin alone.

DAY 121

Romans 7:9–11 *Once I was alive apart from law; but when the commandment came, sin sprang to life and I died. I found that the very commandment that was intended to bring life actually brought death. For sin, seizing the opportunity afforded by the commandment put me to death.*

I think many of us can identify with what Paul is saying here. We are winding our way through life, having a great time, doing what we want, putting ourselves in the best light possible, and really not considering the impact of living for ourselves instead of living for God. Then something happens that snaps us to reality and makes us face the consequences that has resulted from our careless lifestyle. At this point we feel guilt. We feel remorse. We may even feel like we would just like to die, depending on the seriousness of what has transpired.

What produces that guilt? It comes from an awareness that we have done wrong. It may come from a practical joke that turned out not to be so funny. It may be an utter act of rebellion or a break in a relationship with someone we cared about. We don't like the feeling and we want to get rid of it, but it only comes about when we realize we have done something wrong.

This is what Paul is talking about. It was the law, the commandments, that made him aware of "thou shalt not!" When the reality of his sin was confronted, he had no excuse and the thing that he once thought was fun was then a source of pain. Sin produces guilt only when we realize that it is sin, but when that realization comes, it comes on us like a tidal wave.

We used to call this feeling conviction. Do you remember conviction? That time when the Holy Spirit made us aware of God's presence near us and we felt so unworthy to stand before Him. I know the feeling of conviction very well, for to this day the Spirit of God chastises me if I do something that I know I shouldn't do. It's a part of the check and balance system that God places in the life of a believer, but it is also the initial impacting agent when we are confronted with our sin before our repentance.

The gospel is good news, but to get to the good there must first be a dealing with the sin that has been made known to us, and that is always painful. Sin beats us up continually and drags us lower until it is finally resolved in Jesus. Thank God there is relief for conviction, but it is only through Christ alone.

DAY 122

Romans 7:12 *So then, the law is holy, and the commandment is holy, righteous and good.*

It's no surprise for most of us to understand that God is good. Though some may not understand God's ways and turn bitter against Him, most clear-thinking people who know anything about Him at all would agree, He is good.

Have you ever given any thought to the idea of what kind of situation we would be in if God wasn't good? Just imagine Him with unlimited power, presence, and knowledge, and only concerned about making us His toys to be used for His own pleasure. It's too frightening to even contemplate.

Because God is good, He gave Moses His law so that His creation could understand what is expected of us. Without some kind of divine guidance mankind would wander forever trying to figure Him out. That's what all the other religions of the world do. But God gave us instructions that were not only clear, but good for us. There are four that have to do with our relationship with Him, and six that have to do with our relationships with each other. He wants the best for everyone who ever set foot on this planet.

When Paul tells us that the commandments of God are holy and righteous, he is letting us know that we can't do without them. We need guidelines. We need to know how we can please the Lord, and we need to know how to get along with each other. We need a holy path to keep us going the right way.

There is no way to separate the three attributes of the commandment listed, namely holiness, righteousness, and goodness, from God. The commandment is all of these things because it comes from God and He is all of those things.

What we need to remember is the theme that Paul is pursuing in this passage of scripture. He is acknowledging the validity of the law and the lack of his own personal character. He is building a case to show how helpless we all are when we try to be holy, righteous, and good on our own. It's obvious that we fail miserably and need help to put us right. This is where the law comes in. We just have to follow as God leads.

DAY 123

Romans 7:13 *Did that which is good, then, become death to me? By no means! But in order that sin might be recognized as sin, it produced death in me through what was good, so that through the commandment sin might become utterly sinful.*

Do you ever have trouble recognizing what sin is? It's actually a good question because so many people have so many different ideas about what sin is, or if it even exists at all. After all, some may say, "What is sin for you may not be sin for me." Some Christians do things that other Christians think are sinful, but each group still claims to follow Christ.

For Paul, sin was recognized by comparing the action to what God's commandments had revealed. Therefore, stealing was a sin. Adultery was a sin. Coveting was a sin, etc. When he was tempted to break one of the commandments, conviction from the Holy Spirit set in and caused him to recognize that the action or attitude was wrong.

What Paul reveals here is something that many Christians have forgotten, or neglected. The Ten Commandments still are valid for holy living. If they were not, then God would not have given them to Moses in the first place, for God never changes. Jesus said they were important, in fact, indestructible. They will be around when everything else has passed.

The reason they are so valid and important is that they define what God wants us to do or not do. Having no other gods before Him is where they begin and that one in itself should bring conviction to a whole host of people. The problem is that we have gotten so used to putting our own pleasures, our own wants, our own family, and our own way of doing things before God that we overlook the fact that He wants everything about our lives to begin with Him.

The Commandments are good because they bring pain when they are broken so that we will know what not to do again. They bring joy when they are fulfilled because in their wisdom, we find what pleases God. We overlook the Commandments to our own peril. They show sin for what it is and give boundaries by which we can live. No pain, no gain is how the slogan goes. For Paul, no law, no sin, but without knowing what sin is, we are destined to a life of pain without the benefit of relief.

DAY 124

Romans 7:14–15 *We know that the law is spiritual; but I am unspiritual, sold as a slave to sin. I do not understand what I do. For what I want to do I do not do, but what I hate I do.*

Here Paul begins to unravel the complex issue of sin and how it affects mankind. We are born into this world as slaves to sin. We are controlled by what affects "us" and have little concern for the needs of those around us. A baby that is hungry or wet will cry and keep its parents awake at night until its needs are met. The baby doesn't care that the parents may have worked a twelve-hour shift and are exhausted. It doesn't care if the parent is hungry, or even sick. The baby wants its needs to be satisfied above all other matters.

As we grow up this self-interest only intensifies. It is possible through correct child training to teach principles of discipline that may cause the child not to voice his or her interests, but they are there, nonetheless. Until cleansed from the nature of sin and selfishness, we will continue to long to be first in all things that touch our lives. When we see rioters in the streets who are burning someone else's property and looting stores, we are seeing this played out on a larger stage. Sin wants what it wants and will destroy others in order to get its own way.

Paul recognizes that the Law of Moses, given by God, puts a damper on such things. The law says to not bear false witness, but the temptation to do so is so strong if it gratifies and protects the self. We may not want to covet our neighbor's possessions, but when sin rules we have no control. The lust of adultery beacons to the human urge for self-satisfying sex, and even if the urge is not acted upon, the temptation can be very powerful. This is why Jesus said that lusting after another person is just the same as sin (Matthew 5:28). The desire is there, and the selfish "me" wants that urge satisfied.

So, the struggle to do right goes on. What the law says not to do, self wants to do. The good that self wants to do, it is unable to do. The self is confused, frustrated, and constantly in turmoil and conflict. The situation seems hopeless. There is an answer to this problem, but we will have to read on to find it. For now, we must just remember that only through Jesus will we ever find that answer.

DAY 125

Romans 7:16–18 *And if I do what I do not want to do I agree that the law is good. As it is, it is no longer I myself who do it, but it is sin living in me. I know that nothing good lives in me, that is, in my sinful nature. For I have the desire to do what is good, but I cannot carry it out.*

One of the main problems with people trying to be religious, or even trying to live as a Christian, is found in the act of trying. No doubt, effort may be involved to accomplish anything we do, but unless the "want to" is changed, not much else is changed either.

If we come to Christ with our pre-set agendas on how we think a Christian ought to live, then we are most likely in for a rude awakening. Christian living isn't about nice people telling other people how to be nicer. Living as a Christian means going through a radical transformation by the power of God's Holy Spirit and there is nothing ordinary about that experience. We move from death to life, and from what we were into a new creation. Our desires are transformed, or in other words, our "want to" changes.

You see, as long as we want to have our own way, want to run our own show, want to keep our same habits and lifestyle that led us in the way of unrighteousness, we will do so. We usually do what we want to do. If church attendance, Bible reading, and prayer are things that we would rather avoid, then we will probably do just that. If hating our neighbor, cheating to get ahead, and lying to excuse our behavior is still a part of our lifestyle, then it is unlikely that any real change has happened. Salvation is not about a relative change, but a real change.

There will be the work of discipline along the way for any true believer, for like a baby who is born, a person who is born again has to grow and mature. But if we cling to our sinful nature, it means that what was supposed to happen, didn't happen, and we are still living in our sins.

The person Paul is describing in this passage is a person that has not yet had his "want to" changed. Only a true touch from the Master's hand can do that and no imitations are accepted. Until that happens and our rights are given over to Jesus, then we will continue to struggle and often fail in our walk as a Christian. Only by fully surrendering to Jesus can our desires be changed into what He wants them to be.

DAY 126

Romans 7:19–20 *For what I do is not the good I want to do; no, the evil I do not want to do—this I keep on doing. Now if I do what I do not want to do, it is no long I who do it, but it is sin living in me that does it.*

This verse makes very clear the point that Paul has been trying to make in the previous verses. Unless the sin that ravages our lives is dealt with and destroyed, we will live in submission to it for as long as we live. Outside of complete victory through Jesus, we have no hope to win the battle against it.

An incomplete, but perhaps clarifying analogy would be to compare sin to gluttony. Anyone who has ever fought the fight with trying to lose weight knows that the battle of the bulge is something that is not easily won. We know we should exercise, eat mainly fruits and vegetables, and be very consistent in this endeavor if we are going to be successful. However, those donuts just look so good, and fast food is so much easier to afford, especially when our budget is limited. We want to lose weight. We know how to do it, but it just seems like a continual battle that many find themselves losing.

Sin is like that. Going our own way instead of God's way is so enticing when all the world seems to glamorize the dens of iniquity. Sensual pleasures are so attractive, our peers' influence is so strong, and opportunities are so available. No wonder so many succumb to sin's influences. Lying seems to be the opportunity to get away with something that we did that was wrong. Stealing is much easier than working for what we want, and the list goes on and on. We are mastered by our desires when we don't put those desires on the altar of surrender before Christ.

Paul speaks here as one who is in anguish. He shows the futility of will power and determination against the enemy of our soul. We will never be victorious over the traps that destroy us on our own.

Thankfully, Jesus can free us from this dilemma of a perpetual cycle of sin, repentance, and sinning again. Where we are weak, He is strong. Where our will power breaks down, He is there to energize us. He is able to cleanse us completely from this yo-yo of perpetual sinning and backsliding as we try to establish our walk with Him. He alone holds the keys to our victory, and He alone will be willing to truly set us free.

DAY 127

Romans 7:21–23 *So I find this law at work: When I want to do good, evil is right there with me. For in my inner being I delight in God's law; but I see another law at work in the members of my body, waging war against the law of my mind and making me a prisoner of the law of sin at work within my members.*

We are back to the issue of the law again. In fact, Paul is referencing two laws. There is God's law, which is the law of righteousness, and the law of the flesh that is emboldened by devilish influences.

One key idea in these verses is found in that the inner being delights in God's law, but the opposing law dominates and doesn't allow the joy to last. The battle for the mind and the body is continually a problem as the desire for good and the desire for evil fight for control.

Does this sound familiar? For so many people who are attempting to live the Christian life in their own strength, this is a daily experience. The story repeats itself in a multitude of lives as people want to serve God, but the temptations around them don't allow them to have peace. They constantly struggle to stay spiritually victorious because the walk with Christ just seems too difficult for them.

Paul has been beating this drum for several verses, building a case that describes the problem of man and sin's effect on him. It's as though the person who has been freed from sin's hold by grace has become a prisoner again by the very forces that formerly held rule. The words "evil," "law," "war," and "prisoner," that Paul uses here are not just arbitrary terms. They are describing something that is far too common for far too many Christians. These are examples of Christians who are trying to live a holy life under their own power rather than relying on the Holy Spirit to free them completely.

It is a fact that we will be possessed by our desires. If the desires are still tied to the paths of rebellion that brought bondage in the first place, then the result will be that our spiritual walk will be up and down like a yo-yo. Until the break is made, and Christ is Lord over all areas of our life, then we will continually struggle to find joy and freedom in our daily walk. There surely must be a better way for the Christian than this life of conflict. The following verses will explain that yes, there truly is a better way.

DAY 128

Romans 7:24–25 *What a wretched man I am! Who will rescue me from this body of death? Thanks be to God—through Jesus Christ our Lord! So then, I myself in my mind am a slave to God's law, but in the sinful nature a slave to the law of sin.*

This is what we have been waiting for since Paul began his conversation about the struggle with sin back in verse seven of this chapter. At this point he realizes his "wretchedness" and cries out for help. Is there anyone who can free mankind from this up and down struggle with the powers of sin? Thankfully, he finds the answer is yes, but only through Jesus our Lord.

There is a comparison to be made here with the fifth chapter of Revelation, where in heaven there was consternation over the sealed book. Was there anyone who would be able to open the book and reveal its content? Again, like in Romans, the answer is Jesus.

Slavery has never been a path upon which a child of God is supposed to walk. The bonds of sin can't be broken by will power, twelve step programs, or recovery methods. Those solutions may work well for developing and reforming personal habits, but sin can only be conquered by Jesus Himself. He is the one who won the victory on the cross for our full salvation and only as we cast all our cares on Him can we ever be free.

There is no reason to live the Christian life as one that is tied to the old way of existence. Jesus died to free us from our sin, not to give us power to suppress it. The sanctifying grace of God is available for all who will call upon Him and surrender themselves completely to His will and way. Freedom is available for the asking.

The thing that is required of us is that we be willing to put all the life of sin behind us. We can't play with fire and not be burned. We can't dabble in the forces of darkness and not have it seep into our souls. But once we say the final "yes" to Jesus and His will and plan for our life, then we can sing the old song about joy unspeakable and full of glory, with meaning.

Who will deliver us? Jesus will. Who has the power to free us? Jesus does. Who is waiting right now to receive us into His presence? Jesus is. He is all we need, always. Thanks be to God, indeed!

DAY 129

Romans 8:1–2 *Therefore, there is now no condemnation for those who are in Christ Jesus, because through Christ Jesus the law of the Spirit of life set me free from the law of sin and death.*

It's important to understand the full and complete meaning of these words. No condemnation, or not guilty, is the verdict for us as we stand before God, because of our relationship in Christ. That ruling is certainly a wonderful gift that the Father has declared for us. However, not guilty is not the same as innocent. It's not like we never did anything wrong, because there is no one except Jesus who falls into that category, but it does mean that our wrongdoing is held against us no longer.

I think that sometimes people come to the idea that only those who are really saints throughout their lives can have this kind of verdict. They would think that only really good people, like Mother Theresa or Billy Graham, or some really holy person could get such a declaration, but nothing could be farther from the truth.

In I Corinthians 6:9–10, Paul lists a whole bunch of people who had sinned against God. They include the sexually immoral, idolaters, adulterers, prostitutes, homosexuals, thieves, the greedy, drunkards, slanderers, and swindlers—all who stand guilty before God. But in the very next verse he declares, "And that is what some of you were. But you were washed, you were sanctified, you were justified in the name of the Lord Jesus Christ and by the Spirit of our God" (I Corinthians 6:11).

Do you get the idea? It doesn't matter what we have done. Once we have entered into a relationship with Christ, all that sin business is behind us, and we then are declared "not guilty" before God. It's not that we haven't even done anything wrong, for we undoubtedly surely have, but it's because the blood of Jesus cleanses even the dirtiest of us when we submit to Him as Lord of our lives.

Over the past few verses Paul has built a strong case for the sin that is exposed by the law but is not dealt with. In Christ, our sin is not only exposed, but forgiven and cleansed so that we can stand before the Father and hear Him say, "No condemnation!" What a wonderful gift of grace! What a tremendous power of transformation! Thanks be to God!

DAY 130

Romans 8:3–4 *For what the law was powerless to do in that it was weakened by the sinful nature, God did by sending his own Son in the likeness of sinful man to be a sin offering. And so he condemned sin in sinful man, in order that the righteous requirements of the law might be fully met in us, who do not live according to the sinful nature but according to the Spirit.*

Sin is a terrible thing. Though it is often ignored, scoffed at, and even played with, it costs the sinner a terrible price. Even if it looks glamorous and attractive to the viewer, the end result is a broken and destroyed person.

Not only is sin costly to every individual on this planet who is affected by it, but it cost a lot of God too. In condemning sin to be evil and harmful to His creation and knowing that we would never be able to overcome it on our own, He gave of Himself, His own Son to break sin's power through the sacrificial death of Jesus on the cross.

Even though God first gave the law to Moses so that the Israelites could see the way of life, they refused to walk in that way and proved what God knew all along. He knew that rule keeping would never work because mankind doesn't keep rules very well, but He had to give the law to show us what He knew, and we didn't. The Old Testament is a long story of man finding out that our own way doesn't work, and that we are so weak that even when God literally spells things out for us, we still don't get it.

Jesus came to not only give us the perfect example of how we are to live, but personified what God wanted from Israel all along. The key, however, that allowed Jesus to do this, was the infilling of the Holy Spirit all throughout His ministry. He knew that many times our spirit was willing, but that our flesh was weak, and He showed through His life that only with the Spirit's filling could we ever maintain victory and the kind of life God wanted.

This walk in the Spirit was not just something for Jesus, it's for us. It is the power of the Holy Spirit that breaks the power of the sinful nature and gives us the freedom and choice to live victoriously and not in the bonds of sins' chains. We are not to be slaves to sin, but full of the Holy Spirit so that all God wants us to be, can be realized. The law becomes a part of us as we live not according to the letter, but to the spirit of the commandments. The law points to the cross, which becomes our source of power.

DAY 131

Romans 8:5 *Those who live according to the sinful nature have their minds set on what that nature desires; but those who live in accordance with the Spirit have their minds set on what the Spirit desires.*

A lot of what we do in life comes down to the fact of what we want to do. As children we look forward to the time when we will be able to make our own decisions as independent adults, but even then, our will power controls a lot of what we do, and what we like and don't like.

Of course, there are limitations to our abilities and opportunities to set our own courses in life, but the desires we have do dictate much of our behavior. If I want to buy something, I will usually find a way to make it happen. If I want to master a sport badly enough, I will practice until I obtain some degree of proficiency in it. If I want an education, I will find a way to work through the process of getting whatever degree I want, in whatever field I desire.

With all this being said, it is Paul's contention that it is the nature within us that determines, for good or bad, what direction our life goes. If our nature is turned inward, then we will do whatever satisfies the desires of the flesh and makes us feel happy—at least for the moment. If our nature has been changed by God's Holy Spirit then we will work to please the Lord above all things.

This is why it is so important for Christians to realize that serving Jesus is not just a matter of our consecration. Though it is important to confess our sins, to pledge our allegiance to God, and apply spiritual disciplines in our lives to develop productive habits and patterns in our lives, that is not what truly makes us Christian. We become Christian when the Spirit of God enters our being, regenerates us, and makes a new creation. Until that happens, we are still living only on the strength that our human nature can provide and as a result, will find trying to be a Christian impossible. We may act Christian, but it is Christ within us, changing our nature that makes us Christian.

Remember, Paul is talking about a transformation that brings real freedom, not just our joining a new group with a new title. Jesus saves, sanctifies, regenerates, renews, and empowers. He makes us different, our nature different, than it once was. In Him, we are being remade daily and without Him we are just acting out a role. His change in us is a real change.

DAY 132

Romans 8:6-8 *The mind of sinful man is death, but the mind controlled by the Spirit is life and peace; the sinful man is hostile to God. It does not submit to God's law, nor can it do so. Those controlled by the sinful nature cannot please God.*

There is a great comparison being made here by the Apostle. It has to do with what is controlling the mind of man. In simple terms, he says that if the mind is controlled by sin, then death is the end result. But if the mind is controlled by the Spirit of God, then life is the end result. It's about as blatant a difference as can be made.

There are a couple of things for us to consider when evaluating Paul's words. First, it has to do with mind control. Without trying to sound like something from a science fiction novel, we have before us the idea that some force outside of ourselves is controlling our minds. That may seem like a strange way to put it, but it actually makes a lot of sense. We are dealing with spiritual realities here and the powers of darkness and the powers of light are fighting for the dominance of our being.

When we look at what Paul says about the sinful man, we see that not only is he anti-God, and anti-God's law, but he has no choice in the matter of being that way. If we are controlled by the sinful nature, or perhaps better understood as our selfish nature, we do not have the ability to be pleasing to God. We are controlled by another master and are under its authority.

However, if we have been filled with the Spirit of God and are under His authority, we find ourselves in a state of grace that provides peace for our minds and life abundant here and now, as well as in the world to come.

It seems strange that any rational and thinking person would choose the way of death over the way of life and peace. However, though there are many who genuinely don't know of this promise, or understand what it means for them, there are those who are aware of what this choice means and choose selfishly anyway. They are of all people to be the most pitied.

We should give thanks to God that He has provided us with the way of life and peace, as well as made us aware of it. Because of His great grace, we don't have to live in a state of fear, sorrow, or on the path to death.

DAY 133

Romans 8:9 *You, however, are controlled not by the sinful nature but by the Spirit, if the Spirit of God lives in you. And if anyone does not have the Spirit of Christ, he does not belong to Christ.*

Isn't it amazing what a difference a little two-letter, one syllable word can make? Out of this one verse we have the message of the possibility of holy living here in this world, as well as the message of rejection and doom.

It all centers around that little word, "if." First, we are given the assurance that freedom in Christ, because of the Spirit of Christ who lives in us, is possible. There may be some who would doubt that the sinful nature can be removed from our lives, but Paul gives us assurance that such freedom is a possibility. If we have the Spirit of God living within us, then we are controlled by that Spirit, not by the sinful nature that had held us captive for so long. I for one, am thankful for such a reality.

The bad news is that those who do not possess the Spirit of God are not free from sin, and in their sin they will stand in judgment before God, unless things change. This is the basic definition of what it means to be a Christian, for either Christ has come to live within us or He has not.

For far too many times people have equated Christianity with acts of service, church membership, taking communion, or even being baptized as proof of one's faith. The fact is, however, that Christianity is the only religion in the world that is totally based on grace, not on what man can do to earn a god's favor. There is no substitution for a personal relationship with Jesus Christ to have sins forgiven and obtain salvation. Any other means of Christian activity is just an imitation and a false hope.

This is why it is so important that we who know Christ as our personal Savior and Lord, keep spreading the Good News that delivers mankind from sin. We were forgiven from the cross and grace for salvation is available for all, but that gift of God's Spirit must be acknowledged and received for us to be adopted into the family. There will be no sadder words ever heard than for someone to stand before Jesus someday and hear the words, "I never knew you. Away from me, you evildoers" (Matthew 7:23). Thankfully, no one ever has to go that route, for the joy of the Lord abides where His Spirit resides. Thanks be to God!

DAY 134

Romans 8:10 *But if Christ is in you, your body is dead because of sin, yet your spirit is alive because of righteousness.*

The movie-world has made a big deal in recent years of glorifying zombies, or the undead. I've never seen any of these movies, but it seems like the advertising for such things has a tendency to spill over into the non-fiction world too, so I am aware of them.

When Paul speaks of our bodies being dead though, it is totally different because his concern is being dead as a result of sin. Like Adam and Eve in the Garden of Eden, the physical doesn't die immediately usually, but deadness occurs in the spirit, nonetheless. Death within is not always recognized by others, and it is possible that the person who is dead because of sin doesn't even know it themselves, but death has occurred anyway because sin is a living reality.

Of course, the point Paul is trying to get across to all who read this is that there is an option to being dead. As long as sin rules there is no option, but when we are freed by the Spirit of God, we have a new life and the former existence we had truly has passed away.

What we must keep in mind though, is that our new life is only because of righteousness. We must not get the big head, however, for it is not because of our righteousness, but God's. He is the one who is perfect and He is the one who has a perfect plan for our lives. He is the one who makes us aware of our deadness and He is the one who instills new life within us. There is nothing we can do to bring the new birth about on our own, but in Christ, even the dead come alive.

Jesus made this clear in John 11:25–26, where He said, "I am the resurrection and the life. He who believes in me will live, even though he dies; and whoever lives and believes in me will never die." The news was not only for Martha, one of the sisters of Lazarus, but it is true for all of us everywhere.

When we are dead in sin, we have no hope. When we are made alive in Christ by virtue of His righteousness, we are free to live our lives as God intended for us from the start. So today, live as a child of God!

DAY 135

Romans 8:11 *And if the Spirit of him who raised Jesus from the dead is living in you, he who raised Christ from the dead will also give life to your mortal bodies through his Spirit, who lives in you.*

People are always wondering what will happen to us after we die. Usually that question is in the context of what we witness as we go to a mortuary and view the earthly remains of someone we cared about. But maybe we are thinking about the wrong thing and asking the wrong question. What if we focused on what Paul is talking about, and reflect on what happens to us after we die when we truly die to sin? Maybe it would give us a whole different perspective when we consider what happens when our heart stops beating and we stop breathing for the final time.

When we die to sin, we are raised to new life in Christ. That means we are regenerated from the deadness that once possessed us and kept us from being what God always intended us to be. When we die to sin and are raised to new life in Christ, we are fully adopted into the family of God. We are no longer on the outside looking in, but now have complete access to our heavenly Father at any place or time. And it is not just access that we have, but we have access as His child. When we think of how we love our children, just imagine how much God cares about His.

When we die to sin and are raised to new life in Christ, we are justified fully in the eyes of our Creator. He holds those old sins against us no more. It's the ultimate do-over for all of us who have made such a mess of things, as God proclaims our blamelessness for Jesus' sake.

Oh, in days to come we will deal with the questions about what happens to these bodies and our inner being after we close our eyes in physical death, for death comes to everyone at one time or another. But the good news we have to share is that when we die to sin and are raised to life in Christ now, we are just in the initial stages of what we will experience all throughout eternity. The Spirit of Christ comes to live within us, and that same Spirit will be our comfort and guide for all the ages to come. This life will end in death, but since death has been defeated, we can anticipate a resurrection that is going to be like Christ's, and we will live forever.

What good news! What a transformation! I wouldn't miss it for anything!

DAY 136

Romans 8:12 *Therefore, brothers, we have an obligation—
but it is not to the sinful nature, to live according to it.*

Do you like to be in debt? It's not a trick question. I can't think of any sane person who would say "yes!" We usually want to stay as far away from owing others as humanly possible, so if we get the opportunity to pay things off and be free of those monthly bills, we want to do so.

How much more should we want to be free from the debt of sin that we obtained through our sinful nature? Most of us lived in that debt for far too long, but all sin's debts have been cancelled when we put our trust in Jesus Christ to forgive what we owed.

What remains because of our relationship with Christ, is a new obligation. We have an obligation to live as redeemed individuals who have a new mission to spread the glory of God around the world. The job that God first gave to Abraham four thousand years ago, has not changed in its purpose. We are to be influencers on the rest of the world for the glory of God so that all mankind will be able to share in His blessings.

Our obligation begins in our homes, as every married person has the duty to present Christ to his or her spouse in a loving and kind way. It continues on to our children so that they may know the way of life and avoid the paths of sin and death. It carries on to our communities so that we can live in a wholesome place where Christ is exalted as King, and where we as His brothers and sisters can live in harmony and peace.

Because Jesus gave us the Great Commission to take the Good News around the globe, our obligation reaches to the far-off lands and islands of the seas so that our Father may receive the glory.

Yes, we remain under a great obligation, but it's not a burdensome one. Once we have been freed from our addiction to sin, we have our blessing of life to portray as an example to all. Just as we once lived for self and sinful pleasures, our allegiance is now to God and we live out our new life of freedom with abandon.

Perhaps today will be the day that a new door of opportunity will open so that we can share Christ's love with someone else. May it be so for all of us.

DAY 137

Romans 8:13–14 *For if you live according to the sinful nature, you will die, but if by the Spirit you put to death the misdeeds of the body, you will live, because those who are led by the Spirit of God are sons of God.*

Living only on self-gratification is a sure way to be miserable. What pleased us today has to be increased in order for us to be pleased tomorrow. As time goes on, the dissatisfaction with what we have continually grows and leads people to all kinds of pain, and eventually to death. This is the truth Paul writes about.

In contrast to trying to find what best pleases us, we have the option when we are in Christ, to be led by the Spirit. This is one of the greatest joys and perks that Christians have, and we need to always remember that God's guidance is available to us. The choices we make as children of the King can be guided by an unseen force to do what is for our good and for the King's glory.

There have been so many examples of this in my life. The Spirit guided me in where to go to college, what friends and connections to make, what to do for a life's vocation, where to work, and even in the purchases I have made. I must confess that I didn't always listen as clearly as I should have and therefore have made some mistakes along the way. But I have found that when I ask, wait, and listen for the Master to give me direction, I have never been sorry with the outcome.

This is one of the huge benefits in Kingdom living that is often overlooked. So many people consider life to just be the luck of the draw, or circumstances that are out of our control, but that's not the case at all. The world had a definite beginning and is moving toward a definite conclusion, and along the way while we are in it, we can be truly in the midst of God's plan. We don't have to wander aimlessly, hoping to find the right way. We are King's kids, and we can ask when we don't know and expect to get an answer.

We access the Father by faith and move as He directs us by faith. We will not be disappointed when we choose His way over our own preference. Our Father knows what we need and is more willing to show us the way than we are even to ask. This is how we find confidence and courage in the midst of our journey. Ask God, and then trust Him. He will guide your steps.

DAY 138

Romans 8:15 *For you did not receive a spirit that makes you a slave again to fear, but you received the Spirit of sonship. And by him we cry, "Abba Father."*

It seems like we live in a world that is filled to the rim with fear. Every day we meet people who are afraid of getting sick, afraid of going to the hospital, afraid of not having enough money, afraid to face all the unknowns that our world is throwing at them. It's interesting to me when Christians have this reaction to life's curveballs, because over and over the Bible instructs us, "Don't be afraid."

We need to remember that we who are in Christ have been set free from the spirit of fear. That form of slavery was broken when Jesus was hanged on the cross, and there is nothing we are ever going to face that we will have to face alone. We have the Spirit of Christ as our constant companion, and He has already conquered all we have to worry about and more.

Not only have we been freed from the spirit of fear, but we need to remember that we have been adopted into God's royal family. Families are very special units of God's creation because family members have a closer tie to each other than they do with those who are not in the family. Because the blood of Jesus was given for our behalf, we can claim membership in His bloodline as surely as if we had been born a Jew in Palestine two thousand years ago. We who are in Christ are connected in the highest of places.

Children who are just learning to talk are usually encouraged to say, "Mama," or "Dada" as an incentive to get a response. Here Paul reminds us that "Abba, Father," is the same type of endearing term, and we can call upon our heavenly Father as surely as a child reaches out for his or her earthly one. The reason we can do this is because the Spirit within us recognizes God as the one our heart longs for. Just as a baby will cling to his or her own parents much more readily than for some stranger, this is Paul's way of reminding us that because of our family connection we too can call upon the Lord of the universe in the most intimate terms.

We have been freed from fear and engulfed into the family of divine love through Jesus Christ. We are kin with God and that's as good as it gets in this world and the next.

DAY 139

Romans 8:16 *The Spirit himself testifies with our spirit that we are God's children.*

I love this verse! It's one that I have quoted to many congregations over the years, because every time I read these words, I feel a spurt of joy on the inside. It is a promise of a reality that I have come to experience personally and a sensation I wish for every person every born.

I hope you understand the truth that's given here. First, Paul is reminding us of what we already know, namely that God's Spirit speaks to our spirit. How amazing! How indescribable the blessing that the King of all kings, the Creator of all that exists, the Savior of our souls, talks to us. He takes notice of our existence and is interested in our daily walk and interaction with other parts of His creation. He really does care about us enough to communicate with us.

The second amazing truth here is that this communication recognizes us as children of the Almighty God. We are not riffraff that have no place in this world. It doesn't matter what is or what isn't in our bank accounts, or even if we have one. It doesn't matter if we have lots of talent and are beautiful to behold, or if we are barely able to cope with life and are not much to look at. We are royalty! We matter! We have a place right now in the presence of God and He looks upon us as His children. These words should be words of encouragement for every person that understands their impact.

Of course, this promise is conditional. Not everyone hears the voice of God. This relationship of communication and confirmation of grace is only for those who have put their trust in Him and have committed their life to Him. The Spirit calls everyone, for God wants no one to perish, but it is only those who truly belong to Him that get this seal of approval from His Spirit.

This is one reason why it is so important for the children of God to learn to listen to and for His voice. Not only does He provide words of assurance for us, but He also wants to communicate with us on other matters. He speaks to us through His Word, the Bible, and He speaks to us deep within the recesses of our minds. He speaks to us amid the storms of life and He speaks to us in the mundane events that fill our days. He speaks to us. That is amazing, and that is grace! Thanks be to God!

DAY 140

Romans 8:17 *Now if we are children, then we are heirs—heirs of God and co-heirs with Christ, if indeed we share in his sufferings in order that we may also share in his glory.*

There are three very important things that the apostle proclaims in this single verse. First, he tells us that we who are in Christ are joint heirs with Him in relationship to all the Kingdom of God contains. Just think, all that Jesus has received we will receive too. Not only the glories of heaven after we die, but eventually we will receive a new body and a new assignment in the new earth that His Kingdom will produce. It's more than our wee-little minds can comprehend, but fantastic to think about.

Second, he tells us that in order for us to achieve that co-heir status, there is going to be suffering involved. This may seem like some kind of a good news-bad news joke, but it's the reality that is expressed in scripture over and over. Paul said it also in II Corinthians 1:5, "For just as the sufferings of Christ flow over into our lives, so also through Christ our comfort overflows." He references it again in Philippians 3:10, "I want to know Christ and the power of the resurrection and the fellowship of sharing in his sufferings, becoming like him in his death." Jesus told of this in Matthew 17:24, "If anyone would come after me, he must deny himself and take up his cross and follow me." In John 16:33 Jesus reminds us, "I have told you these things so that in me you will have peace. In this world you will have trouble. But take heart! I have overcome the world." To His disciples He said, "No servant is greater than his master. If they persecuted me, they will persecute you also. If they obeyed my teaching, they will obey yours also" (John 15:20). The choice to follow Christ will involve suffering for the follower.

Finally, he reminds us that even though the way to the inheritance we share with Christ is going to be accompanied by pain, there is a glory waiting for us that we will also share with Christ. Paul quotes from Isaiah 64:4 in I Corinthians 2:9 when he says, "'No eye has seen, no ear has heard, no mind has conceived what God has prepared for those who love him'—but God has revealed it to us by his Spirit." We have good days ahead. There may be a cross to get there, but serving Jesus is worth every step of the journey and every hard place we may face. There is no higher calling, no greater challenge, and no more glorious reward that to be a child of the King of kings.

DAY 141

Romans 8:18 *I consider that our present sufferings are not worth comparing with the glory that will be revealed in us.*

Are you having some hard times these days? Do you feel like you are facing an uphill battle and every step of the way gets more difficult with each bit of effort you put forth? Does it seem that good guys finish last, and those who bend and break the rules are the smart ones who always get away with their treachery? Well, I've got news for you; you are not alone. We all feel that way from time to time.

The good news in Christ, however, is that while these things may in fact be true for now, there is another day coming when all things will be as they should be. We as Christians, across various denominational lines, believe in another era where God will have the final say and His way will be just and fair for everyone.

I fully realize that there are people who have had things much tougher in life than I have, or ever will have most likely. I know what it is like to be poor, and I know what it is like to have plenty, and even abundance, but there are many worthy souls in this world who have rarely had even the most meager amounts of good things.

I can't identify with those who have serious physical or mental defects. I can't imagine what it would be like to be raised as an orphan by people who really didn't want me. It is impossible for me to fully understand the trauma of being born with such terrible birth defects that having a normal life is completely out of the realm of human possibility—or of being the caregiver for people in such situations.

There are truly many things in the world that seem unjust and unfair, and we may be tempted to ask where God is in these kinds of topics. What we must remember is that all of this is temporary. The life we live in this world is important, and we must do all we can to help everyone we can in it, but there is another day coming when every tear will be wiped away, and joy will replace the sorrows that so often pervade the minds of so many.

In Christ we have hope. It is in Him that we put our faith. Because of the promises of Jesus, we have more just ahead than this world could ever offer.

DAY 142

Romans 8:19–21 *The creation waits in eager expectation for the sons of God to be revealed. For the creation was subjected to frustration, not by its own choice, but by the will of the one who subjected it, in hope that the creation itself will be liberated from its bondage to decay and brought into the glorious freedom of the children of God.*

We have a tendency to think perhaps that God's concern for what He has made has only to do with the people He has created. We mentally and faithfully affirm that He is responsible for all tangible things that we see, but don't always consider how precious God's total creation is to Him. Some have gone as far as to not care about this planet because they think God is going to burn it all up anyway, so who cares what happens to it?

Nothing could be farther from the truth. Our God is in the business of redemption and restoration. What He made was good and it was man's decision to rebel against God's divine plan that brought about the destruction of God's perfect order and launched the path of sin upon our planet.

But there is a day coming when all creation will be renewed. In Revelation 22 there is a depiction of the River of Life flowing through the New Jerusalem as heaven and earth become one. "On each side of the river stood the tree of life, bearing twelve crops of fruit, yielding its fruit every month. And the leaves of the tree are for the healing of the nations. No longer will there be any curse" (vv. 2–3).

Just as we groan and pray for the salvation of our friends, family, and population of this world, the world itself, as a creation of God, waits for its full restoration back into the Garden that God first created. The curse of sin will be gone, and this world's healing will be complete. Not only will God wipe away every tear from every eye, but the new earth—this world renewed—will be abundant with every good thing as God always intended.

Just imagine a planet with no more pollution, volcanic destruction, or earthquakes. Picture a world where the hurricanes have been tamed and the deforested lands are again teeming with life. Pollution of all kinds will be a thing of the past and we will be able to enjoy eternity in the presence of God there. No, this world is not some place we are just passing through. It is going to be glorious when creation itself has been fully redeemed.

DAY 143

Romans 8:22–23 *We know that the whole creation has been groaning as in the pains of childbirth right up to the present time. Not only so, but we ourselves, who have the firstfruits of the Spirit, groan inwardly as we wait eagerly for our adoption as sons, the redemption of our bodies.*

I am old enough to be of the generation where husbands didn't usually accompany their wives into the delivery room when children were born. Because we lived out of state and away from our family, and because both children came early, sending us to the hospital in the middle of the night, we were alone at each childbirth. The first was a bit of a "rush job" as my wife was taken to the delivery room right after we arrived at the hospital, but with our second child I was able to sit with her through the hours of labor and experience the coming of our son in a way I hadn't done with our daughter. I clearly remember those labor pains as she groaned and travailed over the new life that was about to appear.

In much the same way, all of creation is longing and travailing for its new birth. The old gospel song says, "This world is not my home, I'm only passing through." That's not only a half-truth, it's bad theology. Yes, there is a heaven we will go to when we die, but that is not our final home. There will be a time when heaven and earth will become one and this "old world" will be restored to its original glory.

That's what Paul is writing about as he emphasizes the similarities between this world waiting for its final redemption and we as humans waiting for ours. We have received a deposit, the Holy Spirit of God, who lives within us, but we groan, we stretch, we anticipate the completion of the process of renewal. The divine down payment of His presence placed within each of God's children brings about a longing for when the full reunion will be realized.

Like a couple that have been separated for a long time may be able to talk together over the phone, or even in a face-to-face media communication, the partial connection is not like the real thing when they are finally together again. That's the way we long for the Lord. "Now we see but a poor reflection as in a mirror; then we shall see face to face. Now I know in part; then I shall know fully, even as I am known" (I Corinthians 13:12). Oh, we long for that! Even so, Jesus come!

DAY 144

Romans 8:24–25 *For in this hope we were saved. But hope that is seen is no hope at all. Who hopes for what he already has? But if we hope for what we do not have, we wait for it patiently.*

Hope is a commodity that seems to be in short supply in our world. Perhaps it's because when we look to our media sources we hear and see so much that is discouraging, and the idea of being hopeful appears to be naïve at best.

We who are Christians should have a different outlook on life than what we hear proclaimed from secular sources. We know that we have been regenerated into a new life in Christ and that fact alone opens a whole boatload of hopeful realities. We have hope in the resurrection of our bodies after we leave this world; bodies that will be eternal and free from the ravages of sin and age that we experience now. We have hope that we will see our loved ones who have died in Christ before us and that there is going to be a great time of reunion without end. We have hope that we will be able to join in on the great praise party that is going on around the throne of God right now, and we will be able to sing with the angels and all of creation. We have hope that someday our world will be renewed and be in the state it was when God first created it, and we can inhabit it joyfully for eternity. The list of our hopes could go on and on.

Of course, all these things are not yet here, but somewhere in the future. Like Paul says, "Who hopes for what he already has?" If what we hope for were present and realized, then it wouldn't be hope at all. If what we put our faith in has already come to pass, then it wouldn't be faith. The definition of both hope and faith is found in the idea of not yet having received what we long for.

So for now, we wait for hope to be realized. We continue to trust in the Lord, to work for His glory and purpose, and use the resources He has given us as the best stewards and managers that we can possibly be. We don't know how long it will take for all of our hopes to be realized, but we do believe that they will be realized. That's what puts our faith into action and gives us the energy and drive to keep working in the Kingdom of God here on earth. Work, wait, and hope. It's a pretty good way to spend our lives.

DAY 145

Romans 8:26 *In the same way, the Spirit helps us in our weakness. We do not know what we ought to pray for, but the Spirit himself intercedes for us with groans that words cannot express.*

It is so true that all of us feel weak at times. This is true not only in the physical realm, but also true in the spiritual realm. We get depleted by our continual work, oppression from outside forces, and by the never-ending situations that bring stress into our lives. Sometimes we just want to turn everything off and take a break from life.

Our weakness spills over into our prayer life as well. I think most of us can relate to those times when we have gone to our place of prayer and find that we just don't have the words to express what is in our hearts. Perhaps the pain is too great, the disappointment too overwhelming, or our faith seems to be faltering just at the time we need it the most. In these situations, Paul reminds us that we are not alone. The Spirit of God is available to help us even as we pray, or try to pray.

Some people believe, mistakenly in my opinion, that this verse describes a "prayer language," where our mind goes into neutral and the Spirit begins praying for us in some kind of babbling sounds. Personally, I don't see the scriptural evidence for that kind of prayer, nor have I ever experienced it in my life. However, there have been many times when I am at a loss for words, that I have just waited quietly before the Lord and allowed my heart to communicate with the heart of God. It is not mystical, nor ecstatic, but through my groaning and tears, the heavenly Father hears what I am feeling and is able to convey comfort to my soul.

When we seek after some kind of tangible spiritual experience, we lose sight of the fact that we walk by faith and not by what we see. We are not to seek experiences; we are to seek God. When we set our hearts on connecting with Him, we may not always "feel" like we have been successful, but we can be assured that He is hearing us. Why do I believe this? Because Jesus told us that this is the case, and that's good enough for me.

When those weak times come and we feel like our prayers are only going as high as the ceiling, here are two things to do. Wait in silence and turn to the Bible. God will meet with us and provide us what we need, always.

DAY 146

Romans 8:27 *And he who searches our hearts knows the mind of the Spirit, because the Spirit intercedes for the saints in accordance with God's will.*

There is a God who searches through our thoughts and knows exactly what makes us tick. He knows our likes, our dislikes, our hidden treasures, and our deepest fears. In fact, He knows us so thoroughly that He knows us much better than we know ourselves, for He is able not only to see what is on the surface of our countenance, but even the subconscious thoughts that hide away in our dreams.

That in itself is pretty amazing, but Paul lets us in on an even deeper truth. The God who knows our hearts and minds also knows the mind of the Spirit. Since the Father and the Spirit are one, the intimacy that is shared in the divine Godhead is far more extensive than our finite minds could ever understand. He is just that amazing!

But not only does God know our hearts and the mind of the Spirit, but because that relationship is so close, the Spirit is able to intercede for us in those times when we don't know how we are to pray. Not only does He know what we want and need, but He also knows the Father's mind and what we need to ask that would be pleasing to Him.

It almost seems like doubletalk, but it's not. It is just the reality of what God does for those He loves. He cares, and in His caring, He is not willing that we should be left alone but communicates with us to calm our troubled minds and give us guidance for the decisions of life that we have to make.

When we have those times in which we are searching for direction and clarity, the Spirit is helping us as we pray and pointing us in the direction of what the Father desires for us. We don't have to be left wondering because the God who made us cares for us enough to guide us in the way that will be good for us and pleasing to Him.

Isn't it interesting that so many people struggle when they don't have to? Too often people stress and worry about what direction their life should go, but they don't have to if they surrender themselves to the Father's will for their lives. He is faithful, He is loving, and He will continue to lead us because His Spirit in us makes it all possible.

DAY 147

Romans 8:28 *And we know that in all things God works for the good of those who love him, who have been called according to his purpose.*

Boy, if there was ever a verse that has gotten taken out of context in its use, it is this one. There was a television show that I was watching a while back where the first part of this verse from the King James Version, "All things work together for good," was quoted over and over again. Talk about a misuse of scripture! All things do not work together for good. There are some things that are just bad and will never be good, and to think otherwise is just to distort reality.

What the essence of this verse is saying is that God takes all the things that happen in our lives and can use them to work toward our good if we have dedicated ourselves to His purpose. That's a far different thing than just saying that all things work together for good.

There have been times at funerals when well-meaning people have tried to comfort the grieving by using this verse, but sometimes spin it to sound like the death of their loved one is a good thing that has come from God. That's just not true! Death is an enemy, the last enemy to be conquered and one that we fight against with all the strength God gives us. It doesn't mean that God doesn't help us in times of grief, but it doesn't help to cause people to think that someone's death was God's doing.

When we surrender our complete will and life to God, we give Him the freedom and permission to work things together for our good. Though He doesn't cause death, He can use it and many other events of our life to weave together a tapestry of grace that provides a plan for our life. He is able to make more of what we have than we could ever accomplish on our own.

It all happens when we give up our will and our rights to things and people around us and give them to God. We tell Him that what we have is His and allow Him to work out the details. Once we have surrendered to Him, He will give us a calling for our life that will accomplish the purpose He has for us. The secret to all of this, however, is in that fact that we love Him, and we love Him enough, and trust Him enough that we hold nothing back. We give our best and our worst, our dearest and most precious. He gives back a plan that works for His glory and our good. There is nothing better than that!

DAY 148

Romans 8:29 *For those God foreknew he also predestined to be conformed to the likeness of his Son, that he might be the firstborn among many brothers.*

What is God's plan for our lives? That's an interesting question because in some respects God's plan is as different as there are individuals in the world. Paul will deal more fully with this topic when he speaks of spiritual gifts in the twelfth and fourteenth chapters of this book. But there is one thing that God desires for us all, and it is that we would "be conformed to the likeness of His Son." To put it more simply, God wants us to be like Jesus.

At first, this seems like a hill that is just too high to climb. After all, we may say, "Who can be like Jesus? He is the Son of the living God! He lived in this world without sin!" It seems impossible that anyone living in our wicked world could ever hope to even come close to living as Jesus did.

But Paul uses a very descriptive word here. He says that we are *predestined* to do so. It is God's plan and will for us. He wants us to be made of the same stuff that Jesus is made of. He wants us to be filled with the Spirit, live a life of love, and be free from the bondage of sin. Is all that really possible?

On our own, of course it is not possible. But if God wills it, and He does, and if God knows us intimately, and He does, then God will create a way for us to be able to do and be what He wants us to do and be. Remember, Jesus is the firstborn of all of us who have put our trust in Him for our salvation. Just as Jesus was raised from the dead to never die again, so too, we will be raised from the dead at the final resurrection, never to die again. Because Jesus led the way, we have an example of how we are to follow in His footsteps.

Some may object, "But He was God when He walked here on earth as a man, and I am not!" That is true for all of us, but we have to also remember that though Jesus was fully God, He was God in the flesh, meaning that He was also fully man. He was faced with the same temptations we are faced with and had to deal with life's challenges just like we do. The key here is in the filling of the Spirit. As we are filled, then we can live as God wants us to—and that is to be like Jesus. It is the predestined will of God for us all.

DAY 149

Romans 8:30 *And those he predestined, he also called; those he called, he also justified; those he justified, he also glorified.*

This is what I would call, a stairstep verse of scripture. God predestines, God calls, God justifies, and God glorifies. Let's briefly look at each of these terms one at a time.

The idea of predestination is often misunderstood. Some consider this to mean that God controls everything minutely and that whatever happens has to happen, so we have no choice in the matter. That isn't Christianity though; that's fatalism. Whatever will be will be isn't what life in Christ is about. In this context, God predestines, or God desires, everyone to be conformed to the image of His Son. God wants us to be like Jesus.

Concerning the issue of being called, here we are called to repentance and to be committed to God with our whole hearts. We are all called, but not everyone answers that call in a way that pleases God. If we do, then there is a blessing that God gives us.

That blessing is justification. Regardless of how far away from God we may have been, God erases the charges against us and brings us into His family of faith. We don't have to listen to the enemy's charges against us any longer, for the Divine Judge made His ruling in our favor. This, of course, is based on answering His call and putting our trust in Christ for our salvation.

The last word is about glorification. The truth is, we are not there yet. Jesus, our elder brother, has already gone through the pains of death though and has come out on the other side of that experience in a glorified state. No longer do the rules of earth bind Him, for He is free to live eternally without fear, pain, or sin. He does this to show us what we can expect when we are glorified. God will raise us from the dead just like He raised Jesus and then we will see Him just as He is.

Predestined, called, justified, and glorified. It is all through the hand of God and only He can make any of these things happen. He has all these things planned for those who love Him. We are not out here on our own, for God has a wonderful plan for our lives. We won't see it all fulfilled in this life, but this life is just part of all that there is. The best is truly yet to come.

DAY 150

Romans 8:31 *What, then, shall we say in response to this? If God is for us, who can be against us?*

In order for verse thirty-one to make any sense, it has to be tied to the previous verses, particularly verse thirty. Because the plan of God has predestined, called, justified, and glorified the work of His hands, it calls for a response. This response comes in the form of a question that asks, "If God is for us, who can be against us?"

Of course, the obvious answer is, "No one!" When God acts there is no power anywhere that has any ability to counter that action, and since His action involves His plan for us, then we have the most powerful ally in all the universe.

This should give us hope regardless of whatever situation we may find ourselves facing. Knowing that the Almighty God has our backs and that He never sleeps or leaves us, should provide comfort amid dire circumstances or even in pleasant times.

We must always keep this verse in the context for which it was intended though. It does not mean that we can throw caution to the wind and act foolishly. It doesn't mean that we should flaunt the grace that has been provided to us and act as is we are invincible, for it is God that is invincible, not us. It also does not mean that we cannot break the relationship, rebel against God's direction for our lives, and expect that there will be no consequences for our choices.

God is always for us. It is always His will that we should be like Jesus, and if we strive to do so, then all His assuring promises are true for us. But our walk with God is a relationship. Relationships have good days and bad days. God never changes, but we do. It's important for us to keep our hand in His always, for it is in that context that no one can stand against us.

What this does mean is that I can face any challenge that the enemy of my soul can throw at me. I have the protecting hand of the Triune God covering me and providing me with the needs of life that I have. He will never forsake His own and He will never go back on His promises. We can live securely in our walk of faith for all our days because God is always faithful.

DAY 151

Romans 8:32 *He who did not spare his own Son, but gave him up for us all—how will he not also, along with him, graciously give us all things?*

I can't even imagine what it would be like to give up my son, or my grandson, nor do I even want to think about it. I have lost people dear to me over the years, as most people have, and it is never a joyous parting. Even when I have confidence that better things are ahead for them, I rejoice in their homegoing, but still hurt in the loss it produces in my life.

Our heavenly Father put into play the most painful thing of all time when He sent His Son to pay the ransom for our sins. To leave the glory of the heavenly court to endure life as human with all of its challenges is a huge transition in itself, but to suffer and die for a world of people who did not deserve the sacrifice is a price no Father should have to ask of his son.

Yet, God did it for us. As Paul puts it, He "gave him up for us all." Such love for His creation goes beyond words and we should daily give thanks for His generosity toward us. Countless songs, poems, and books have been written about this amazing grace, but the half has not yet been told.

This is exactly the point that Paul makes here. If God was willing to do such a thing for our benefit, how much more will He give us what we need to fulfill His plan for our lives and bring us to the place He wants us to be. Remember, Paul has been writing about how God predestined, called, justified, and glorified us in Christ (vs. 8:30) and now reminds us that He truly will bring it all to pass.

This is a joint gift from the Father, Son, and Spirit in our lives simply because we are so loved. Grace cannot be explained with mere words, for it goes beyond the ability of mortal man to describe what only God can do on this scale. But it is provided freely and without any conditions. He only asks that we put our trust in Him to accept this gift and see it fulfilled to completion.

There will be a day when this will all make sense to us, I am sure. Someday we will enjoy knowledge and perspective that we can't even picture now. But until that day comes, we will stand in awe as undeserving creatures that benefit hugely from the matchless love of God. Charles Wesley said it well, "O for a thousand tongues to sing, my great Redeemer's praise."

DAY 152

Romans 8:33 *Who will bring any charge against those whom God has chosen? It is God who justifies.*

Because we are flawed creatures, we have personal histories that haven't always shown us in the best light. In fact, Paul has made it clear back in Romans 3:23 that we have all sinned, and it is sin that separates us from the God who wants to commune with us. If we would focus our thinking only on the things we have done that disappoint God, we could find ourselves in a perpetual state of depression.

Thankfully, we who are in Christ have put those things behind us because we have confessed them to Him and have received His forgiveness for our actions and attitudes. We have been given a wonderful gift of grace directly from the hand of God.

This is why we don't need to worry about past sins, though we can always learn from them, because God has justified us and pronounced us free from any penalty for those sins. It's all because Jesus broke the bonds of sin, death, and the grave on our behalf, and now we can look forward to living with Him throughout eternity without fear of retribution.

The enemy of our souls, that evil accuser, doesn't want us to understand this though. The powers of darkness want us to cower in fear and not claim the liberty we have received through Christ. If we can be led to doubt what God has done in us, then we are weakened in our faith and in our stability that we enjoy in the Spirit.

Paul gives a perfect line to us when anyone reminds us of our past and accuses us of being less than what God expected us to be. We can say, "It is God who justifies!" This wasn't our doing, or the preacher's doing, our parent's doing, or anyone else. It wasn't that some family member said that we should be let off the hook and not have to pay for our sins. "It is God who justifies!" He is the highest authority that could ever be considered, and He pronounces us "clean." That settles the matter once and for all.

What a blessing it is to know that our sins are not only not held against us, but to know that when the day of our judgment before God rolls around, the matter has already been dealt with and settled. In Christ we are justified!

DAY 153

Romans 8:34 *Who is he who condemns? Christ Jesus, who died—more than that, who was raised to life—is at the right hand of God and is also interceding for us.*

This is the second of three questions that are asked by the Apostle Paul concerning our station in Christ. In the previous verses he was asking who it was that brought charges against the ones the Lord has chosen. Here he asks who has the right to condemn us, and the answer is no one but Christ Jesus—and He has already forgiven us and is interceding for us.

It reminds me of the story in the Gospel of John, chapter eight, where after all the accusers of the woman who had been caught in adultery had left the scene, Jesus asked if there were any who condemned her. Her answer, "No one, Lord!" When we are asked about who can condemn us, we can have the same reply, "No one!" If Jesus holds us to be righteous, then no one else's opinion matters at all.

There are a few things in this verse that we need to consider, however. First, Paul's claim that Jesus died and was raised to life. He rarely missed an opportunity to tell the story of the resurrection of Christ, for it is in the resurrection that gospel story has its foundation and power.

Second, it is significant that Jesus was not only raised to life, but now sits at the right hand of God in a place of ultimate glory and power. As He occupies the Almighty throne, He has total control over the affairs of this world and is not stymied by any circumstance, power, or personality.

Finally, we see that Christ's purpose at the right hand of God is to make intercession for us. This is almost more than we can grasp. We have most likely been in meetings, whether church or otherwise, when people have made prayer requests on behalf of someone else. How much greater is it that Jesus is asking the Father on our behalf concerning things that affect us? Jesus has been given all power and authority and yet He still concerns Himself with the things that matter to mere mortals like us.

We are so blessed. All charges against us have been dropped. We are free from the threat of condemnation, and Jesus intercedes on our behalf. It just doesn't get any better than this!

DAY 154

Romans 8:35–37 *Who shall separate us from the love of Christ? Shall trouble or hardship or persecution or famine or nakedness or danger or sword? As it is written: "For your sake we face death all day long; we are considered as sheep to be slaughtered." No, in all these things we are more than conquerors through him who loved us.*

This is the third of the three questions Paul asked in these verses to reinforce his focus that we are secure in our walk with the Lord. It is also the passage that gives us the answer in full to all those questions.

I can only imagine what was going through the apostle's mind as pen was put to paper. Hardship? Yes, he had experienced plenty of that. Since he had to toil to support his ministry, there were no doubt many long and tiring days. Trouble? Yes, just keeping up with all the churches that he had started, carrying the load of problems that each one would produce, and having a burden for their success would have been so hard.

Few people knew persecution like Paul did. He was in prison more than once, he was beaten, he was stoned, and he suffered greatly for the task to which he had been called. He knew what it was like to go without good and proper clothing. He knew what it was like to be in danger from shipwrecks, and to be chained, and under guard by the military. Paul was not just pulling idle thoughts from the air. In each illustration he gave, he was not just trying to comfort the Romans, he was speaking from personal experience.

The truth that he found through it all though, was that the love of Christ traveled right along with him everywhere that he went. From the day when Paul first met Christ on the road to Damascus (Acts 9), Jesus had been his constant companion in good times and hard times. They had formed a bond that allowed Paul to sense the love of God that came from such a relationship.

It is this love relationship that he wanted to pass on to the church at Rome and by doing so, he passed it on to us as well. There is nothing that can separate us from the love of Jesus, and because of that love, we are more than conquerors as we take on the challenges that are put before us. We may not have to experience the same stuff that Paul did, but Christ's love for us is just as real. We can be conquerors today through Christ our Lord!

DAY 155

Romans 8:38–39 *For I am convinced that neither death nor life, neither angels nor demons, neither the present nor the future, nor any powers, neither height nor depth, nor anything else in all creation, will be able to separate us from the love of God that is in Christ Jesus our Lord.*

This is one of the very great promises in the Bible. It's worth reading over and over again on a regular basis, or perhaps committing to memory. It is the declaration of faith that has held many saints secure through various storms of life and has provided them hope for their journey.

The inspiration of the Holy Spirit is all over this passage, for it produces in Paul the heart of a poet and the authority of a prophet. The love of God is the one thing that we can be sure about no matter what else happens in life. His power is unlimited, and His reach is immeasurable. There is nothing that can block the love that He has for His children.

This is a good opportunity for us to look carefully at our lives and consider the mountains and challenges we are facing. We may be looking at trials greater than any we have ever faced before, or we may be dealing with uncertainties for which we can see no answer. However, the good and wonderful news here is that we will not face these things alone. If our heavenly Father cares enough for us to provide His amazing grace for our lives, then He cares enough to walk with us through those things that appear so large on our horizon.

Some people live in fear of separation. They are afraid of being separated from their spouse, from their children, from their parents, from their health, or even from life itself. They see the future as so uncertain and events that make the headlines so complex and difficult that hope must be only found in the foolish.

But the child of God knows better. We know that we are on the winning side, and we know that the God who began everything will bring it to its proper and timely conclusion on His schedule, and in the meantime, we have His unfailing love to help us ride the waves of whatever storms we may go through.

How great is the love of God! How blessed we are to be family with Him!

DAY 156

Romans 9:1–2 *I speak the truth in Christ—I am not lying, my conscience confirms it in the Holy Spirit—I have great sorrow and unceasing anguish in my heart.*

These two verses speak volumes to me. It's not because they uncover some great theological truth or shed light on some spiritual warfare controversy. They speak to me because they share something that used to be so common, but something that is almost totally forgotten in far too many churches today. What I am speaking of has to do with "great sorrow and unceasing anguish in my heart."

We used to call it carrying a burden. We would sing a song in church services that went, "Lord, lay some soul upon my heart, and love that soul through me. And may I always do my part, to win that soul for Thee." It's been a long time since I've heard that song sung in any church, and I wonder if folks today even know it.

As Paul goes on in this chapter, he bares his soul. But it's important for us to grasp at the start of it that he begins with a sense of grief and burden concerning the welfare of the people who have missed out on the grace and peace that Christ offers. We sometimes meet in worship to celebrate, and we meet to clap our hands as we get excited about Jesus, but the numbers of people who come together in quiet places to weep, pray, travail, and plead to the Lord on behalf of their lost family member are few.

Call for a movie night at church with popcorn and soft drinks and you will get a crowd. Plan a concert with the latest gospel hit maker and you may fill up your building. Have a church potluck and you will often wonder about having enough food to feed all those who would come. But call for a night of prayer and fasting for the lost, and most churches would be able to count those who meet on their fingers and have fingers left over.

Back in my first pastorate I wrote a song, and the words of its chorus go as follows: "Show me the picture of my brothers bound by sin; let the weeping for their rescue fall from me. Let me bear their load like Jesus bore when He prayed in Gethsemane. Don't send down blessings, send a burden, for the lost to me." If we don't return to that kind of concern, the world will never change.

DAY 157

Romans 9:3–4 *For I could wish that I myself were cursed and cut off from Christ for the sake of my brothers, those of my own race, the people of Israel. Theirs is the adoption as sons; theirs the divine glory, the covenants, the receiving of the law, the temple worship and the promises.*

I really don't think I am there yet. I would like to be, but if I understand what Paul is saying here, he is wishing he could be cut off from God and lost eternally if it would cause the people of his family, his race, to be saved. Now folks, that is bearing a burden. I would certainly give up my life in this world for another without a millisecond of a thought, but my eternal destiny. No, I don't think I have reached that point of sacrifice yet.

He saw so much potential in his heritage. The family line of Israel enjoyed all the blessings that God had to pour out. They were chosen by God, they experienced the presence of God, and they had a contract made between them and God. They were the direct recipients of the Ten Commandments, were given the temple as God's symbolic throne room, and most important of all, they were the people who received the wonderful and endless promises that flow from the presence of the Divine.

It must have been agony for Paul to realize all these benefits that belonged to his heritage and to see so many of his family neglect and ignore them. How is it possible for people to be so favored and yet so negligent in their obligation to their benefactor?

Uh, but wait a minute. What Paul saw in his generation we can also acknowledge in our own. We may not have had the exact same history as the people of Israel, but today our world is blessed far beyond the dreams of those ancient Jews. We have medical and technological advances that were previously beyond the scope of imagination. We have freedom of travel and access to riches that would have made kings of previous centuries envious. Most of all, we have the availability of God's Holy Spirit to lead us, protect us, teach us, and cleanse us. We too have an amazing heritage from our God.

May the burden that Paul felt toward his family become the burden that we feel toward our own. May we be as serious about souls for the kingdom as we are about our daily bread. May we suffer loss that others may gain Christ.

DAY 158

Romans 9:5 *Theirs are the patriarchs, and from them is traced the human ancestry of Christ, who is God over all, forever praised! Amen.*

Paul never made a genealogy list, as did the Gospel writers, Matthew, and Luke, but it's hard to imagine that as he thought over these words that his mind didn't go back to the stories he had heard from childhood. He would reflect no doubt on Adam and Eve in the Garden of Eden. He would remember the lessons on Noah, and on the spread of mankind over the face of the known world.

Of course, what every Jew would remember with delight were the stories of Abraham, Isaac, and Jacob, and not just the stories of their life's adventures, but especially their interactions with God, and how He took such a special interest in this one race of people.

Paramount to all the stories of these men were the bigger than life impacts made on these men in relation to the covenant God established with them. Abraham received the covenant (Genesis 15) and later it was confirmed between Isaac (Genesis 26) and Jacob (Genesis 28). From those points in history the Jewish community had not only drawn their strength, based on the promises made, but actually confirmed their identity as God's chosen people. Everything else in their lives could be turned upside down but knowing that they belonged to the living God who made heaven and earth and chose them out of all the peoples of the planet to be His useful vessel for His divine purposes, gave them reason to persevere and thrive.

As the apostle ruminates on these things, we have to remember that this feeling of pride and hope that comes from his heritage is contrasted by the previous verses, where he carries such a great burden for them. It's as though he is saying, "How could they have received so much for so long and yet have thrown it all away to go after their selfish pursuits?"

I'm sure that many of us could ask the same question of people we know. We know people who have experienced the great blessings of God, but in foolishness have turned their backs on the one true Gospel to find one that fits their itching ears. How can people be so blind? The result is that we are left with the same task as Paul. We are to be burden bearers. We are to carry the load for our families. It's the Christian thing to do.

DAY 159

Romans 9:6 *It is not as though God's word had failed. For not all who are descended from Israel are Israel.*

Paul is very confident of one thing: God's Word does not fail! Though all the world may seem like it has turned upside down at points in our lives, God's Word remains constant. It is our anchor, our guide, our teacher, and our comfort.

The next sentence may take a little more investigation, however, when he said, "not all who are descended from Israel are Israel." When the average churchgoer speaks of God's chosen people, they will almost always refer to the nation of Israel, but Paul shows that there is a flaw in that kind of thinking.

Perhaps we could understand what he means better if we said, "Not all church members are Christians." At this point a light bulb goes off in our heads and we start to understand his meaning, for we can usually agree that it is possible for people to associate themselves among believers without becoming a true believer in Christ themselves.

The Jews are known as Abraham's children, but children who are of the bloodline only are not children of faith. It has been wisely said that God has no grandchildren because every new generation must enter into a covenant with Him just like the believers of old previously did. Our children must be taught that it is not in our church attendance, membership, or baptism, that one is made righteous before God, because each person has to enter into a personal relationship with Christ if he or she is going to be saved.

Paul saw that there were many who were Jews by heritage of bloodline that had departed from the faith of the covenant God had provided with Abraham. That's why he says that not all who claim Abraham actually belong to him. It is a covenant of faith with God that brings one into the family of God or makes an Israelite truly an Israelite.

My personal heritage in America goes back to 1673, and every generation of my branch of the James line since then has lived here. I am an American through and through, but I am also a child of Abraham. My relationship of faith in Christ makes me a true Israelite, even though I have never been to the land of Israel. In Christ I hold a dual citizenship.

DAY 160

Romans 9:7–8 *Nor because they are his descendants are they all Abraham's children. On the contrary, "It is through Isaac that your offspring will be reckoned." In other words, it is not the natural children who are God's children, but it is the children of the promise who are regarded as Abraham's offspring.*

To make clear the difference between national citizenship and spiritual citizenship, Paul continues his focus on Abraham's descendants. His focus here is on Isaac and what the birth of this son to Abraham meant in God's plan.

Isaac generally doesn't get as much attention as does his father, Abraham, or even his son, Jacob, or Israel. The truth be told, there isn't a lot written about him in the Genesis account, and if you asked the average churchgoer what they know about him, they would probably point you to either Abraham's sacrifice of him on Mount Moriah, or the story of Jacob stealing his blessing from his brother, Esau. Isaac remains low-key and almost a footnote on the pages of most Bible lessons.

However, Isaac has one thing going for him that other biblical characters don't, for Isaac is the son of promise. Though it was a big deal when Ishmael was born to Abraham (Genesis 16:15), and quite extraordinary when Abraham fathered six more sons by his second wife after Sarah died, Isaac being born to ninety-year-old Sarah was nothing short of miraculous. The other children came the normal biological way, but Isaac's birth was foretold and blessed by God before it ever happened. Ishmael was a product of man's lust, but Isaac's birth was a product of God's promise.

In the same way, Paul reminds us that it is not those who are born that are necessarily the children of God, but those who have been born again. It is for those who have realized the spiritual birth from above that can declare that they are also Abraham's offspring. We in Christ are children of promise. The promises are not only for a world to come, but for all the things that God promised to Abraham's descendants in this world, the most important being that we could have fellowship and be a friend with the Living God.

Isaac may not have drawn much press, but his way is the better way. Being a child of Abraham is not just a title; it is a promised position of family.

DAY 161

Romans 9:9 *For this was how the promise was stated: "At the appointed time I will return, and Sarah will have a son."*

Many of us know what it is like to have children, or as specifically mentioned here, a son. Most of us didn't have a divine messenger convey the news to us though, and yet we have been impacted by that huge event almost as much as if we had.

When Abraham received this notice back in Genesis 18, he was already a father. He had sired Ishmael through his wife's servant, Hagar. That had happened when he was eighty-six years old and I am sure it was the talk of the town and the countryside too. We are never told what age Hagar was, but we get the idea that she was young enough for childbearing, so the real event was that Abraham, in his old age, was able to be a father.

However, by the time God reveals to him that Sarah, Abraham's wife is going to have a son by him, thirteen years had rolled by. Abraham was now ninety-nine and Sarah was eighty-nine. No wonder the scripture records that both Abraham and Sarah laughed when they heard the news, because it truly seems beyond the realm of possibility.

As a matter of fact, it was. Biologically, Sarah was far past the days when she could even imagine bearing a child. From all that the eye could see, Ishmael, that son of her servant, was going to be the only child that Abraham was ever going to father. It must have been almost unbearable to Sarah to have to face that reality.

The beauty of the story and the beauty of scripture shows us that nothing is impossible with God. He can raise the dead, bring rain into a drought, calm storms, and do whatever He wants whenever He wants to do it. In this case, it was His plan to show everyone that this child, Isaac, was not just a son, he was in fact, THE son. He was the heir of the bloodline of God's people.

God's promises mean everything. We may not see how He is going to work things out, and we may even laugh to think that He might, but God always honors faithfulness, and He always keeps His Word. Abraham could trust in that and we can too. He's the same, yesterday, today, and forever.

DAY 162

Romans 9:10–13 *Not only that, but Rebekah's children had one and the same father, our father Isaac. Yet, before the twins were born or had done anything good or bad—in order that God's purpose in election might stand: not by works but by him who calls—she was told, "The older will serve the younger." Just as it is written: "Jacob I loved, but Esau I hated."*

Could that be right? Does God love some and hate others? That's certainly how a lot of people see God today. It almost seems like Paul agrees with this idea, but before we draw any conclusions, let's look a little closer at what the Bible is saying.

First, Paul goes back to the old story of when Isaac's wife, Rebekah, gave birth to two sons, as recorded in Genesis 25. The point is made that because God is God and is sovereign over everything, He can do whatever He wants to do. In this case, while the boys were still in Rebekah's womb, God made the decision to alter the custom of Abraham's society concerning the rights of the firstborn son and allow the younger to rule over the elder. Paul's point is that God's choice was not based on the goodness of Jacob or the badness of Esau because their births hadn't even occurred when the decision was made.

From the Genesis account, Paul leaps to the last book of the Old Testament and quotes from the writings of the prophet Malachi, chapter one. Here God is disgusted with Esau/Edom because they rejoiced when Babylon destroyed and pillaged Judah, even though their national roots ran back to the same source. It's a bit like having a family member cheer as your sister is being raped. Their actions were disgusting in God's eyes.

The words "love" and "hate" here are used to show the contrast of care God has for His chosen people. God is emphasizing His love for Judah regardless of how others may perceive them.

So back to the question, "Does God hate some people?" The simple answer is "no." God loves everyone. However, God's blessings fall to those who acknowledge His Lordship and serve Him faithfully. Others are also recipients of His love, but they never know it because they are bound up in hate that makes God seem irrelevant or at worst, evil. God cares about you, your neighbor, and your enemy. We see His love because we know Him.

DAY 163

Romans 9:14–15 *What then shall we say? Is God unjust? Not at all! For he says to Moses, "I will have mercy on whom I have mercy, and I will have compassion on whom I have compassion."*

Here is another idea that many times comes to the masses of our society as they proclaim, "God's not fair!" When things go wrong or our desires turn upside down, God is often the first one who catches the blame. Of course, this often comes from a skewed idea of who God is and what He is like, but it is no secret that people often doubt God's justice as it relates to their world.

Paul doesn't mess with words here. He makes it clear that God is not unjust. The reference he uses to prove his point takes us back to Exodus 33, where God and Moses are having a conversation. Moses was in transit with the motley crew of ex-slaves from Egypt known as the Israelites. It was just after the incident of the golden calf, and it appears that God was ready to wash His hands of the whole deliverance idea. However, Moses interceded for the people of Israel, and a conversation between he and God ensued where he asked three things of the Lord. He wanted God to teach him about how he is to do this great job of leading such a wayward people. Second, he asked the Lord to go with them and to allow His presence to be prominent in their midst. To both these requests God answered in the affirmative, but then Moses had one more request. He wanted to see God. It is at this point that God made the statement that Paul quotes above.

We've all been there. We know we want God to show us His way, to go with us, and if only He would allow us a little glimpse into His person, we just feel we could be so much better off.

God's response though is one of mercy. His mercy is extended so that Moses will not die. He asks for something that would be destructive for him and God cares too much to allow that to happen.

God's mercy and compassion are perfect examples of how much He cares for His own. We don't have to have a special insight into God because He knows that would damage our faith as well as our existence. He just wants us to trust Him, follow Him, and allow Him to do in us and through us as He wishes. When we do, we find God is not unjust. In fact, He's always looking out for us in every way possible.

DAY 164

Romans 9:16–18 *It does not, therefore, depend on man's desire or effort, but on God's mercy. For the Scripture says to Pharaoh: "I raised you up for this very purpose, that I might display my power in you and that my name might be proclaimed in all the earth." Therefore God has mercy on whom he wants to have mercy, and he hardens whom he wants to harden.*

I've always found the story of Moses and Pharaoh a fascinating account. Here played out in the book of Exodus, is the power struggle between good and evil on an epic scale, and neither side is willing to give in. As the plagues start to mount and the Egyptian people find that keeping the Israelites is inflicting a terrible toll on them individually and on the nation as a whole, they start pleading for Pharaoh to send those slaves away, but he doggedly holds on to his reins of power until the deaths of the nation's firstborn sons.

What is especially of notice to me is how the story progresses. From the time that Pharaoh first refused to grant Moses's request for the freedom of his people in Exodus 5, a pattern begins to develop. After each plague we see the words, "Pharaoh hardened his heart," or "Pharaoh's heart was hard." But by the time we reach chapter 10, the wording changes. Here we read how "the Lord hardened Pharaoh's heart." God did to Pharaoh what Pharaoh had been doing to himself all along, but when God did it, the work was final.

Throughout my life I have witnessed how many people have played games with God. They get in trouble and God delivers them, but they harden their hearts against God anyway. The pattern is repeated again and again, but eventually the hardness of their hearts becomes permanent and they don't hear the wooing of the Spirit any longer.

God is God and He has mercy for all, but He doesn't guarantee us that our opportunities to respond to His grace will last forever. God will do what brings glory to His name, and He is not one with whom we can trifle. He provides opportunities, but also can withdraw them, for He answers to no one. He allows people's lives to contrast against other lives, showing His grace and mercy to those who will listen and allowing those who won't to suffer the consequences.

We are not saved by our efforts, but by God's grace. We should never forget such mercy, or that in God alone our eternal destiny is determined.

DAY 165

Romans 9:19–20 *One of you will say to me: "Then why does God still blame us? For who resists his will?" But who are you, O man, to talk back to God? "Shall what is formed say to him who formed it, 'Why did you make me like this?'"*

It would seem that Paul loves to anticipate questions as to his theology when he teaches the church by Roman mail. In these days we have found that circumstances often keep us from being face to face as we study and grow in God's Word, but this is not unique to us today. Paul faced long-distance teaching and learning long before the internet.

The argument being made is basically saying, "Well, if God is sovereign over everything and I really have no say in what He does, then why should I be blamed if I do something He doesn't like? If God hardens my heart, why is that on me?"

He answers this question by quoting from two separate sections of the writings of the Prophet Isaiah. In the first, Isaiah 29:16, God is presenting the case that He is right to pronounce judgment on Jerusalem because of their waywardness. In the second quotation, Paul references Isaiah 45:9, where the object of God's focus is Cyrus, the king of the Persian empire. Again, the first quote concerns the Jews; the second, a pagan Persian king. In the first case God is displeased with the backsliding of His people, and in the latter reference God is showing His glory by using a pagan king to accomplish His purposes.

This may be a little confusing, so let me spell it out clearly. Paul proclaims, "God is God, and He can do whatever He wants to do." If He chooses to assess blame to the unfaithful, He can. If He chooses to use people whom others may not think would be qualified to be used for God's purposes, He can. God answers to no one, but His actions are always consistent with His ultimate plan and nature.

What does this mean for us? For one thing, it reminds us that our heritage doesn't protect us from God's wrath when we sin. It also tells us that He can raise up people from anywhere He chooses, to do His bidding if we should decide to not walk in His way. God will always be sovereign and will always do right. We had best do our part to keep up with where He is going.

DAY 166

Romans 9:21 *Does not the potter have the right
to make out of the same lump of clay some pottery
for noble purpose and some for common use?*

Picture this for a moment if you will. You find yourself down at the local lumberyard as you planned your next woodworking project. You buy some two-by-fours, some two-by-tens, some plywood, some wood screws, some roofing nails, a roll of tarpaper, and some shingles. The idea you have is to build a storage shed out behind your house and these new purchases should give you everything you need to complete your project.

But when you get to your backyard and begin surveying the setting, you find that your present shed really isn't in all that bad of shape. What you really need is to just make some sturdy shelves on the inside of it so you can store more materials. So, you use the materials you purchased to build the shelves and store the excess materials on the newly built structures.

Now this isn't at all what you first intended to build, but after all, you are a free spirit and can change your mind whenever you want to. It's your shed, it's your purchase, you are the contractor, and you make the decisions. No one would blame you for doing something other than what you first intended to do.

This is the case Paul makes about God. He is the Master Planner, He is the producer of all the materials, and He is the One who knows best how it will all come together. When He is working with our lives, He is able to do what is best for us and send us in directions we didn't expect, because, after all, He is in charge.

This may seem like a silly comparison, and it probably is. Still, I think the point is made. It's what Paul has been saying for a good part of this chapter. God is God. He is sovereign and in total control over everything and it is His own prerogative to do as He wishes. If He wants to put one man in a high station in life and another man in a lower one, who has a right to gripe? The fact that we have life at all is because of His creative genius and grace.

What this means is that our surrender to God's will for our lives needs to be complete. He will do what is good for us and what will bring Him glory. We may not see it or understand it, but after all, He is the one is charge.

DAY 167

Romans 9:22–24 *What if God, choosing to show his wrath and make his power known, bore with great patience the objects of his wrath—prepared for destruction? What if he did this to make the riches of his glory known to the object of his mercy, whom he prepared in advance for glory—even us, whom he also called, not only from the Jews but also from the Gentiles.*

I am reminded of the story in the second chapter of the Gospel of Luke of how Jesus was taken to the temple in Jerusalem when He was eight days old for the ritual of His circumcision. While He was there, a man named Simeon saw Jesus and blessed His parents but told them that the child would be the cause of the falling and rising of many in Israel.

That thought is not far from what Paul is saying here. Just as no one ever rises who has not fallen, no one can know the way back from God's wrath who has never experienced it. Basically, he is telling the Romans that perhaps God poured out His wrath on the Jewish people so that He was able to offer them mercy and provide salvation when they saw the dire contrast between the two options.

This is true not only for the Jews, but for all people everywhere. Sin is a terrible taskmaster, and the Lord allows everyone to be a free agent of their own choices in order for us to see just how badly we can mess up our lives when we don't follow the guidelines for living, He has given us. By showing us the options of wrath vs. mercy, we hopefully will choose mercy and turn from the path of destruction that we walk down without Him.

God always has a plan, and He always has a reason for doing what He does. Even to this day I understand that when hard times come my way in the form of injury, sickness, financial stress, or some other malady, it is another opportunity for me to testify to His grace and remember that He causes all things to really work together for good, as we are called according to His purpose (Romans 8:28). Life may not always be easy, but it always points to the fact that His way is the best way.

We may be born headed for the precipice of destruction, but because of God's grace we are turned aside from that cliff of sin and shown a better way in Christ. We don't always walk in the light given to us, but when we do, we find God has been waiting for us, for our best, all the time.

DAY 168

Romans 9:25–26 *As he says in Hosea: "I will call them 'my people' who are not my people; and I will call her 'my loved one' who is not my loved one," and, "It will happen that in the very place where it was said to them, 'You are not my people,' they will be called 'sons of the living God.'"*

The story to which Paul refers is a fascinating one. It's the story of how God instructed one of his prophets to marry a prostitute, so that the story of God's love for a wayward people could be visualized for all to see. When children came to that union, they were given names that meant, "not loved," and "not my people." How would you like to go through life with those names branded upon you? It was a sad state of affairs for the people who had once been so close to their Redeemer.

However, the story doesn't end there. A time came when, in the course of the book, God would call His people to Himself and their names would be changed to "my people," and "sons of the living God." What does it mean? Well, it's a story about redemption. It's a testimony to a God who loves His own so much that He is not willing to let them go. He will go to any and every length possible to redeem us for our good and His glory.

That's the way it still is today. We who have enjoyed a relationship with God want all people everywhere to experience what we have experienced and know what we know. We want people to understand that even though they may have been born under a cloud, there is a bright light of hope still available for them. God has provided His Son, Jesus Christ, as an answer for the sin that plagues our world, and all who will come to Him will find freedom, forgiveness, and a new start in life.

Along with a new start is a new name. Where once we were called a sinner, in Christ we are called "Christian." We are among those who have been blessed with a way to see life more abundantly, just like Jesus promised. We who felt like we were not loved by God are now loved by God, and we who felt like we didn't belong to anyone, anywhere, are now called sons of the living God.

This is what God does. He is in the redeeming and restoring business. He takes the broken and makes it whole again. He is working for our good and longs to bring us home. He so loved the world that He gave us His Son.

DAY 169

Romans 9:27–28 *Isaiah cries out concerning Israel:*
"Though the number of the Israelites be like the sand by the
sea, only the remnant will be saved. For the Lord will carry
out his sentence on earth with speed and finality."

When I came into this world, there were about 2.7 billion people on this planet. As of 2020 there were almost 7.8 billion people covering much the same area. That's a lot of population increase over my short lifetime. Because of the television, radio, cell phones, and the internet there seems to be a lot more of the earth than there used to be when our communication was much more isolated. The world may be getting smaller because of our access to it, but we are a long way from being united as one.

These numbers are staggering, and are increasing every day, but still we hear the Word of the Lord declaring that only a remnant will be saved. When God decides that time shall be no more and the wheels of judgment and justice are rolled into place, it won't matter how many people are alive or how many have lived, for all will stand before the King of kings.

There are always self-ordained prophets in every generation who claim to have some special insight as to when all these things will occur, and even people who truly mean well by their love for the Lord can get caught up in the speculation. I guess all we truly know though is that the Lord will return, and judgment will take place. Everything else is just opinion.

So, what are we to do with this knowledge? It behooves all of us who know the saving grace of our Lord Jesus Christ, to carry a burden for the lost masses of humanity who do not know the redemption Christ can provide. In our families alone, there are so many people who are among the number who may miss out on God's plan of salvation unless something happens to convince them otherwise. Let us be the salt that makes them thirsty for the grace of God. Let us be the light that points to a consistent path of righteousness. Let our feet walk the highway of holiness ahead of them so that they will have a model to follow.

If most will be lost and judgment is coming, it's time to take this warning seriously. It will be to our eternal shame if we have the words of life and neglect to share them with those who need them most. May God open the doors for us to be agents of life for those He puts in our paths.

DAY 170

Romans 9:29 *It is just as Isaiah said previously: "Unless the Lord Almighty had left us descendants, we would have become like Sodom, we would have been like Gomorrah."*

Paul is quoting here from the Prophet Isaiah, chapter one, verse nine. It's the same chapter that begins with the Lord declaring that even though He had nurtured and raised up Judah and Jerusalem, they had rebelled against Him, and as a result they would suffer the consequences for their attitudes and actions.

It's actually a statement of grace to which Paul is referring as he addresses the Romans. He is telling them that the same pattern of rebellion witnessed by Isaiah was being made evident with the Jews of his day as well. Because of God's great grace and mercy, He was leaving them a remnant rather than wiping them out. In both Isaiah's time and Paul's time, the faithful were few in number, and the penalty of judgment was falling heavily upon them.

Flashforward to our present age and situation. Can we say that today that God's people have been proven faithful for our world? Certainly, there are true believers on every continent who continue to proclaim the Lord's majesty regardless of the societal pressure not to do so. But it doesn't take a social scientist or religious expert to recognize that the nations of the world have been very guilty of not giving God the honor and prominence He is due. Even the church that bears His name, and is supposed to be fulfilling His Great Commission, has too often grown anemic by an insufficient diet on the whole Word of God, and distracted by infighting as it tries to compete with the standards of the world.

What Isaiah proclaimed about the Jews of his day and what Paul saw throughout the Jewish society of the first century, we many times see repeated in our Christian circles. We are in the midst of spiritual warfare and unless God is merciful, we too, as a nation, and as a called-apart people will face the judgment and justice of God. We too could become like Sodom and Gomorrah if God weighs us in the balance and finds us wanting. There is a better option. Isaiah wrote of it too: "Seek the LORD while he may be found; call upon him while he is near" (Isaiah 55:6). May the Lord show us favor, mercy, and revival one more time.

DAY 171

Romans 9:30–31 *What then shall we say? That the Gentiles, who did not pursue righteousness, have obtained it, a righteousness that is by faith; but Israel, who pursued a law of righteousness, has not attained it.*

G race is certainly an amazing thing. Those who didn't look for it, found it, and those who pursued it—on their own terms—missed it altogether. That seems to be the message Paul is espousing here. He will deal with that thought more completely when we get over into chapter ten of this epistle.

It's a bit like a tale of gold miners. Some who went searching for gold, who panned, dug, and blasted to find it, came up empty in their quest. But it's also the story of men who were walking along a creek bank and looked into the water and saw tons of gleaming riches just lying there for the taking.

I believe the lesson that we need to take away from this idea is that no one finds God on their own. It's not like we went out searching for God one day and by accident, or by purpose, stumbled upon Him. He is the one who initiated the search, and He is the one who has been leaving the breadcrumbs for us to follow so that the path into His presence can more easily be found. He is the Good Shepherd who has been watching out for His sheep even when we didn't know we were being watched.

Of course, this doesn't excuse the church from its responsibility in spreading the Word of God. We are to do our job in sowing the seed, cultivating, and caring for what we have planted, but we must always remember who the Lord of the harvest is. It is His seed and the produce belongs to Him as well. We are just the laborers He has called to work in His field.

A person may ask, "If the Gentiles found God without looking and the Jews looked and missed Him, why don't we just let folks find Him on their own, like the example Paul gives?" The problem is that the Gentiles didn't find God in a vacuum. Every person that comes to faith arrives at that point by a combination of the Spirit's leading and the witness of workers in the harvest field. We do not produce life, for only God can do that, but we can be helpers to make the field as ready for the gospel as possible. Someone prepared the way for the Lord to speak to our hearts, and it is our job to prepare the way for the Spirit to speak to others.

DAY 172

Romans 9:32 *Why not? Because they pursued it not by faith but as if it were by works. They stumbled over the stumbling stone.*

Paul is making reference here to the fact that the Jews did not seek righteousness by faith, but by their own natural abilities. The problem with what they did is the same problem that people have with serving the Lord today. They want to do it their way. The way of the Christian is always to be a way of faith. It will no doubt play out in physical ways, but our relationship with Christ is first and foremost a faith walk. If we try to earn our way to righteousness, we will end up just like the Jews of whom Paul is speaking.

Our walk with Jesus really does come down to doing it His way. Where mankind gets in trouble is when we think we can change the direction He gave us and follow our own preferences rather than the way of faith. This is why we have the Holy Scriptures as our guide. When we ignore what they say or interpret them in such a way that their intended meaning is distorted, then we fall over the stumbling stone once again.

Living the Christian life is all about learning the ways of the Kingdom of God, which are paradoxical to the normal way of doing things. In this kingdom the poor are rich, the weak are strong, the helpless have power, and the undeserving are justified. In the Kingdom of God, the highest rank is the one of the lowest servants, and the one who has the most is the one who has given all. These things seem so backwards to the post-modern world and therefore they trip over the stumbling stone once again.

A faith walk is just that—one without sight. When we have to put spiritual things into physical categories, we have missed the point of trusting without seeing, and that blinds us truly to what God is doing. The Lord is continually putting out the call for followers who will cast all their cares on Him and follow at His word. It's a big risk, but with such a risk comes big rewards.

To recap, righteousness is not achieved by what we do, but by who we are, or more importantly, *whose* we are. We are people who have been redeemed, but not because of anything we have done. We walk by faith, live by faith, plan by faith, and love even our enemies because faith in Christ has made it possible to do so. The world will never understand it until they experience it, because until they do, it's the way of the stumbling stone.

DAY 173

Romans 9:33 *As it is written, "See, I lay in Zion a stone that causes men to stumble and a rock that makes them fall, and the one who trusts in him will never be put to shame."*

There is an old saying which states, "You can't die on every hill." As a minister of the gospel in local churches since 1974 I have come to understand that statement far better than most, because there are so many causes one could choose for which to fight, but not all of them are worth dying over.

Christianity has often made the mistake of falling on its own sword in this area. Because many Christians think that showing the love of Christ means being all things to all people, they try to bend every which way to please folks, but most of the time end up not making anybody happy and themselves miserable.

As Paul quotes from Isaiah once again, he is claiming that Christ is the Rock of our salvation and following Him requires looking at our world with different eyes, a new Christ-space worldview, if you will. By trying to be Christian through bending to accommodate the world, we only cheapens the grace that we have received, and makes us weak replicas of the people Jesus wants us to be.

Here is some guidance for the thoughtful Christian. First, place yourself totally under that lordship of Jesus Christ. He is the King, and we are the servants. We cannot allow anything to mess with that chain of command. Second, pour yourself into the study of God's Word, the Bible. It's not enough to know what it says, but it must be understood in the context as it was written, and for the audience who was intended to receive it. A good rule of thumb here is to remember that though the Bible was written for us; it was not written to us. We must keep in perspective that difference as we look to legitimately strive to interpret its truth for our lives today.

Finally, it is vital that we approach all people with love. Some may rail against Christians, our God, and our Bible, but that comes with the territory. By following these simple steps, we can help others to keep from stumbling over the Rock of Christ and falling for every wind of doctrine. In doing this we will never be put to shame or bring shame to the name of Jesus.

DAY 174

Romans 10:1 *Brothers, my heart's desire and prayer to God for the Israelites is that they may be saved.*

Over the years as a pastor, I have been in many prayer meetings where prayer requests were made publicly by members of the congregation. It is not unusual to hear requests made for people who have cancer or some upcoming surgery. I often heard requests made for safety in travel for some loved one. There are many times requests are made for financial needs, or a request for a job. The topics can be as varied as the number of people who are in these kinds of meetings.

The request of God that is much less frequently made is for the souls who are lost and need a Savior. There have been some occasions when people were grieved enough to share such needs with the body of Christ, but far too often we keep these kinds of things to ourselves.

That seems strange to me, especially in light of what the apostle is saying. How could it not be our heart's desire to see sons, daughters, spouses, parents, and friends find forgiveness for their sins and freedom in Christ. It's not that they are going to be lost someday, they are lost right now! Do we not believe that they are lost? Do we think that God is going to make a special exception for them because they are related to us? Why don't we carry a burden for the spiritual needs around us as much as the physical needs that are more public?

I'm not sure that there is any one answer to those questions, but it is pretty evident how Paul feels about the matter. His "desire and prayer to God for the Israelites is that they may be saved." It's not just his immediate family that causes him to grieve, but for the race of people of whom he is a part.

Perhaps what we need to do is to begin with those we know, but then branch out to public officials, community leaders, the local firefighters, or the police department. What if we prayed for our president, our national leaders, and all those who are in authority? Would it make a difference? I don't know, but I know it couldn't hurt. I do know that carrying a load for others in prayer to be saved has the possibility of changing lives for time and eternity. It may begin close to home, but we are building the Kingdom of God as Christ builds His church. The way forward in doing that always begins in prayer.

DAY 175

Romans 10:2 *For I can testify about them that they are zealous for God, but their zeal is not based on knowledge.*

Have you ever wanted to believe something so badly that you want to believe it even if it is proven to be false? In this atmosphere of political unrest that surrounds many people, this becomes a way of life. When I was young, I wanted to believe that I could be an Olympic runner, but as time and events of life went on, I had to come to the realization that I just didn't have what it took to be that kind of an athlete.

Dreams for which we are zealous die hard, and there is no time when this is truer than when it comes to spiritual matters. Religion is such a contentious topic that most families don't even want to bring it up at family reunions or holiday gatherings. The most fervent advocates of whatever branch of belief that is pushed, can make life miserable for those who don't want to argue over such things.

Paul knew what he was talking about. He had been a hardline Pharisee, the strictest of the Jews, and he pushed his belief system on all who would listen. But when he met Jesus on the road to Damascus, everything changed in his focus. He remained as fervent as ever, but his direction changed to see Jesus as the Messiah he had been longing for all his life. His contemporaries naturally didn't understand this transformation, and those who had been his friends turned against him. His zeal and their zeal met like a warm front and a cold front that produces a thunderstorm.

In the church today, folk theology runs rampant. Because preachers are trained by different people, and they have different levels of training and different years of experience, one pastor's theology can be almost completely opposite from another pastor's theology. Obviously, they can't all be right, but this discrepancy causes great confusion among the laity that listen to them week after week. Many just preach what they have heard others say, without studying for themselves, and errors abound. This is preaching with zeal, but without knowledge. It's a dangerous thing because it leads to bad theology and leads people astray.

Paul loved his family, and we love ours, but facts and truth must always trump zeal. If not, then we are in a worse state than unbelievers.

DAY 176

Romans 10:3 *Since they did not know the righteousness that comes from God and sought to establish their own, they did not submit to God's righteousness.*

I remember hearing both Frank Sinatra and Elvis Presley each singing a song entitled, "I Did it My Way." It was a hit for both of them because it seemed to resonate with the basic core of human nature. It is sometimes even sung at funerals, as if the person in the coffin wants to say one more time, "No one is going to tell me what to do. I did it my way."

Unfortunately, that's the way too many people live their lives. Unwilling to bend to new ideas or new ways of doing things, they spend their years stuck in their stubborn attitude and staying ignorant of any new light that might come their way.

Apparently, the Apostle Paul saw this attitude among the Jews of his generation. They sought after righteousness, but not being willing to find it through God's direction, they continued to flounder on trying to figure out divine things with human wisdom. The result is not only historical, but sad. The blessing of being God's ambassadors to the rest of the world was passed to the church as Jewish religious zealots refused to bend to the new thing that God was doing in their midst.

There is so much we can learn from this. Although it has been said that nobody enjoys change except a wet baby, change is inevitable in our world. It's also inevitable in the church. If the Covid-19 pandemic of 2020-2021 should have taught us anything, we should have learned that what we are used to can be turned on its head in a moment. Styles of worship will always need to change with the generations that pass. Stretching our understanding is always because no one has all the answers. Our very bodies change every cell of our make-up every seven years, so when we stop necessary changing, we die.

You know who doesn't change? Jesus. The Word of God doesn't change either. We can trust in the relationship we have with Him and trust His Word to guide us into the paths of true righteousness. We can rely on the fact our growth in grace depends on our closeness to our Savior, and by understanding this we learn that His way, and not our way, is the best way.

DAY 177

Romans 10:4 *Christ is the end of the law so that there may be righteousness for everyone who believes.*

The goal that God has for every one of us is righteousness and He wants us to understand that He only has our best interest in mind whenever He does anything. The law that was given to Moses many generations ago was given so that people could learn a framework of what righteousness before God looks like. The only problem with the law was the fact that man in his natural state doesn't possess what is necessary to keep it. The desires for selfish gratification push to the forefront, and corrupt what God intended to help us be holy.

This is where Jesus comes in. He doesn't destroy the law, but instead, fulfills it. Where the law could only lay out a pattern of what God expects from us, Jesus is able to transform our hearts and minds into new creations that can free us to live for God's glory. Selfish desire and its nature of sin can be put to death by the infilling of God's Holy Spirit, where we are freed to live as we were intended to live.

The key to this freedom goes back to the simple concept of belief. Being righteous before God is not possible in our trying to do good or be good, but belief in the fact that Jesus' death on our behalf creates a new path to God. We can be as God wants us to be because Jesus made it possible.

Our own historical record shows that we don't operate too well on our own. Even when we are trying to serve the Lord, we often walk blindly because we try to do it without divine guidance. But the Spirit of God within us is there to direct us as to how we should live, as He gently nudges us and checks us concerning what is pleasing and displeasing to the Father. As we learn to recognize the Spirit's work in our lives, then we conform more to the image of Jesus as we progress on our journey.

God is providing all we need to live righteous lives before Him. We have His instructions, we have the example of Jesus, and we have the Spirit of Christ within us to help us on our way. Without Jesus, the way to righteousness is incomplete, but with Him we walk in lockstep with God's plan for our lives. This is a great gift that none of us deserve, but because of God's great care for us, we can be made righteous today in His sight.

DAY 178

Romans 10:5–8 *Moses describes in this way the righteousness that is by the law: "The man who does these things will live by them." But the righteousness that is by faith says: "Do not say in your heart, 'Who will ascend into heaven?'" (that is, to bring Christ down) "or 'Who will descend into the deep?'" (that is, to bring Christ up from the dead). But what does it say? "The word is near you; it is in your mouth and in your heart," that is, the word of faith we are proclaiming:*

This passage of scripture can be a bit confusing because Paul bounces around in the Old Testament books of Leviticus and Deuteronomy. These are two books of the Law, or Torah, upon which the Jewish people base their belief system.

However, the first quotation from Leviticus 18:5 has to do with adherence to specific practices that would keep the people clean before God. The rest of the quotations come from Deuteronomy 30:12–14, where Moses is recapping the choice of life or death for the people of God, depending on how obedient they will be to the Lord's commands.

What Paul is dealing with specifically though, has to do with man's righteousness before God. His reading of Jesus into these Old Testament passages is meant to reinforce his arguments for the life of faith, but because of the context, it's a little hard to grasp his intent.

Basically, here is what he is trying to get across to the Romans as well as those who would read this after them. Though actions often speak louder than words, it is not so much action that is required. It is the word of faith that is necessary to be right in God's eyes. If all is well with the heart, then the right actions will follow.

Don't we see this today? Some people spend their lives trying to promote worthy causes, even spiritual causes, but without transforming faith to set them into a new status with God, they are fanning the air without much lasting effect. The words that are in our mouths, the words that come from our hearts, are life changing when they are the words Christ has placed within us. When they are just our words, they will fall on deaf ears, or what they promote will eventually pass away. When Christ makes us holy, our lives change, and words that reflect that life of faith will follow.

DAY 179

Romans 10:9–10 *That if you confess with your mouth, "Jesus is Lord," and believe in your heart that God raised him from the dead, you will be saved. For it is with your heart that you believe and are justified, and it is with your mouth that you confess and are saved.*

Within these two verses are the core components of the gospel message. The process of salvation on our part begins with the simple instruction to believe. We are to believe that Jesus is Lord of all. He is not just simply a lord, or even a god. He is Lord of lords, King of kings, and God of gods, for He will not take a back seat to anyone, anywhere, or at any time. God the Father has exalted Him to the highest place and our belief in that fact is where our faith journey begins.

We also have to believe in His resurrection. Every other religious leader throughout the history of the world has died and left their human remains behind as proof of their humanity. Jesus, however, was as dead as any of them, but then was resurrected to not only eternal life, but with a glorified body that will never wear out. He is the firstborn of the resurrection and we who trust in Him will be resurrected someday in like manner.

What this belief produces is our salvation. It is not from our good works, our good looks, our intellect, our talents, or our contribution to society and the history of the world. We are saved by faith in Jesus Christ; nothing more and nothing less.

As Paul elaborates here, we are justified by the dictates of our heart. Naturally, he didn't mean that blood-pumping muscle that lies within our chest. No, for the ancient world, the seat of our emotions was driven from our inward being and it is the totality of our rational focus that is intended here. With this kind of belief, we are judged as righteous, or justified, before God and are made a member of His kingdom.

The final step of the salvation process is to speak the words of faith with our mouths. This is why we ask for a testimony when people are baptized and why we encourage believers to share their story with others. First, it proves that we are not ashamed to be numbered with the people of God, and second, it gives us opportunity to help someone else understand God's work in our lives. The end result is salvation. Thanks be to God.

DAY 180

Romans 10:11 As the Scripture says, "Anyone who trusts in him will never be put to shame."

It's really hard to find things in life in which you can put your full confidence without any fear of being let down or disappointed. We don't have to put many years under our belts before we realize that people will sometimes let us down, no matter how well intended they may be. We know that we can't trust the red tape of governmental affairs, and even our own minds and health fail us if we live long enough.

That's why this verse is so refreshing. Paul has been talking about how our faith enables us to enter into a relationship with God through His Son, Jesus the Christ, and here we are reminded that when we have a relationship with God in this way, it is solid and secure. We don't have to worry about God changing His mind and letting us down just when we need Him most. He is always faithful.

I remember visiting with a saint of the church who was a couple of years past 100 in his birthday celebrations. His family was all gone and as he faced long days alone, and his body was failing his faith wavered as well. I'll never forget him telling me, "I'm starting to think God doesn't want me." He was serious. Even though he had served the Lord for many decades, his mind was weakening and causing him to doubt whether he had been good enough to be pleasing to God.

With joy I assured him whenever I would visit, that God hadn't forgotten him and that he could count on the faithfulness of the Holy Spirit to see him through all the way into eternity. He finally did go on to his reward, and I know that the grace that saved him brought him into the arms of Jesus, just like the Master promised.

It is so easy to be disappointed in people, systems, and relationships. We fail at times because none of us is perfect, and our flaws sometimes get the best of us. But it's not that way with God. He is always faithful, always trustworthy, and always there for us in all situations. We can stand on His promises with confidence and be assured that whatever He has in store for us will come to pass, and it will be for our good and His glory. We can relax today in the arms of Jesus, knowing He will never let us down.

DAY 181

Romans 10:12–13 *For there is no difference between Jew and Gentile—the same Lord is Lord of all and richly blesses all who call on him, for "Everyone who calls on the name of the Lord will be saved."*

There are many people in our modern societies who love to play the race card whenever they run out of facts to back up their arguments. No doubt some have genuine grievances because there is a lot of bigotry and sin in the world, and sometimes people really do end up on the short end of the stick.

That's not the case with real Christianity though, because when it comes to grace everyone is equal at the foot of the cross of Jesus. He died for people of all races and colors, and no one can ever rightly accuse Him of favoring one people group over another. But with this consistent level of equality, there is one thing that needs to be considered. Even though all are loved, it is only those who consider Him Lord of all that can receive the full blessings that God has available to them.

When we give up our personal rights into the hands of Jesus, He is able to direct us in the way we should live our lives, and as a result of His direction we find blessings that we would never find otherwise. Having the mind of Christ, which always puts God first and others before ourselves, causes us to make decisions and treat people in such a way that only benefits our own lives in the long run. It is true that what goes around comes around.

We must realize that this doesn't mean all of our life will be problem free and without challenges. Sometimes having the direction of Christ means that we will be placed right in the midst of the storms of life, but Christians have found that even in such places there are blessings that we would never have experienced if we hadn't been to such places. But along with those blessings there is one more benefit that we need to consider. When we call on the name of the Lord, He provides salvation for us.

There is no double-talk here. Everyone means everyone. Every person regardless of their race, their color, their social status, their financial situation, gender, or marital situation will be saved when they call upon Jesus and make Him Lord of his or her life. The gospel is free for all and to all who will follow after Christ, and that is the good news that will never change.

DAY 182

Romans 10:14 *How, then, can they call on the one they have not believed in? And how can they believe in the one of whom they have not heard? And how can they hear without someone preaching to them?*

Somewhere in the world, in fact, in too many places in the world, there are people who have never heard the name of Jesus. They not only don't know that He is the Savior of the world but have no idea that He exists or ever has existed. For many more people, they know the name, but it is often just used as slang or in swearing and have no real idea of His life and mission here on this planet.

When we live in a church cloistered bubble we hardly think about such things. We know that the world is in need, and we know that sin is running rampant in the nations of the world, but sometimes we either ignore or hide from that fact. Evangelism is not an issue that we concern ourselves with because after all, that is for the professional clergy folks.

Paul is making a plea here. "How can they call?" "How can they believe?" "How can they hear?" These are not idle or unimportant questions because they strike right at the core of who we are as Christians.

It is time for the Church of Jesus Christ to answer these questions by praying in and raising up a whole host of preachers who will take the gospel to our cities, our country sides, and to the nations of the world. It is time for the church to accept the burden and responsibility of carrying such a burden, that our youth and even our children are impacted by the need to save souls and feel the call of God to do something about it.

When I confirmed my call to preach, I was in my first year of college. I had considered being a preacher throughout the latter part of my high school days but could never find the courage to accept such a mission. But when I finally announced God's call on my life, there were others who already knew, and were just waiting for me to hear God's voice on my own. The saints of my church had been praying for me and trusting God to confirm in me what He had already confirmed in them.

Are we praying for the children and teens of our churches to hear the voice of God? If not, why not? How will the world hear without a preacher?

DAY 183

Romans 10:15 *And how can they preach unless they are sent? As it is written, "How beautiful are the feet of those who bring good news!"*

Here is a question that should cause most church people of our land to seriously ponder. How long has it been since God has called someone out of your congregation to preach His gospel? If you can say that God is choosing people out of your group on a regular basis, then I congratulate you and rejoice in what you are experiencing. However, sadly, that is not the case in most churches of which I am acquainted.

In many of our religious schools there is a serious shortage of ministerial candidates, and even of those who do attend to prepare for this life's work of service, there are many who never finish their education. Of those who do graduate from such schools, the dropout rate among clergy within the first five years of service is staggering. The years of preparation and training is often not adequate to get new pastors ready for the rough and tumble life of living within a church setting fulltime. Add to this the effect such pressures have on a spouse who has not been trained in such matters, and one can see why divorces among parsonage families are on the rise.

This is a lesson for all who are not called to serve in such a capacity, but who are definitely called to support those who are. Many a pastor is made or broken by the congregation he or she is called to serve. Often churches expect near perfection in areas of preaching, teaching, counseling, administration, music, technology, human resources, and a myriad of other parts of a church's ministry. When the pastor is not given time to learn the job before being bombed with criticism, the pressure often is just too much.

Here is something church folks need to remember. If a pastor has been sent to you to preach to you, remember who it is that called and sent that pastor. God's plan for God's man or woman deserves consideration at the very least. Remembering that their "beautiful feet" have been commissioned by the God Most High should cause us to pause before we criticize.

God calls and God sends, but churches often do make or break pastors. Support for developing clergy is critical in such times as these and if we want to have more generations of preachers to share the good news, we need to back them beginning right now.

DAY 184

Romans 10:16 *But not all the Israelites accepted the good news. For Isaiah says, "Lord, who has believed our message?"*

It's sad to say, but it is a true saying that there are always going to be people who will not believe the message of the cross. There are so many people who have barely heard the message, so many that have heard the message distorted, and so many people that have basically misunderstood that message, that the odds against reaping a harvest for our King are greatly increased. Added to this number are the many who have heard, understood, and rejected the message, so again, we see that we don't have an easy task.

Paul pulls part of a verse from Isaiah 53 here to emphasize the state of the Jewish people of his time. He would no doubt, be the first one to say that unbelievers are legion in number, but acknowledging this never seemed to diminish his efforts to change the odds that were stacked against him.

Here is where we can learn much from the apostle. Even though, "not all the Israelites accepted the good news," there is a silver lining shining through this cloud. It must be that some did accept the good news—and that's what gives us hope.

Just look around where you live. It's most likely true that there are many people who are your neighbors that live out their days in denial of the gospel. But even in the midst of many who may never believe, there are some who will believe—if they are given the opportunity to hear the Word of God explained to them on the level they can understand. This is our mission field. We are not going to win everyone for Christ, but if we spend the rest of our lives trying to win people one person at a time, we will never run out of prospects for eternal life.

In fact, I am convinced that God puts us where we are, regardless of where that may be, and when are supposed to be there, regardless of how old or young we may be, for the purpose of living out the gospel before our peers. There is not a family who doesn't need Jesus. There is not a school child who doesn't need Jesus. There is not a marriage, a retirement home, a government building, or any place that contains people, that doesn't need Jesus. Our work is cut out for us, and we'd better get busy. We will not win them all, but by God's grace we can win some, for His glory.

DAY 185

Romans 10:17 *Consequently, faith comes from hearing the message, and the message is heard through the word of Christ.*

When did you first hear the message of Christ? It may not have been the first time you ever heard it preached, because until the Spirit of God quickens our hearts through our ears, we never really hear the good news.

For me it was on an August Sunday evening back in 1960. I had been attending church services more than regularly for most of my life. Every week I was in Sunday School, morning worship, Sunday evening service, Wednesday night prayer meetings, plus two-week revivals, and two-week children's Bible school were a steady diet. I know I heard the message over and over, but if the truth were known, lots of church didn't cause me to hear.

It happened just after my sixth birthday that the Lord used all those other services as primers to get me ready for that Sunday evening. I was sitting on the front row in the middle of the sanctuary with my dad. The altar was about three steps in front of me. I couldn't tell you what the preacher said or even what book he preached from, but all at once I knew I didn't know Jesus like others knew Him, and I knew that I needed to.

Those three steps to kneel at an altar at the close of a Sunday evening preaching service brought a six-year-old boy into the Kingdom of God. From that day to this I have never doubted the experience with Christ that took place that night. My life was changed forever because Jesus did something in me that I couldn't do myself.

My faith came about because I heard the message. I heard the message because the church had its doors open on a Sunday evening so I could be there. My parents made sure that their kids were always there whenever the doors were open. I don't know if I ever sat in the seat on the front row of the church again, but that night all the pieces fell into place, and I became a new creation in Christ.

Faith came to me by hearing the message, and the message was heard through the Word of Christ. My story is different from others, but alike in one special way. Whenever the church does its job to share the message, the Holy Spirit has an opportunity to offer anyone a new life—and He will.

DAY 186

Romans 10:18 *But I ask: Did they not hear? Of course they did: "Their voice has gone out into all the earth, their words to the ends of the world."*

In this verse, Paul quotes from Psalm 19:4, and the point in context is that people everywhere, and the Jews in particular, had received ample communication from God about His existence. The psalmist was declaring that "the heavens declare the glory of God; the skies proclaim the work of his hands," (Psalm 19:1). The general revelation of God's creation should wake everyone up to the fact that He truly is the King of kings!

However, we know that is not the case. Even though mankind sees the wonders of the universe around us, the human tendency is to try and find some rational and finite way to explain it all. There is nothing wrong with honest curiosity, but when it is honest and complete it will lead us right back to God every time. When it is self-serving and God denying, it only displays the ignorance of the investigator.

This is why Paul is making the case that preachers are needed. Everyone should see, but everyone doesn't see. Everyone should be convinced by the grandeur of the work of God's hands, but everyone is not convinced. Because of this, God uses men and women to accomplish His purpose to communicate and convince people of His majesty.

So, this takes us back to verse fourteen, "How can they hear without someone preaching to them?" We never want to downplay the role and power of the Holy Spirit working in a person's life, for God can reach anyone, anywhere as He chooses to do so. But it seems that His chosen method of reaching the world of men and women is through other men and women, who are empowered by the Holy Spirit. Prevenient grace can draw a person to God, but in order for more people to be touched by the words of life, God uses us to reach others.

As a result of this truth, Ephesians 4 states that God still calls apostles, prophets, evangelists, pastors, and teachers," to do the work of touching people with the words of life. We have been given the Great Commission by Jesus and our time is limited as we work to fulfill it. The world may see the natural beauty God has created and be awed by it, but each of us is needed to share the good news of salvation with words, so let's get to work.

DAY 187

Romans 10:19 *Again I ask: Did Israel not understand? First,
Moses says, "I will make you envious by those who are not a nation;
I will make you angry by a nation that has no understanding."*

The quotation given by Paul here is from the last part of Deuteronomy 32:21. The occasion is when Moses is declaring God's wrath against Israel if they should become wayward and cease from following the one true living God. The picture painted for the unbelieving and apostate followers of self rather than God is stark and warns that if the people of God turn their backs on God, He will use others who have not had the same privileges as the Israelites to accomplish His purposes.

History has recorded how this all played out. The book of Judges itself is a documentary of God's favor, man's laxity and rebellion, the overthrow and oppression by Israel's enemies, pleas for mercy to God, God's deliverance and favor, and then the process starts all over again. By Paul's time, this scenario had been played out countless times, and was proof that God always keeps His promises.

This is where the church comes in. The Israelites continued to be unfaithful, and God grafted in the Gentiles to accomplish His plans. His will is unstoppable, and His options are endless as His schedule rolls right along through the ages.

These words should serve as reminders that if God was willing to set aside His original plan to use the bloodline descendants of Abraham, to use spiritual substitutes known as Gentiles, He can and will do the same with the modern church if it becomes unfaithful to Him.

Our world is populated with many church groups who claim the title but have denied God's instructions and power. Factions may splinter off and go their own ways, but God will use whomever He chooses to retain a church that will do His bidding. This is not something to gloat about, but to grieve over. Anytime the church forsakes the clear instruction of scripture to run after current trends and idolatries, it will pay a bitter price. God will not be mocked, and He will not be outwitted by people who think they know better.

Therefore, be faithful. Let's be true to our King. Let's be real Christians!

DAY 188

Romans 10:20 *And Isaiah boldly says, "I was found by those who did not seek me; I revealed myself to those who did not ask for me."*

The passage to which Paul refers in this verse comes from Isaiah 65:1, and it gives a pretty good description of God's dealings with Israel from the time of Abraham on to the church of the present day. All of us have one thing in common, and that is in the fact of God's matchless grace upon us.

We have no record in scripture of Abraham asking to find God. We likewise can find no one today who has ever initiated a relationship with God. He always has and always does make the first move when it comes to a divine-human connection. We may like to think that we found Jesus, but in truth, He found us. We wouldn't even know where to start looking.

This is an amazing fact that we will never be able to fully understand or explain. Why would the King of all that there is, be concerned enough about anyone to begin first contact and establish a relationship of love? It's a mystery, but one of which the wise take full advantage, and enjoy a life of fellowship and interaction with God. Those who are foolish ignore God's offers of intimate connection and think that they have all they need to get by without God's involvement. Some even go so far as to deny God even exists. It's like the pot saying that the potter never had a hand in its' being. It's ignorance and foolishness at its highest level.

Those of us who have entered into a relationship with God through Christ by the power of the Holy Spirit, know that we are the weakest partner of such an affiliation. We don't bring anything to the bargaining table that God needs. Anything we do have; He gave to us anyway. We come as empty vessels, but vessels that are available for Him to fill and use for His glory.

As we continue in our walk with Him, we find that not only do we benefit by the association, but we begin to see Him reveal His plan for our lives. He works through us to develop other relationships and provides circumstances that put us where we need to be in order to see His hand at work. It may or may not be apparent to others, but no one who puts their trust in Him will ever be put to shame. God reveals Himself through the workings of His hands and provides for us in ways we often don't see coming. What a blessing it is to be counted as a child of God!

DAY 189

Romans 10:21 *But concerning Israel he says, "All day long I have held out my hands to a disobedient and obstinate people."*

I don't think nearly enough has been written or said about the patience of God. We often think about His power, His creative ability, His wrath, and even His love, but His patience, in my opinion, certainly doesn't get enough press.

There are numerous examples throughout the Bible of this attribute when He is dealing with people. From Adam and Eve in the Garden of Eden all the way through the apostles, we see the mercy of God at work as He holds back His hand, when He could have rightfully punished much more severely than He did.

We look at how Jesus spoke to His enemies. He didn't mince words with them, but just as He opened the eyes of the blind and even raised the dead, He could have blinded the Pharisee and struck the teachers of the law dead in their tracks. He didn't do that because God is patient.

Paul reflects on this fact from the words of Isaiah. God extended His grace to Israel in a marvelous way, only to be rebuffed and rejected time and time again. We have to wonder why He didn't just do away with them all and start His plan over with another group of people.

Or how about us? How many times have we walked away from God's perfect plan for our lives and rejected His grace before we finally came to faith? Do we think that we deserve any less punishment than those who reject Him in the Bible? No, God is patient, and we should forever praise Him for that attribute.

Just as the fruit of the Spirit in our lives produces love, it also produces patience. It works in us that way because patience is of God, and He manifests Himself in our lives by causing us to exhibit His fruit. He makes it possible for us to be patient also because He is patient, and He is transforming us into His image day by day.

No one deserves grace, but we all get it. God has been faithful to us and has been more than patient with us all. May we follow His example and allow such the flower of patience to bloom in our lives for our good and His glory.

DAY 190

Romans 11:1 *I ask then: Did God reject his people? By no means! I am an Israelite myself, a descendant of Abraham, from the tribe of Benjamin.*

Tribalism is a cultural phenomenon that is understood in many parts of the world, but almost totally unknown—at least by that name—in much of Western society. If someone in the United States speaks of someone's tribe, they are usually referring to a group of American Indians, such as Apache, Cherokee, or some other native group. Some may think of groups of families in Africa, or some people groups connected with far off or ancient civilizations, but we are not usually identified by our tribe in the twenty-first century American culture.

Paul was very much aware of his tribal history though. He was in the linage of Benjamin, as was Saul, the first king of Israel. Benjamin was the second and final child of Rachel, who died giving him birth. Rachel was the wife of Israel, one of the patriarchs and namesake of the nation. Benjamin means, "son of my right hand," a title that was given him by his father after the death of his mother. To be a Benjamite was a big deal for Paul. It was a heritage in which he took great pride.

Because the apostle has been writing about his Jewish heritage and carrying such a burden because of their waywardness before His heavenly Father, one might get the idea that God had just written the whole nation off and had turned His back on them in favor of the church. Paul says emphatically, "By no means!" God made a covenant with the people of Israel and God never goes back on His word.

The very fact that Paul was both a Benjamite Jew as well as a Christian tells the story that God still had a plan for His originally chosen people. His purpose is to redeem all people everywhere, not choosing to eliminate anyone from His desired purpose for their lives. As God loved Abraham, God loved the Jews of Paul's day, as well as the Jews of our time.

The difference between the old covenant that had been established with Abraham and the new covenant that was established with His church is found in the person of Jesus Christ. He is the linchpin that pulls the old and the new together under the umbrella of God's love. Jews can be saved, and Gentiles can be saved through the amazing grace Jesus provides.

DAY 191

There are times for everyone when circumstances of life tend to get the better of us. We have medical problems, we lose valued possessions, we have relationships that fall apart, and life can be a real challenge that has many diverse chapters.

Elijah was having some of those bad days, in the story to which Paul is referring. After defeating the 400 prophets of Baal by the power of God on Mount Carmel, and at the Lord's command bringing rain to a land that had been in drought for three years, Elijah found himself running for his life after the wicked queen Jezebel threatened to have his head removed. She had been responsible for the deaths of many other Jews and Elijah knew she wasn't bluffing, so he ran.

When God finally got Elijah's attention, Elijah began to complain and make excuses before the Lord for his actions. He was afraid, he was depressed, and he was depleted physically, but most of all he felt like he was all alone in his fight against evil and things weren't going well at all.

I'm sure you have been there. I know I have. Maybe you are there now. Maybe this is a time in your life when you feel like the world is against you and you don't know how much more you can take. These bodies of ours are human and our minds can play tricks on us, especially if we are alone and feel like no one else cares.

This is a good place to remind you that you are not alone. Even if there is no other physical presence in the room with you right now, you are not alone. Our Savior, Jesus Christ, promised that He would never leave us, and He has never gone back on that promise for any of His followers down through the centuries. Even when circumstances seem, and perhaps are, very bleak, Jesus is there for us and is holding us in His arms.

Perhaps today you just need to reach out to Him, cry out to Him, and hold on to Him. When you are at your lowest, He is with you and holds you tight.

DAY 192

Romans 11:4 *And what was God's answer to him? "I have reserved for myself seven thousand who have not bowed the knee to Baal."*

This verse is the rest of the story that connects Paul's reference to Elijah. Elijah, who felt so alone, with only the presence of the Lord to strengthen him, found out that God's presence was enough. God was also able to open his eyes to see that he was not actually alone, but that God had a remnant of people that were still faithful to their Divine King.

We all find ourselves going through periods of despair at times. We like to think of the church as being a safe place where everyone always gets along, and everyone has the same focus for ministry to advance the Kingdom of God. However, anyone who has been involved in church ministries very long finds out that we all have feet of clay, and that there are no perfect churches. Sometimes people with good intentions say and do the wrong things, and sometimes, let's just be honest, there are people who are not spiritually qualified, but have positions of leadership that they shouldn't have. There have been too many situations where people have been "iced out" of service because godliness took a backseat to personal privilege and ego. When this happens, we may feel very, very alone.

There is good news for us though. God will always have a people. The local church can disappoint us, the governments of the world can try to close Christian movements down, and circumstances beyond our control can cause us to feel alone and isolated, but God will always have a people. We are on the winning side, and our King's mission cannot be stopped or foiled by any earthly entity, and because God is always faithful to us, we can rest in His care no matter what comes along.

Paul used these words to encourage the people of the Roman Church. Christianity was still in its embryo stage at that point, and people had no idea what was coming down the line for them in the years ahead. The reminder Paul provides, of God always having a people, has kept believers secure through the centuries.

Even today, we are not alone. We are more than conquerors through Christ who loves us and we can count on God reminding us of that fact on a regular basis. In tough times, hold fast. God never forsakes His own!

DAY 193

Romans 11:5–6 *So too, at the present time there is a remnant chosen by grace. And if by grace, then it is no longer by works; if it were, grace would no longer be grace.*

Grace is such a marvelous thing. It is the undeserved favor of God on our lives. We didn't and can't earn it because there is no way we could ever be good enough or do enough to be equal to its value. It is a gift leading to salvation that God makes available for every person ever born.

The fact that it is freely given by God to us doesn't stop some people from trying to earn their way into the Kingdom though. In fact, every other religion in the world is based on what the devotee does or is, but Christianity is different. With Christianity we are totally dependent on a God who chooses to show mercy to us but doesn't have to. If He gave us justice then we would all be in big trouble, but because His being is the ultimate essence of love, He continues to be gracious to us in every way.

Paul knew this to be the case and because God is so giving and loving, He provides a remnant of believers to stand in the gap for the rest of the world. God's grace chooses us to be more than we could ever be on our own and more than we could ever earn. Literally, we have received the gift of life and life everlasting.

This is why we don't build up credit with God by going to church, reading our Bibles, praying, sharing our faith, or doing any of the spiritual disciplines. All these things are beneficial for us and for the glory of the Father, but they do not move us any closer to attaining His favor. We could be the most pious or the most wicked of all people, but what God provides for us is a gift with no strings attached. He loves us. He offers to redeem us and gives us every opportunity to make a relationship with Him happen. All we must do is accept His offer of life by faith and follow Him as He leads. It's the best deal anyone is ever going to get.

The nation of Israel in Paul's time just didn't get it. People today often don't get it either. How could something so precious be absolutely free? Too many times faith is hindered when the offer just seems too good to be true, but in this case the salvation and freedom that is provided is real and genuine. We should always give thanks to a God who cares that much!

DAY 194

Romans 11:7–8 *What then? What Israel sought so earnestly it did not obtain, but the elect did. The others were hardened, as it is written: "God gave them a spirit of stupor, eyes so that they could not see and ears so that they could not hear, to this very day."*

It's frustrating for anyone when they try so hard to achieve something and continually fall short of the mark. Paul puts Israel in this category because although they recognized God's favor on them as a people, they could never seem to get their act together to live like the people of God. Some tried, but others just gave up and got bitter because they couldn't live up to the standard of the law that was always before them.

For those who turned away from searching after the Lord, their attitudes and lives show a picture of hardness. God does what He always does, which was to give them what they truly desired, and that was their own selfish ways.

This brings up an interesting point for discussion. Does God really harden the hearts of those who turn their backs on Him? Well, yes and no. He gives everyone an opportunity to find Him and serve Him, but when they refuse and choose their own path, He allows them to reap what they have sown. Closing our eyes to the ways of the Lord produces spiritual blindness and eventually that blindness becomes so permanent that we can't see what God longs for us to see.

It's so important for us to develop a tender spirit and discerning ears for the Lord's voice. There are so many entities throughout our world that shout for our attention and try to draw us into their deceptive webs. Only when we learn through days, weeks, months, and years of continually coming to the Lord in our quiet places and quiet times, can we genuinely begin to hear the clarity of His voice amid the clamor and din of society.

Church services are wonderful and needful for all believers because fellowship with other believers is a necessary part of our spiritual growth and development. However, just singing songs, praying congregational prayers, and hearing sermons once a week leaves us in a weakened and vulnerable state if such practices are not followed up with meaningful private devotion and prayer time. Then God will meet with us and help us to avoid the sad situation of the spiritually hardened. It's a benefit of belonging to the elect.

DAY 195

Romans 11:9–10 *And David says: "May their table become a snare and a trap, a stumbling block and a retribution for them. May their eyes be darkened so they cannot see, and their backs be bent forever."*

To put Paul's quotation from David in context, we have to go back to Psalm 69:22–23. He was explicitly referring to those who were his enemies that were mistreating him. David was in a perilous place and sought the Lord's help and judgment against his foes.

Paul took David's words and used them in a completely different context. He was not referring to people who were attacking him personally like David was, but people who had turned their backs on the holiness of God and had been spiritually blinded as a result.

Many times, when we are frustrated, we have a tendency to lash out at those who are making our lives difficult, and like David hope that God will balance the scales of justice for our situations. We may not see the spiritually impaired in that same light, but their situation is actually more dangerous because their eternal soul is hanging in the balance.

I see Paul's use of God's judgment on those who do not see, as a means to an end. It is possible that those who fall over the stumbling block of faith in Christ to be brought low enough for them to see the error of their ways and rebound from their darkened eyes to see the light of the gospel.

It's become clear to me that no one ever gets up unless they realize that they are down. It sometimes takes the hard breaks of life to help people to realize that they are not God, and that they can't run their lives as if they were. Sometimes it's in the pain of failure that eyes are turned upward so that the shackles of sin's bondage can be removed.

I have no problem praying for God to bring people low in order for them to see the error of their ways so that they can be lifted up. In fact, I think that is the purpose of intercessory prayer. To pray the words, "Whatever it takes," for the spiritually blind to receive their sight, and the spiritually broken to be healed, seems like truly the Christian thing to do.

May we not pray for judgment so that we will be vindicated, but so that people will be redeemed. After all, that's the business God is really in.

DAY 196

Romans 11:11 *Again I ask: Did they stumble so as to fall beyond recovery? Not at all! Rather, because of their transgressions, salvation has come to the Gentiles to make Israel envious.*

It is amazing how God works out His plan for our world by using different methods? We usually think of someone's downfall as being a bad thing, because when we are put into dire straits it seems very painful. However, God specializes in doing the unexpected, and making something very wonderful and precious out of what would normally seem a very bad event.

When I had my motorcycle wreck back in 2017, it seemed like a very bad thing to everyone who viewed the situation. A driver who was three times over the legal limit for drunk driving pulled out in front of me when I was traveling at sixty-five miles per hour. Having no time and space to avoid the collision, I hit the driver's truck so hard that the back axle was knocked from beneath the truck and my bike—and me—were left in a broken mess in the middle of the road. I should have been killed by the impact, but apparently God had other plans for me.

Immediately after regaining my senses while lying on the ground, I found that there were multiple people surrounding me. A nurse began to care for me right on the spot. Another man stood over me to block the blinding sun from being in my eyes. Some stopped traffic on the busy four-lane highway so that the situation wouldn't be made worse by having another collision.

Eventually, there was an ambulance and EMT's, an emergency room with doctors and nurses, a trip to a trauma center, and more doctors, surgeries, and treatment. It was an experience I will certainly never forget.

However, through it all God began to work. Healing eventually came to my body, and I was out of the hospital within a week, and back preaching from a wheelchair within another week. Since that time God has allowed me to tell the story to many people and give Him praise for His protecting hand and healing grace. This would never have happened without the accident.

Paul shows us here that unfortunate things sometimes happen so that God can receive glory from them and work them out for our good. His way is always the best way, and through Him even stumbling can lead to recovery.

DAY 197

Romans 11:12 *But if their transgression means riches for the world, and their loss means riches for the Gentiles, how much greater riches will their fullness bring!*

Sometimes bad things happen to us, and from our limited perspective we may initially truly see these events as nothing but bad. It is a fact, however, that for those of us who have put our trust in God, things don't happen in our lives without the watchful eye of the Almighty seeing everything that is going on, and Him finding a way to bring good to us and glory to His name because of what we endure. That doesn't mean God causes bad things to happen, or even that He doesn't grieve when pain comes to our lives, but He always is able to take broken things and find a way to put them back together if we will let Him.

When I lost both of my parents within five weeks in 2016, when I had a bad motorcycle accident in 2017, when I had two major surgeries in 2019 and 2020, or when our home was complete destroyed by fire during the Covid-19 Pandemic, some might look at these events and think that these things were unbearable. However, I have found through a life of walking with the Lord, that whenever hard places come, He has a way of not only bringing us through them, but also knows how to provide grace for us to be able to see that He is strengthening us daily instead of mistreating us. He always has our best interest in mind.

Paul is stating that though Israel was unfaithful and caused God to grieve, their very unfaithfulness provided an opportunity for the Gentiles to be grafted into His plan of salvation. What started off as something bad, allowed God to turn it into something wonderful, and as a result all the world has been offered the way of life everlasting. Again, God specializes in taking broken things and circumstances of life and making them whole again.

It may be that things are upside down in your world right now. It could be that you are frustrated, tired, sick, and discouraged. You might even wonder whether God has forgotten you. Here is a secret that provides a way out of your dilemma: Praise the Lord. Sing to the Lord amid of your pain. Praise Him when you are going through the hard and dark places. God inhabits the praise of His people, and He will see you through your storm.

DAY 198

Romans 11:13–14 *I am talking to you Gentiles. Inasmuch as I am the apostle to the Gentiles, I make much of my ministry in the hope that I may somehow arouse my own people to envy and save some of them.*

Have you ever considered your existence vital to someone else? If you haven't, you certainly should. No doubt there are family members, friends from across the years, co-workers, schoolmates, and neighbors who value you in more ways than you could possibly imagine.

But have you also ever considered that your role in this world is vital to God's plan for the Kingdom He is building? You may think, "Well, what can I ever do that would be important to God?" The answer is, "Being the best you that you can be, is what God needs."

When Paul was addressing the Romans in this letter, he was jumping back and forth, as first he would address the Jews, and then later he would address the Gentiles. Sometimes it gets a bit confusing as to which group he is referencing at which time. Here he makes it very plain though. "I am talking to you Gentiles." He is telling them—and us—that they/we have a very important job. It is our job to make others jealous.

At first blush, this doesn't sound like a very Christian thing to do but look a little deeper. Paul is encouraging those who are Gentiles to live in such a way for God, that the Jews will be hungry to have the same kind of relationship with Christ as they have. Hopefully the Jews will recognize that holy oneness and want such a relationship for themselves.

Jesus said that His followers were the salt of the earth. Salt has many properties such as the preservation of food, and at one time was even used as money. But the main thing we notice about salt is that it makes us thirsty. Just try to eat a spoonful of salt without following it up with a drink. A little bit of it can go a long way as far as having an effect.

That's what Jesus meant, and what Paul is after in these verses. We are to live in such a way that people see what we have in Christ and desire the same relationship for their lives. We can only do that if we are filled with the Spirit of God so that Jesus can be seen in us. It is the biggest and most important job we will ever have.

DAY 199

Romans 11:15 *For if their rejection is the reconciliation of the world, what will their acceptance be but life from the dead?*

In life, everyone has choices. Some choices lead to great things and other choices lead to sadness and despair. Thankfully, some of the bad choices we make are not permanent, because God's grace finds a way to bring hope out of chaos.

It was a poor choice for the people of Israel to reject Jesus as the Messiah for whom they had been waiting for centuries. Their stubborn refusal of God's plan has led to all kinds of grief for them right up to this very day. But in their refusal to follow God's way, they opened an avenue to life for all the rest of the world. Love always finds a way, and there is no love like God's love. Those of us who are Gentiles should always be grateful and live in awe that God allowed us to be grafted into His family.

The outcome of this is life everlasting. It is not just that we go to heaven after we die, but someday there will be a bodily resurrection from the dead and we will live eternally on a redeemed earth in the immediate presence of God and His holy angels. This is not a dream, but the fulfillment of God's promises to all who put their trust in Him through Jesus Christ by the power of the Holy Spirit.

I can't even begin to imagine what the resurrected life will be like. I don't know what kind of bodies we will have, but most likely they will be similar to the resurrected body of Jesus. I don't know how we will appear as pertaining to age, to occupation, or our standing in God's social order. I do know that it will be perfect, and it will be forever. Perfection forever doesn't sound like too bad of a deal to me.

All of this comes about because of one choice we can make right now. We can choose to confess our sins, turn from our wicked ways, and follow after Jesus as His devoted disciple. It's not a one-time action, for being a disciple is a lifelong commitment that requires nurturing, growing, and facing challenges in the name of the Lord. But whatever price is required of us, we can be assured that when this age ends, it is going to all be worthwhile. Though we were once rejected, now in Christ we are accepted, and transformed to join with the redeemed of God throughout eternity.

DAY 200

Romans 11:16 *If the part of the dough offered as firstfruits is holy, then the whole batch is holy; if the root is holy, so are the branches.*

A person's bloodline tells a lot about the person. The scientific breakthrough of mapping one's DNA has opened lots of doors for researching one's family tree and heritage. I have often wondered what my ancestors were like. I would love to meet John James and his first wife, Elizabeth, the first James's of our branch to set foot on what would be Virginia's American soil in 1673. What kind of people were they? What caused John to leave Wales at fifty years of age and chart a new path for himself and his descendants? How did he cope when Elizabeth died in childbirth with Thomas, the first child to be born to the family in the New World, just one year after their arrival? I'm sure the conversation would be as fascinating for him as it would be for me as we compared the historical notes that tie us together.

As important as my human bloodline is to me, my spiritual heritage has an even greater value. I am not who I am only because I was born, but more importantly, I am who I am because I have been born again. The holiness of God flows through my veins and continues to transform me and renew me into His likeness. This is nothing I can take credit for, or boast about though, because it is by the grace of God that my life is as it is. The King of kings has adopted me into His family, and that has made all the difference. Had I not come to Christ as a child, my worldview would be very different.

When Paul was relating the importance of God's holiness in the lives of the Roman church folks, he was emphasizing how God's work in them would be life changing. The Jews would be considered the firstfruits here because God originally offered them the privilege of carrying His message that would redeem the world. When they balked on that mission, He then grafted in the Gentiles as branches who would carry the message that the Jews had refused to recognize and propagate.

Certainly, we Gentiles have dropped the ball many times ourselves, but God has allowed us to be picked up and restored in our labors. His line of holiness that runs through us is our guiding light and empowering presence. Because God is holy, His presence in us is making us holy too.

DAY 201

Romans 11:17–18 *If some of the branches have been broken off, and you, though a wild olive shoot, have been grafted in among the others and now share in the nourishing sap from the olive root, do not boast over those branches. If you do, consider this: You do not support the root, but the root supports you.*

It has been said that the ego is a fragile thing. If a person is too harshly criticized or if he or she suffers abuse, then that person's confidence can take a tumble, or be even permanently damaged. This is why raising children or discipling new believers both require wisdom, patience, and much prayer for guidance.

However, the opposite of a damaged ego is an inflated one. When a person's opinion of his or her own self-worth is out of balance, it can cause pride and overconfidence, which is usually unfounded.

Paul was warning the Gentile Roman Christians about being prideful because of their being chosen by God over the Jews to accomplish His purposes. He didn't want them to forget that just as God chose them, He could choose others if He so desired. He also wanted them to remember that it was the Gentile branches that were grafted into the vine and not the other way around. Christians will always have a debt of gratitude to pay to the Jewish people because it was through them that God provided a way for all men to be saved.

I don't believe that it is too far out of context for us to consider what this means for our local churches and the workers that are given tasks to do for the Kingdom's sake. We should always remember that we stand on the shoulders of those who have labored before us and that we owe much to the heritage we have received. Sometimes with changes in music styles, church structures, styles of dress, and administrative renovations there are some who look at the latest fads as THE WAY, and look at former practices and beliefs as outdated, old-fashioned, or immature. It would do us well to take Paul's words to heart and realize that it is the "wild olive shoots" that were grafted in, not the root that produced life originally.

When we are tempted to be proud and full of ourselves, a step back to revere those who came before us might be the best way forward.

DAY 202

Romans 11:19–21 *You will say then, "Branches were broken off so that I could be grafted in." Granted. But they were broken off because of unbelief, and you stand by faith. Do not be arrogant, but be afraid. For if God did not spare the natural branches, he will not spare you either.*

Paul here uses a common object that everyone could recognize, a tree. If we have lived very long, we have seen limbs that have been removed from many trees. Sometimes it is for the good of the surrounding landscape that such pruning is done, and sometimes it's for the good of the tree itself. Lopping off branches then, can be a very good thing if it is done for the right reason.

The obvious comparison that Paul is making, considers the tree to be the plan and Kingdom of God. When Israel disobeyed God's will and veered off from His plan, He pruned them as one would cut branches from a tree. In their place, the wild branches that were grafted into the tree after branches from Israel were removed, are represented by the Gentiles. So, what we have as a result, is that the plan of God and the Kingdom of God is growing with both Jews and Gentiles being added to complete His great act of mercy toward His creation.

Unbelief in God's plan caused the Jews to need to be disciplined or chopped from their place in the original plan. However, just because removing some of the limbs (i.e., the Jews) made room for new growth to be grafted in (i.e., the Gentiles), neither group has a right to feel overly confident or proud of their status. For just as God could exclude some in order to bring others on board, He can exclude those late to the party also. It all comes down to a matter of belief rather than one's national or ethnic background.

The Kingdom of God is a kingdom of faith, and only the faithful will walk in it and be a part of it. His plan will not be thwarted, and His Kingdom will not be stopped. He can do as He wishes to bring about His purpose with or without whomever He desires. This is why no one should take their place of fellowship with Him for granted. God is faithful always, but especially to His own nature and purpose.

His love will conquer all in the end. It is our choice as to whether we will be on the winning team when He concludes all things or be added to the losers.

DAY 203

Romans 11:22 *Consider therefore the kindness and sternness of God: sternness to those who fell, but kindness to you, provided that you continue in his kindness. Otherwise, you also will be cut off.*

Perhaps it needs to be spelled out, so here goes: There is no free lunch in the Kingdom of God. There is free grace, the love of God that we can never deserve, but there is no freedom to ignore that grace without reaping the pain that comes with such a choice. God's kindness is equaled by the sternness of His justice, and He will never be taken for a fool. When we put our trust in Him, He will always be there for us, but if we turn away, we will face the consequences of that action as well.

The reason that this needs to be stated and understood is because there are too many people who think that God is playing some kind of ritual game with us when we come to Him. There are those who believe that if we say the right words of confession, are baptized, and join a church where we will attend regularly, that we are forever secure in our relationship with Him no matter what else we may or may not do. Paul tells us that this is not so as he admonishes the Romans not to take their relationship with God for granted.

Our walk with our heavenly Father is much like a marriage. Most marriages start off with the couple being in a loving relationship and a oneness that completes their connection. However, we all know that over time we find that the relationship requires nurturing, planning, giving, and taking if it is going to continue to be successful. Far too many people take their vows for granted and assume that the other person is always going to be there, but sadly find out that such is not the case. Marriages can and do fall apart, just as a person's walk with God can sour.

God never leaves anyone, but we can choose to leave the relationship with God. It doesn't mean that He doesn't love us anymore, for He cannot deny Himself His nature, and that is one of perfect love. It does mean that He will not continue the relationship when we choose not to honor Him, serve Him, and love Him. God, the perfect gentleman, always gives us what we want.

So, if we choose to abide in Him, we will find His kindness complete in every way, but if we choose to ignore Him, He will cut the relationship off. That's not being cruel; it's being just. God is God and He will always be in charge. His grace and His mercy are not to be taken for granted.

DAY 204

Romans 11:23 *And if they do not persist in unbelief, they will be grafted in, for God is able to graft them in again.*

There have been so many times that we as humans have made mistakes in judgment and wished that we had a do-over. For the most part, our lives are the results of our choices, and those choices can be very, very wise, or very, very foolish, and often just fall somewhere in the middle of that range.

The beautiful and wonderful thing about the Gospel of Jesus Christ is that we have a King of the universe who is the King of the do-overs also. There is no person too broken but whom Jesus cannot repair. There is no situation so desperate that we cannot turn to Him and find Him available. Jesus knows our griefs and our pains, and He knows how to help those who are willing to hear His voice, to get back on the right track.

Like so many topics of which the Apostle Paul writes, this again comes down to a matter of faith and belief. By faith we come to Christ to receive forgiveness and salvation. By faith we walk with Him and have our being in Him. But when a person's faith lapses, that doesn't mean that the Almighty is through with him and washes His hands of our entire mess. When we fail, but turn back to Jesus sincerely, He is able to give us a new start and point us in the direction we need to go again.

This doesn't mean that we can take His mercy for granted and throw caution to the wind because we have assurance of God's divine nature of love. Every move we make that is not done in faith can lead to our downfall and eventual destruction. God is not one with whom we can toy and disrespect without penalty. But when circumstances of life get the best of us, and we look away from our power source in Christ, we become like Simon Peter, who was willing to walk on the water to meet Jesus, but then lost his faith. When this happens to us, we need only to cry out with the sincere prayer that Peter uttered, "Lord, save me!" We will find our Savior ready and waiting to wrap His arms around us and pull us close to Him.

This is grace at its highest point. This is the love that reaches out to we who are imperfect and creates a new opportunity for life in us. Jesus forgives and is able to provide us with a do-over in the area of our faith. We don't need to fall, but if we do, Jesus is waiting to help us get up again.

DAY 205

Romans 11:24 *After all, if you were cut out of an olive tree that is wild by nature, and contrary to nature were grafted into a cultivated olive tree, how much more readily will these, the natural branches, be grafted into their own olive tree?*

We who were on the outside of a walk of faith for too long, have been blessed beyond our ability to understand how God would care so much for us, and bring us into fellowship with Him. Paul's words here, "wild by nature," describes many of us pretty well. Some have lived for years in selfish desires before later in life coming to faith in Christ. Others of us may have been raised in the church but were wild in our spirits and unwilling to yield to the calling of Christ upon us. It is a miracle of grace that any of us are saved.

Therefore, it should not be a surprise to us to understand that God's grace—which has been wonderfully extended to "the wild ones," should also be given to those who once had been a part of the family of faith, but have somewhere along the way, turned away. If people without faith are given the gift of faith by God, then those who have had faith, and left the faith, can also be brought back into the fold, and be reunited with the Savior who loves them. God always loves to the uttermost.

This is a great lesson for those of us who deal with everyday church life. In lots of churches similar scenarios are played out on a far too often basis. People come into the church, profess faith, then lose faith and leave the church, but then someday want to come back. We may feel like it would be just to deny them entrance back into the family of God, but if we do this we stop acting like God. Jesus made it very clear that if a person sins against us and then comes and asks for forgiveness, then we are to forgive them no matter how many times it has occurred. It doesn't mean that we should throw caution to the wind and put the returners back into positions of leadership, but how can it be Christian to deny grace to anyone, anytime?

People who sincerely come to faith at whatever stage they are in along their life's journey, need to be welcomed into the family. After all, we were once "wild by nature," and God let us in. If others were in, then went out, but want back in, how can we do less than God. Grace is always grace—and it's always free.

DAY 206

Romans 11:25 *I do not want you to be ignorant of this mystery, brothers, so that you may not be conceited: Israel has experienced a hardening in part until the full number of the Gentiles come in.*

God always knows what He is doing. In fact, God has a plan that is going according to His design, and He is not sweating the fact of whether or not we agree with it. In our own limited wisdom, we often find what we consider to be irrefutable facts, but God has the oversight and foresight to do whatever He wishes and makes our human wisdom seem like foolishness.

Take the issue of Paul's topic here. God hardened the hearts of the Jews so that they would make room for the Gentiles to be a part of the Kingdom of God. That doesn't seem right. It doesn't seem fair. It doesn't even seem possible, but God is the God of the impossible. By capitalizing on Israel's unbelief, He opened the door for Gentiles to be full-fledged members of His divine family. No wonder people of Paul's generation had such a hard time understanding this.

We are not told what the full number of Gentiles is. We don't have an exact mathematical figure, but it seems that as long as there are people who are outside the gift of salvation, there is still time for us to reach them and work for us to do. We don't know how long God will hold off on closing the pages of time and setting into motion all the events that will usher us into the new age, but we do know that our time is limited. If we lived to be 100 years old, we still would find ourselves with work to do in the evangelism of the world.

Paul says that God has hardened the Israelites "in part." That means salvation may have been stunted for a few, for some period of time, but it also means that both Jews and Gentiles now have access to the Good News and to the family of faith. The hardening of the one led to the saving of the other, but though it may seem odd, it was what God chose to do.

In the time and strength that we have remaining to us, we need to share the gospel with as many people as possible. The opportunity for eternal life is before us, because there are so many people who do not yet realize God's grace, and their lostness should produce our motivation to bring God's light into their lives that have been in the dark for far too long. Just as grace has been extended to us, we need to extend it to others.

DAY 207

Romans 11:26–27 *And so all Israel will be saved, as it is written: "The deliverer will come from Zion; he will turn godlessness away from Jacob. This is my covenant with them when I take away their sins."*

In this passage from Paul, we find he is making references to the promises God made to the people of Israel in Isaiah 27:9; 59:20–21; and Jeremiah 31:33–34. If you would take the time to read through those passages carefully, you will indeed find that our heavenly Father promises that all of Israel will be saved when they turn from their sin and follow the Most High God in faith.

What we have to remember though, is that Paul has been declaring that there are Jews and true Jews, much like John the Revelator did in Revelation 2:9. All who have by faith, staked their lives on the Lord Jesus Christ as God's promised Messiah, fall into the camp of the true Jews, or New Israel. Those who merely have the bloodline lineage of Abraham, but not saving faith in Jesus, may be nationalist Jews, but do not enter int the camp of the redeemed. It is in this sense that Paul believes all Israel will be saved. That doesn't mean every person who claims an ancestral father-figure will be saved, but those who confess their sins, turn from their wicked ways, and put their trust in Jesus for their salvation will be saved.

When Paul wrote these words, Mohammed's religion of Islam would not be concocted for another 500 years. However, they too claim the bloodline of Abraham and their views are anything but Christian. Paul is not saying that all who claim Abraham will be saved, but all who put their trust in Jesus will be saved. They are the true Jews.

The words of these verses have caused confusion among the body of Christ for generations, but this is why it is so important that all scripture be kept in context. These verses without the surrounding verses to prove Paul's point, lead us to conclusions that He did not intend. Proof-texting may be advantageous when doing a research paper as one tries to build a bibliography, but disastrous for true biblical understanding. We must remember the old adage, "A text out of context is nothing but a pretext." Another good one to remember is, "The Bible can never say what the Bible never said." All Israel will be saved—but by faith—not by bloodline.

DAY 208

Romans 11:28–29 *As far as the gospel is concerned, they are enemies on your account; but as far as election is concerned, they are loved on account of the patriarchs, for God's gifts and his call are irrevocable.*

God has a very long memory. Because He is not bound by the restrains of time and space, His conversations with Abraham, Isaac, and Jacob are continually current. He talked and talks with them often I am sure, and they must smile together as they consider the divine plan being enacted for the rescue of the faithful.

Though it surely grieves the heart of God whenever His children are abused, as were the Christians of Paul's day, it never stops His love for the abused or for the abuser. Paul knew that God's passion for His chosen people would not be stopped because some rejected the truth and decided on living as enemies rather than friends.

To this very day God is in the business of caring for His followers by providing them with gifts and giving them a calling in life. The gifts are too many to name, but among them are the tools needed to advance His cause and promote our good in this world. The call that He provides is to follow after the pattern of His Son, Jesus, to live in such a way that God is glorified, and His Kingdom is being established in our world through the work of His church.

Perhaps He has gifted you with musical ability, a brain for numbers, a homemaker's heart, or a thirst for knowledge. It may be that you have an ability to speak to multitudes, work in a children's nursery, or have the strength to shovel snow for people who need help. Whatever He has gifted us with in life, our calling then is to use that gift to increase God's influence in our world and provide a way of hope to others as we become blessings in their lives. It really isn't all that complicated. God provides us with abilities so that we can use those abilities to help others. As a by-product of our helping others, God gets the credit and is glorified.

Today there will be opportunities for us to use the gifts He has provided for us to fulfill the calling He has for us. The question is whether we will be cognizant of those opportunities that come our way or not. It's certainly something to think about and something for which we should prepare.

DAY 209

Romans 11:30–31 *Just as you who were at one time disobedient to God have now received mercy as a result of their disobedience, so they too have now become disobedient in order that they too may now receive mercy as a result of God's mercy to you.*

Within these verses is a picture of the circle of life. It is also a story of how people change their behaviors when confronted with an Almighty God.

Most of us have as a part of our Christian testimony, at least one example of a time when we were disobedient to God. Most of us also know of people who had once been on the front lines in the church's fight against the powers of darkness, but for some reason, along the way they dropped out and stopped being faithful in their walk with Christ.

It's a true statement to say that God would have been well within His divine prerogative to squash us all like a bug when we veered off from what He had planned for our lives. Earlier on in this book we read that "the wages of sin is death ..." (6:23). Allowing our own desires to trump the will of God is not a very smart thing to do.

A beautiful part of the gospel message though, is the rest of 6:23, "but the gift of God is eternal life in Christ Jesus our Lord." Mercy is what God does best and we should be thankful that such is the case. When we walked in disobedience, God was merciful to us and allowed us time and opportunity to make things right and get on the right track with Him.

As for those who once walked with God and later walked away from Him, their absence in Kingdom work opened opportunities for those of us who came after them to pick up the baton and carry on the race. If they had not left, then we might not have had the opportunity to serve as we do. Even in a loss of manpower, God is gracious.

But those who walked away from God have received God's mercy too. Our hope is that they will come back to faith and resume their previous commitment to their Savior. Maybe our filling their shoes will cause them to be jealous enough to want to be back in the race. At least we hope so. In any case the love of God is spread across those who once were disobedient and those who presently are. God always has His best in mind for His kids.

DAY 210

Romans 11:32 *For God has bound all men over to disobedience so that He may have mercy on them all.*

I am convinced that the conviction of the Holy Spirit is one of the greatest gifts that God has ever provided to mankind. It is because of the conviction of the Spirit that we ever turn our hearts toward Jesus, repent of our sins, and find the freedom that only He can give. It is because of the conviction of the Spirit that we are drawn into a closer relationship with the Father to the point where we desire to have our hearts cleansed and made free from the desire to sin against Him. It is because of the conviction of the Spirit that we have guidance for our daily walk as He gives us the checks and nudges that govern our behavior and keeps us living as Jesus wants us to live.

When Paul wrote these words, he was speaking from personal experience. He no doubt remembered when He walked in opposition to the will of God as he persecuted and prosecuted believers of the new way in Christ that many of his generation were experiencing. God allowed him to walk that path only long enough to understand just how disobedient he was, but then the light from above and the voice of Jesus on the road to Damascus brought him into the path of mercy and grace.

No one gets up until they have fallen. No one really sees until they realize they had once been blind. No one walks in obedience to God or man until they recognize the difference between obedience and disobedience. God makes it possible for us to not only have a learning experience, but to be transformed from that experience. He is the ultimate good and loving Father that cares always for the best we can possibly experience.

Today, as we take a new look at our world, let's remember these words from Paul. If we watch people carefully, we are going to see that there are some people who walk in obedience to God and some who are walking in disobedience. The obedient are walking as directed by the Spirit of God and the disobedient are those who have not yet been enlightened by the Spirit, or have rejected His teachings. This should give us cause to pray for the disobedient, that they may be quickened and come to faith. It should lead us to pray that those who are bound, will receive and accept God's mercy. As we pray God will hear, and lives can be forever changed.

DAY 211

Romans 11:33 *Oh, the depth of the riches of the wisdom and knowledge of God! How unsearchable his judgments, and his paths beyond tracing out.*

D o you ever find yourself just breaking into song? In my family, it's hard to bring up a topic about anything without someone starting to sing some tune that is associated with it. I know that in my own prayer time, I like to walk. When I walk, I often find myself singing words of the great hymns and gospel songs I have memorized over the many years of my church experience. Putting voice to our praise is usually therapeutic for us and I'm sure it always sounds good to God, regardless of our musical capacity.

We aren't told anywhere in the Bible about Paul's singing voice. We don't know if he would have been a star soloist or a person who couldn't carry a tune in a bucket with a lid on it. We do see from his writing though, that he was a person given to praise on a regular basis. Maybe he didn't sing it, but his heart just seems to always be filled with an overflowing appreciation of the Savior's grace and power.

In this verse he probes the boundaries of God's wisdom and God's knowledge. He comes to the conclusion that both are off any scales of measurement that we could ever produce. The reasons behind the decision He makes are God's alone, and there is no way that anyone in this world could ever figure out His purposes unless He chooses to let us in on His plans. When He does it is glorious but looking on from the outside all we can do is stand amazed.

This is not the only place where Paul emphasizes the difference between God's wisdom and ours, but it certainly is a profound spot. Nobody has ever figured Him out and nobody is ever going to. In man's level of wisdom, we usually try to reason things to a point of understanding that we can explain. If we can't produce a purpose behind something God has done, then we find ourselves conjuring up our own answers for the questions that can't be answered.

Paul doesn't go down that road though. He just looks at God and how He works in our lives and is overwhelmed. He knows that the King will always have the last word and we can put our trust in Him for all we ever need. Some things require us to wait till we can ask Him, but it's worth the wait.

DAY 212

Romans 11:34 *"Who has known the mind of the Lord? Or who has been his counselor?"*

I don't have the reputation of being one who can think quickly on my feet. I can make snap judgments about things, but I often wish I had taken a little more time to examine the thing I was considering before I made up my mind. I like to ponder things, turn them around in my thoughts, and consider options before making decisions. When I don't take that path, it usually turns out that I wish I had.

God is not like that. He knows everything about everything, always. He doesn't need my advice or my information. He knows about my prayer requests before I ever ask them, and He knows what His response will be before the situation that concerns me even arises. He is an all-knowing, all-powerful God, who has no equal anywhere.

Some may ask then, "How then should we pray? Or even, "Why should we pray? If He already always knows, then why bother?" These questions come from the person who perhaps doesn't understand what prayer is all about. Prayer is not our quoting off a list of requests before God and begging Him to answer them so that our needs will be met. Prayer actually goes much deeper than that.

The highest quality of prayer time that I have ever experienced is when I have just found a place to be alone and sat quietly in the Lord's presence and waited on Him. Sometimes I will follow the advice from Eli to young Samuel in I Samuel 3:9, where he says, "Speak, LORD, for your servant is listening." It is in those times that I truly begin to understand that my advice is not needed by God, but I sure do need Him to be my counselor.

Waiting on the Lord is hard to do because it goes against the grain of our training in society. We have a hard time listening to others because we are already thinking of a response to what they are telling us. But when we wait on the Lord, in silence, He is able to speak truth to our hearts and provide us with the information and guidance we need. His divine word may not come to us instantly, but often over time. It probably won't be audible or visible, like a bolt of lightning. But if we will wait, God will speak, and we will know it—and when that happens, nothing else matters.

DAY 213

Romans 11:35 *"Who has ever given to God,
that God should repay him?"*

When I was about seven years old, my parents started giving me a weekly allowance. My brother and I each got fifty cents, but it came with some stipulations. First, we had to put back twenty-five cents into a savings account for the rainy days ahead. Second, we had to pay ten percent tithe to our church from the entire amount, which amounted to five cents. That only left us twenty cents per week to spend, but in a time when I could go to the local drug store and buy a hot dog for fifteen cents, a coke for five cents, and a large milkshake for twenty-five cents, it seemed to be enough.

Inflation has taken its toll and fifty cents won't buy what it once did, but that simple act of financial training from my parents has stayed with me and guided me in how I should handle money even to this day. It's important to save, and it's important to have money to spend, but the non-compromising part of my financial planning always involves paying my tithe and an offering beyond that as God provides.

That seems very noble and conservative to some people, but here is what I have learned from my giving experiences throughout my life. Regardless of how much I give, or what percentage I give to the Lord, it doesn't begin to pay God back for all He has done for me. As Paul said in I Corinthians 13:3, "If I give all I possess to the poor and surrender my body to the flames, but have not love, I gain nothing." God doesn't owe me anything, but I owe Him everything. I'll never be out of debt when it comes to my account before Him.

Why do I give then? Because giving tithes and offerings is not about giving God what benefits Him; it's about developing what benefits me. Just as my parents never profited financially from giving me an allowance, God doesn't benefit from Him giving to me or me giving back. Money is a training tool for me to determine where my true allegiance actually lies. I can spend all I received any way I want to, but I find that God is pleased when I put Him first. When I do put Him first, then He finds ways to bless me as His child and provide for my needs. He doesn't have to do it, and the blessing may or may not come back to me in financial ways, but He always gives me more that I can repay, so my debt gets greater the more I give, but the blessings pile higher as well. What a wonderful circle of abundant life He provides!

DAY 214

Romans 11:36 *For from him and through him and to him are all things. To him be the glory forever! Amen.*

Some of the most important words in the Bible are in the first sentence of it, where is says, "In the beginning God created ..." We as Christians base everything we know about God and our universe on the fact that He is the one responsible for it. There will always be discussions and viewpoints about exactly how and when He brought His creation to pass, but surely, we as people of faith can believe that He is the force behind it all.

It is also true that everything goes on under His watchful eye. A deist would have us believe that once God put the earth into play and the planets into motion, He then sat back to watch us to see how it would all come out. That kind of a view makes God a spectator of our lives rather than a participant. Paul claims that God is involved and active through it all. He isn't distant from His creation but is imminently and creatively connected to all that goes on in our world. Jesus reminded us in Matthew 6 that there is not a sparrow that falls or a flower that blooms that doesn't have the attention of our heavenly Father. He even sent His Son to be *Immanuel*, "God with us." He couldn't be any more involved than He is.

Also important is the acknowledgment that all things are *to Him*, as well. That means that everything that He made, everything that He sustains, and everything that we do is to be for His honor and glory. Much of mankind has neglected this truth, to their own peril, and have made idols of other men, statues, money, and power. Paul reminds his readers that everything has been brought to pass to bring glory to God. From the beginning of time until its end, He is to be credited with every good thing that has happened or will happen. It is only when people step outside of His plan and purpose that bad things happen, for God is always good and His actions reflect that character.

For this reason, Paul proclaims that God is to receive glory all the time and everywhere. Our purpose as Christian people is to make sure that He gets the credit, and we do that best by living out lives that have been transformed by His personal touch. We remember that He caused it all, works in the midst of it all, and receives credit for it all. He is God, and He has no equals.

DAY 215

Romans 12:1 *Therefore, I urge you, brothers, in view of God's mercy, to offer your bodies as living sacrifices, holy and pleasing to God—this is your spiritual act of worship.*

There is so much preaching material in this single verse. It's as though the Apostle is pleading with the readers in the most emphatic terms to be more than just a nominal follower of Christ. The verse is truly a watershed mark in the life of a Christian believer.

But this is also a watershed mark in this particular book. Up to this point Paul has been laying out his theology and giving the readers the reasons for what they are to believe as far as their relationship with Christ. It has some practical applications, of course, but in doctrinal categorizing, the first eleven chapters would fall into the theological camp. Beginning with this verse, the practics of Christian living is spelled out. Chapters one through eleven tells us the *why* of Christianity, but now Paul shows us the *how*.

It all begins with the word, "Therefore." The old rule we follow when we see this in a sentence, is to back up and see what it is "there for." In other words, in light of what Paul has been saying in the first eleven chapters, this is now what we should do about it. What we should do as our very first act as Christians, is to give ourselves wholly over to God as a sacrifice to Him.

There are some things we should note about sacrifice. First, it is a complete *commitment*. Anything or anyone that is fully sacrificed loses all possibility of withdrawing that commitment. Of course, as humans we can change our minds anytime, but if we would do so the fellowship with God would be broken. Second, sacrifice in this sense is *voluntary*. God is not making us do it, though He desires it more than anything. He never takes away our free choice in the matter. Third, this sacrifice leads to *holiness*. All our rights are given up at the foot of the cross of Jesus, and the path that we pursue from that time on is one that is totally devoted to God.

It is not something we should consider lightly. Being a living sacrifice requires everything we are and everything we have. Being put on the altar of God's service causes us to join the ranks of servants and not equals. We are completely put forward as tools for whatever God wants to do with us. Not everyone will commit to it, but those who do will never be sorry.

DAY 216

Romans 12:2 *Do not conform any longer to the pattern of this world, but be transformed by the renewing of your mind. Then you will be able to test and approve what God's will is—his good, pleasing and perfect will.*

The first bit of instruction given here seems like a nearly impossible task. We do live in this world, we are a part of this world, and we are continually influenced by events and powers of this world. How could we ever break free from what has such a huge effect on us to do otherwise?

Paul relates to us that there is only one possible way—we must be transformed. We must be made into something that does not happen naturally, which of course leaves only the supernatural influence on our life to consider. We are to be changed by a power that is outside of us. This is necessary because we don't have the will power strong enough to break the connection we have to the pattern of this world. As Paul earlier mentioned in chapter seven, in our natural state we are slaves to this world.

The answer to this dilemma is in the renewing of our minds. This doesn't come from reading books or studying theories. This happens when we do what Paul spoke about in verse one, namely we become a living sacrifice that is given over to God's will and work. Only then can the Lord take what we offer and remake us into new creatures that can break the bonds of earthly entrapment. We are given a renewed mind to see what we couldn't see before, to understand what was muddled before, and to be empowered to reason on a level that only God could provide for us. New creations in Christ get a new mind, the mind of God.

Then and only then, can we begin to test and approve what it is God has for us to do. Up to the point of self-sacrifice we are living for our own desires and interests, but when Christ becomes our all, then we are able to live and act in such a way that pleases God. We learn how to recognize His voice, how to test the spirits to see if they are of God, and how to sense the checks and prodding's of the Holy Spirit as we live out our life for God and others, instead of ourselves.

We can only accomplish things for the Lord when we have been given a new start, and that comes with a new mind. Only then can we really taste and see that the Lord is good (Psalm 38:4).

DAY 217

Romans 12:3 *For by the grace given me I say to every one of you: Do not think of yourself more highly than you ought, but rather think of yourself with sober judgment, in accordance with the measure of faith God has given you.*

If there is one thing that all people everywhere should agree upon, it is the fact that everyone, every person born on this planet, is important. We have been created by the Divine Artist of the universe and each person is fearfully and wonderfully made.

I am fairly sure that the Apostle Paul would echo that sentiment, but he cautions us here not to take ourselves too seriously. Since it's true that we are important, but also true that everyone else is important, we should not consider ourselves special or deserving of special privilege in life. All people should be proclaimed as equals, and especially so in the church and in the eyes of God.

However, human nature being what it is, we have a tendency to elevate certain individuals above others. We rate people according to their looks, their education, their personality, their wealth, and even what part of the world they come from. While it may be true that natural man does this according to their own measuring scale, Paul admonishes Christians not to be prideful concerning their own importance in life. Pride is a sin, and sin separates us from God, so if we are going to rate people, it should be by using a scale, or measuring tool, that God gives to us.

Paul sees this measurement system to be connected to our faith, and in doing so he reminds us of some very important facts. First, whatever faith we have, God has given it to us. In Ephesian 2:8, we are reminded that "it is the gift of God." Earlier in this book (Romans 10:17) Paul states that "faith comes from hearing the message, and the message is heard through the word of Christ." We have no reason to gloat over something given to us. Second, our faith is measurable. We are told to consider our importance in accordance to the measure of faith we have. The world looks at the outward appearance and at our possessions and talents, but God considers our value as measured by our faith. So here is the question: Since God rates us by our faith, and God is the one who gives us our faith, how do we see our value rating today? It's certainly something to think about.

DAY 218

Romans 12:4–5 *Just as each of us has one body with many members, and these members do not all have the same function, so in Christ we who are many form one body, and each member belongs to all the others.*

Paul's use of the body as an analogy is widely understood now, but that recognition has developed over time. Most likely it was not original with him because it is such a simple concept for man to grasp. However, his use of this idea in relationship with the people of God in Christ is unique. Through his eyes we see a new way for us to understand Christ's plan for His church.

Along with this unique perspective is the fact that the many people of faith in Jesus are to be truly one. An outsider could look on and wonder if that really is true because churches have had a long history of division over doctrine, personal preference, and societal influences. However, the ideal remains the same. There are few who take the name of Christ who believe that there will be dividing walls in heaven to mark off territories for the various denominations and independent groups in Jesus. We see ourselves as each doing our best to build the Kingdom of God in this world, as we try to aid the Master in the building of His church.

Perhaps it is in the varied denominational example that we get our best view of what God is doing and what Paul is meaning here. Toes don't look like eyes and feet don't look like stomachs. Not only do they not look alike, but they also have completely different functions and purposes. In the same way many of our church groups look very different. Some meet in cathedrals and some meet under trees. Some build their buildings out of brick and mortar and others meet in homes. They are divided by different names like Baptist, Pentecostal, Catholic, Lutheran, Friends, Nazarenes, Methodists, Wesleyan, and hundreds of other names. In our efforts to serve the Lord we can sound and look very different.

This is exactly the point Paul is making. We don't have to look alike, sing alike, dress alike, worship alike, or preach alike to accomplish God's purpose. As long as we love alike, we are on the right track. We are one family who belongs to Jesus, the Head of church, and we each go about our service to the Head as best we understand our duty. Our diversity only divides us if we let it. In Christ, our unity is solid, and our goals are the same.

DAY 219

Romans 12:6–8 *We have different gifts, according to the grace given us. If a man's gift if prophesying, let him use it in proportion to his faith. If it is serving, let him serve; if it is teaching, let him teach; if it is encouraging, let him encourage; if it is contributing to the needs of others, let him give generously; if it is leadership, let him govern diligently; if it is showing mercy, let him do it cheerfully.*

The body of Christ is a wonderful and diverse entity. We come from so many different backgrounds, have so many different life encounters, and as Paul states here, we have so many different gifts. Since these gifts are given to us by God, we are expected to use them for His glory and for the good of His church. Also, since the gifts are given by God, He doesn't expect us to be working in areas other than where He has gifted us.

I hear of people experiencing burn-out after extended times of working in the Master's service, but I often wonder if our burn-out comes from trying to do things for which we have not been gifted. For example, if I had to work in the nursery with the babies, or if I were responsible for cooking meals for others, my burn-out limit would be reached after about ten minutes. However, if I am given an opportunity to stand before people to preach and teach, I never get tired of it. When we work where we are gifted, our service becomes a source of joy, not a dreaded task that has to be endured.

At times people have asked me, "How do I know what my spiritual gift from God is?" I have a four-step equation to help answer that question. *First, what do I like to do?* God is not going to ask you to dedicate your life to something that makes you miserable. Where your greatest joy meets the needs of people around you is a good place to locate your gift. *Second, what am I good at?* What talents are evident in your life that show a level of skill and expertise as well as brings you joy? Your gift may need to be developed, but if you are an artist, a mechanic, a computer nerd, or a strong-backed ditch-digger, your gift may be staring you in the face. *Third, what do the people of the church say about me when I am using my gift?* If it is positive, then take note of that. If it is negative, notice that as well. *Finally, what doors are opening for me to use my gift?* God has a way of putting us where we need to be, when we need to be there for the good of others, and for His glory. When we work at where we are gifted, good things usually happen.

DAY 220

Romans 12:9 *Love must be sincere. Hate what is evil; cling to what is good.*

D on't you hate phoniness? When someone tries to be something that they are not for the purpose of personal gain, it drives most of us nuts. We like people to be honest and trustworthy, especially when it comes to personal relationships.

This is why genuine love is such an important part of the Christian life and experience. There are always people who are looking for reasons to call believers hypocrites, and sadly there have been too many Christians who have given them fuel for their fire. Paul realized this and warned the church at Rome to be better than that. He urged them to be real and to be sincere with the love they projected to the world. There is nothing that our societies need more than love and genuine love can only come from God. We are to be the ambassadors and dispensers of that love.

This is one of the few times in scripture where we are instructed to hate. It almost seems out of character for Paul to say such a thing, until we understand what it is that he hates. He hates evil. He hates deception, lies, and works of darkness. No doubt he has had plenty of opportunities to see evil in action during his days of traveling the Roman empire, and he understood evil to be the direct opposite of the love that only God can provide. God can never be evil. He can never be cruel or unfair. He is always just and full of love.

That's why it is important for believers everywhere to hold tight to all the goodness we can grab. Because there is so much evil in our world, we are to hold forth the light of God's love so that those around us can witness the alternative to what the enemy of our souls has to offer.

In these days of Covid-19 we are often separated from the ones we love most. Some are children of parents in nursing homes, or in hospital situations, and the isolation in such times is great. For me, I miss the hugs of my grandson. If I could, I would hug him for as long as he would let me, just because he is so special to me. That's the way we in Christ are to hold on to what is good. We are to embrace it, strengthen our grip on it, and defend it with all our might. It is one of the most important jobs we will ever have in this world, and the generations to come will judge how well we do it.

DAY 221

Romans 12:10 *Be devoted to one another in brotherly love. Honor one another above yourselves.*

The task that Paul assigned to the church in Rome was to be about the work of "philadelphia." That's a Greek word that literally translated means, "brotherly love," hence the name of our large U.S. Pennsylvania city. In order for them to do this, however, there are two things that need to be considered. They were important in the first century, important in our time, and would greatly benefit Philadelphia, the city, if they were to act on his guidance.

The first instruction is that the people of the church should be devoted to each other. We don't know exactly how large or small were the churches Paul was addressing. What we do know though, is that regardless of their size, they would never be effective as representatives and ambassadors of Christ, unless they really cared about each other. One thing that becomes a problem as churches grow and get larger is the tendency for people to become numbers, even if it is done unintentionally. Being devoted to one another means we not only have to know each other's names, but what they like and don't like, where they live, how they live, and how we can impact their lives. In other words, we must build relationships with people so that the prayer that Jesus prayed for us to become one will be fulfilled. Being devoted to one another means trust building, and that kind of relationship is essential for a church to function as Christ intended.

The key to building such a relationship is found in the practice of honoring others above ourselves. This concept should be understood without having to say it, but with many people the carnal nature runs deep, and they have to be reminded that the way of the cross is the way of selflessness. If we always have to win, or are always trying to win, or get in the last word, we will have a hard time building the devoted relationship that honors the Lord.

Here is where we need the grace of God. We should not expect that we can have brotherly love until we are fully surrendered to the Lord and have been showered with His divine-agape love. As we are filled with the presence of the Holy Spirit, loving others above ourselves becomes much more natural, for God is love. May we love God completely so that His love for others flows through us to those who are around us.

DAY 222

Romans 12:11 *Never be lacking in zeal, but keep your spiritual fervor, serving the Lord.*

I remember from many years ago, reading an article by the late Dr. Neil Strait, who was a great pastor, district superintendent, and writer, that was entitled, "Beware of Passionless People!" I can't remember the full account of the article, but the title stays with me still because the warning is so real for every generation.

That must have been the case during the life of the Apostle Paul also, because he recognizes that being zealous, when it is for the right cause, and done in the right way, is essential for those who would be servants of the one true God. Trying to live without passion is not only ineffective, but really a pretty boring and sad way to live one's life.

It's important to understand that zeal is not necessarily tied to emotion. I have never been accused of being overly emotional about anything by people that know me. I keep my cards pretty close to my vest and it takes quite a lot to get a hardy laugh from me. However, that doesn't mean that I don't have zeal and passion for the things that are important to me. At the top of my list always is the work I do for the Lord. I love to preach, teach, write, and travel, and I can get pretty intense about any one of those things because the purpose behind them all is my desire to see the Kingdom of God come to pass on earth as it is in heaven. Whatever I can do to help that process along motivates me in a big way. As a result, I will plan, pray, study, work, and do whatever it takes for me to be about the Master's business.

Paul was urging the Roman church to be likeminded and the same should be presented to the church everywhere today. We cannot be satisfied with just going through rituals or the spiritual motions of ministry. We need to be intense in our pursuit of holiness and alive in action for the Kingdom to come.

With this idea in mind, perhaps this would be a good time for us to do an evaluation. In what way are we zealously serving the Lord? If we follow up on the gifts God has given to us and use those gifts to the best of our abilities, then having spiritual fervor will come naturally to us as we work for the betterment of mankind and the glory of God. Perhaps it's something for us to think about, to pray about, and give over to God today.

DAY 223

Romans 12:12 *Be joyful in hope, patient in affliction, faithful in prayer.*

This verse falls amid a series of admonitions that Paul is giving to the church at Rome. Each one of them is good advice and we would do well to heed the directions the Apostle is giving.

Here he states the importance of not only having hope but being joyful in the midst of it. That's not always an easy task because even when we are hopeful it is so easy for doubt and fear to sneak their ugly little heads into the midst of our thoughts. Try as we might, focusing as strongly as we can, and believing good thoughts, we still find ourselves struggling.

This is why the first word of this verse is so important. It should be remembered that we can't always *do*, but we can always *be*. Remember what Paul wrote about in verse two of this chapter? He said to be "transformed by the renewing of your mind." Transformation is not something that we do, it's something that God does. We can't transform anything; we aren't that smart or that talented. However, God specializes in making things new, and that is just what He promises to do by the power of His Holy Spirit. He knows that we can't, so He does what we can't do.

Once God transforms our lives into the likeness of His Son, Jesus, then we can be the overcomers that He promised us we could be. So, when Paul says, "Be joyful... be patient... be faithful," we can breathe a sigh of relief and know that as long as we relax in the care of our Lord, fully trust Him in all situations, and follow Him as He leads us, we don't need to act out the part anymore. We actually become joyful, patient, and faithful. We have hope, we can endure affliction, and we can continue steadily and faithfully in prayer. It's the gift from God that keeps on giving.

It may sound like I am looking at the world through rose-colored glasses, but that's actually not the case. Our outlook on the world comes from our worldview. If we have a Christian worldview because of Christ's transforming power, then we will realize Romans 8:28 is true when it says, "that in all things God works for the good of those who have been called according to his purpose." He is continually remaking and remolding us for His glory. If that doesn't cause us to be joyful, patient, and faithful, I don't know what does, because God always does things right.

DAY 224

Romans 12:13 *Share with God's people who are in need. Practice hospitality.*

There is an old saying that proclaims, "Kindness never goes out of style." It is so true. Even our pets can tell whether we are kind to them.

How much more should we be considerate toward people! Whether it would be sharing financially, sharing food, sharing shelter, sharing a ride, or just sharing a smile, people in need always deserve for us to do what we can to help them along.

Somewhere we picked up the idea that it is the role of the government to care for people. I know that social programs and social justice is all the rage these days, but I have to wonder if the huge dependency on national governments that our world has developed, may have come about because the church found it much easier to just kick the can of responsibility over to elected officials.

Obviously, nations have more financial capital than individuals or individual churches do. We can't provide many of the big-ticket items that society is clamoring for continually. But is it possible that people keep wanting more because they believe that someone owes them more? Sometimes our evening news seems like Proverbs 30:15, "The leech has two daughters. Give! Give! They cry." Certainly, we will never run out of people's selfish desires because that is the nature of sin.

The caveat here is that we are instructed to "share with God's people who are in need." If we take care of the area of ministry that God has given us, then perhaps others will follow the example and more needs will be supplied.

Throughout my ministry I have had many people from outside the church come to my church office, looking for money. My first question to them is always, "Where do you go to church?" When I find that they don't, I answer them, "This is one reason why you should." We do all we possibly can do to help people of the congregation, but even hospitality requires responsibility if we are to be good stewards of God's resources. Paul's guidance for giving here is not universal. We do what we can with what we have where we are. I believe God will be satisfied with that.

DAY 225

Romans 12:14 *Bless those who persecute you; bless and do not curse.*

This is so hard. Blessing those who make life miserable for us and cause us continual grief is such an unnatural thing to do. I mean, who does that, really? Who is able to really bless and not curse when troublemakers come our way?

Well, Jesus said that His followers would do that. It is in fact not Paul who came up with this idea, but Jesus Himself. Listen to His words, "But I tell you who hear me: Love your enemies, do good to those who hate you, bless those who curse you, pray for those who mistreat you" (Luke 6:27–28). This command comes from the highest source possible—Jesus!

While it may seem unrealistic and even impossible to many, it becomes the norm when we stop running our lives and let Jesus take over. It is not our spirit and our experiences, or our attitudes that make such a demonstration of grace possible, but the Spirit of Christ who wants to come into us and empower us to be "kingdom kids" for the glory of God.

Again, we need to understand that it is natural to curse. It is natural to hate. It is natural to want revenge on those who do us dirty. No one is really disputing that. I don't even think Paul or Jesus would deny that such attitudes and actions are the natural things to feel and do. However, Christianity is not about experiencing the natural, but the supernatural. If we could, by our own will power, love our enemies and continually be a blessing to everyone we meet, we probably wouldn't need Jesus at all. In fact, He could have just avoided the whole cross thing and even skipped the incarnation altogether. After all, if we can do it, why do we need Him?

The truth is though, we can't. We can't love as we should love. We can't have an attitude of praise continually within our spirits, and we can't give thanks in all circumstances, as Paul reminds us to do in I Thessalonians 5:18. We need Jesus. We need His forgiveness. We need His sanctifying grace. We need His mercy, but most of all we need to be transformed by His power into the disciple He wants us to be, one that is endowed supernaturally, rather than naturally. If we could do it all on our own, then we wouldn't need a Savior, but we can't, and He knows that, so He is here for us. He alone, in us, can cause us to bless and not curse our enemies.

DAY 226

Romans 12:15 *Rejoice with those who rejoice;*
mourn with those who mourn.

This verse has always bothered me a bit. Maybe it's because my emotion intelligence meter is broken when compared to most folks, but it is a direction from the Apostle Paul, so I must consider all that it means for my life, as well as for others.

It should be an easy thing to rejoice with those who rejoice, because everyone likes to have a good time. We live in a culture that seems to want to party more than they want to do anything else, so whether it is at a wedding, the birth of a child, a graduation from some school or course of study, or spiritual victories, it is a good thing for us to join in on the celebrations.

Mourning with those who mourn is not nearly as desirable because grief is a terrible taskmaster. Only those who have spent time in that pit of despair, or the valley of the shadow of death, can fully identify with those who mourn, and can offer genuine empathy in times of crisis.

As I said before, these things are hard for me. At the very least, expressing emotions is work for some of us introverts, but it is something that I believe God provides grace for, just as He does in other areas. When times of celebration or grieving come to pass, it is not that we don't appreciate the hilarity or the gravity of the situation, we just have trouble reflecting it. It is a cross I have borne for many years, and I truly can't say I am joyful about it.

But in areas like even our emotions, Christ can help us to be more than conquerors. To have the mind of Christ and to be filled with the Spirit of Christ is the answer to help us relate to others as a person within whom Christ dwells. It is His joy that flows from us and His peace that provides comfort in us, so as we count on Him in all other areas of life, we trust Him to help us rejoice with those who rejoice, and mourn with those who mourn.

There are probably a lot of people who don't understand this, but I have a feeling that there are other introverts out there who know what I am talking about. Remember this: whatever we face, in whatever area of life we face it, whether physical, emotional, financial, spiritual, or whatever, Christ will always be enough. And that's good news for the rest of us.

DAY 227

Romans 12:16 *Live in harmony with one another. Do not be proud, but be willing to associate with people of low position. Do not be conceited.*

If this weren't such a serious subject, it would be easy to poke some fun here. One could consider our being "willing to associate with people of low position" could just mean that we who are taller should hang out more with shorter people. However, though that is a great idea, I think Paul means something else here.

Our world is being rocked by the friction between the haves and the have nots. I suppose it has been that way as long as there have been people that were able to accumulate more in the way of earthly treasures than others. Some people have good looks, lots of money, superior intelligence, good and productive jobs, and seemingly a higher quality of life than others. Some have, and some don't have, that's just an earthly reality.

However, we must remember that when Paul is writing these words, he is addressing the church. He is telling them that we as Christians are to get along with everyone as well as we possibly can, and we should do that by treating everyone equally. If we are ever tempted to do otherwise, we only need to remember that we are all equal at the foot of the cross, and that the grace that has been dispensed by God to us is more than enough to compensate any inequality we may feel toward others.

The reason understanding this is so important is because it has to do with the Kingdom of God that He is bringing to the earth, as it is in heaven. In God's Kingdom, all people are on the same social and economic level. In God's Kingdom, the lowest of the low is raised in value to the highest of the high. In God's Kingdom, the servant of all will be the most important of all.

That's the way it will be someday here on earth, but as we wait for God to consummate His plan, and for Jesus to return in power, we are to be doing our part to bring that Kingdom to pass in the here and now. Every time we pray the Lord's Prayer and say, "Thy will be done on earth as it is in heaven," we are vocalizing our vocation and our reason for doing what we do in life. Someday we will fulfill this verse without thinking, but until then, we are to show others that this is the way of the coming Kingdom; the way Christ wants us to live.

DAY 228

Romans 12:17 *Do not repay anyone evil for evil. Be careful to do what is right in the eyes of everybody.*

This is perhaps one of the telling observations of Christianity in action today. We are so used to people standing up for their "so-called rights" that we have come to expect repercussions when those rights are violated or offended. Because people tend to wear their feelings on their sleeves these days, it's pretty hard not to make someone upset about something, regardless of which side of an issue one takes a stand.

Though we may all be different in different ways, and believe different things about different issues of life, for the Christian there is always one standard that must remain in our center focus. That issue is the matter of love, God's love that He has poured on us, into us, and with which He has filled us. That love is to be so abundant in our lives that we should splash over on someone whenever we move in any direction.

When Paul says that we should not pay back evil with evil, he is not calling for something that we can accomplish on our own. Our natural tendency is to "put people in their place," to "give them a piece of our mind," or to not let people "run roughshod" over us. Our whole world is screaming to get its own way, and God help anyone who gets in its way. Civility is often the first thing sacrificed in our post-modern society.

That's why we must understand that only by the filling of our lives with the Holy Spirit of Jesus, sent from the Father, can we ever be able to avoid taking the path of revenge when people do things to us that are evil. The Spirit always leads to a way of love, for that is the makeup of the Father. The Spirit reminds us that God is the judge and jury over the works of His creation, and He will settle the scores if any need to be settled. Any natural response from us will glorify the flesh, but the supernatural response will glorify the Father. He is the only one that can make it possible.

Trying to do what is right in the eyes of everybody is a nice thought, but in reality, we are do what is right in the eyes of God and allow Him to deal with those who might disagree with us. No one can please everyone all the time, but in Christ, we can show love to all people and give God the credit for it, for He is the one who truly makes it possible.

DAY 229

Romans 12:18 *If it is possible, as far as it depends on you, live at peace with everyone.*

There are some key catch phrases in this sentence. The goal of living at peace with everyone is the focus, and certainly that should be the Christian hope in every situation. However, I think that even Paul understands that is not always going to be possible, so he leaves us a couple of caveats that we should consider.

First, we look at those words, "If it is possible." Let's face it, there are some people with whom we are never going to be able to live in peace because they simply won't let us. We are so divided as a society that having an opinion that differs from others often ends up being the cause for hatred and anger being spewed our way. Whether one leans to the left or the right causes the other side to have characters that will never be satisfied with our thinking differently.

That's why Paul included the words, "as far as it depends on you." This is where we have an opportunity to truly represent Christ to those who are around us, as well as those who are watching us from afar. We can't control how other people think, how they treat us, or what obstacles they will put in our paths, but we can control how we react to others. We who have the mind of Christ should remember that representing Him is the most important thing we will ever do, so love should be our guiding key and focus for living and reacting to our enemies as well as our friends.

The problem is, *we* like to react to people who differ from us also. Whether on Facebook, Twitter, Instagram, or some other means of social media, people get our attention when they say something outrageous, and we just don't want to let it stand. We have to add something, put our own two cents in, and set the record straight. Though there may be times when this is appropriate, especially when our response is loving, this can be a trap that leads to more division than healing.

Others have suggested a way to respond in the form of questions: Is it true? Is it necessary? Is it helpful? Will my response bless or agitate? Thinking before we speak helps us to do our part to keep civility in the world. Christ died for all, so as much as we can, we need to get along with folks.

DAY 230

Romans 12:19 *Do not take revenge, my friends, but leave room for God's wrath, for it is written: "It is mine to avenge; I will repay," declares the Lord.*

Though the idea has been around for a long time, it was the 1982 Star Trek movie, "The Wrath of Khan," that made popular the saying, "Revenge is a dish that is best served cold." Of course, the idea is that delayed gratification intensifies the pleasure that comes from giving payback to someone who deserves it.

Sadly, I am afraid that too many Christians think this way, even if they never say it. We have situations that arise in which we are taken advantage of by someone, and we secretly hope that God zaps them with a lightning bolt, or that something bad happens to them because of their evil behavior. We may never reach the point where we would take action ourselves, but we sure are eager to see God really burn the perpetrator.

Now it is true that God is the ultimate and all-wise Judge who will eventually right the scales of the universe but wishing bad things to happen—even to bad people—is not the Christian way of life. In fact, in His Sermon on the Mount, Jesus made it very clear that it is not the act alone that God will judge, but also the intention of our hearts. Could we be guilty of wishing for the same thing to happen to others like they have just done to us, even when it caused us pain? Such an attitude doesn't sound like the Christ who said from the cross, "Father, forgive them, for they know not what they do."

This goes back to the state of our hearts. If the natural will is left to dominate, then we will be forever rooting for bad guys to receive bad stuff in their lives. But if we have truly been transformed by the power of the Holy Spirit, then our desire is that everyone would be saved and come to the knowledge of Jesus Christ. That is the way Christians are to handle conflict. We do not pray for the destruction of our enemies, but for their transformation and salvation so that they will receive good, and God will be glorified.

May our prayer always be that God would protect us from harm in the midst of the attacks from life, but also that God would transform the person doing the harm. God is in charge, and He will have the final say, but wouldn't it be nice if those doing us wrong would be changed from Saul into Paul instead of our getting revenge on them. Love is a dish best served at any time.

DAY 231

Romans 12:20 *On the contrary: "If your enemy is hungry, feed him; if he is thirsty, give him something to drink. In doing this, you will heap burning coals on his head."*

In this verse, Paul is alluding to Proverbs 25:21–22. Let's look at it as it is fully depicted: "If your enemy is hungry, give him food to eat; if he is thirsty, give him water to drink. In doing this, you will heap burning coals on his head, ***and the LORD will reward you for it***" (emphasis mine). Could it be that Paul is using a passage out of context? Well, I think the setting and the word usage in the original language needs to be considered before we make such an accusation, but that's for another time and place. There is something that we can take away from this right now though.

The idea behind providing kindness to our enemies is not so they will have burning coals put on their heads and be harmed. That's not God's way of doing things, and I don't believe He wants us to act with an attitude that is different from His. However, we could take this to mean that when we do kind things to others, they will notice and by seeing how we respond to them, they may be convicted of their own actions so that their need for repentance and change will be clearly demonstrated.

In my book, *The Fifteen Flavors of Love*, I give a definition that fits very well here. "Kindness is the act of being nice to living beings, whether they deserve it or not." I go on to say, "You see, just as God is love, God is kindness personified and exampled for us in the person of Jesus Christ. Just as patience is a fruit of the Spirit, so is kindness. Kindness comes from God because God is kind and when His Spirit enters our lives, kindness enters our lives. In other words, to be Christian is to be kind, and without kindness there is no Christianity."

True love is very durable but going through the motions of love without having the real thing is very fragile and temporary. We need to pray for God to fill us with the real thing so that the people before whom we live will see the difference between our life and theirs and want what we have. We are in the business of making people hungry for God by them seeing what He has done and is doing in our life. To whom can we show God's love today? It might even be the enemy He has allowed to be placed in our path.

DAY 232

Romans 12:21 *Do not be overcome by evil,*
but overcome evil with good.

We are bombarded by bad stuff on every side. To venture outside the safety of our homes is to take a chance on any number of situations that could do us harm. There are people who could hurt us, a virus that could kill us, and accidents that could befall us. Life is a very uncertain thing.

What we must remember is that everyone is in the same boat. We live among a world of citizens who also have to face whatever life throws at them, and they don't know what is coming next any more than we do. Evil can rear its ugly head at any time.

This is why we are to be overcomers when facing evil, so that we can offer goodness to those who are in need. It's not just a matter of our being victorious over the powers of darkness, we need to be the source of goodness and grace that can be applied to the ones God puts in our path.

It is through the grace and power of God that we can overcome the evil of the world, but with every victory we experience we have an obligation to be a dispenser of goodness, so that others can see just how good the Lord is. By our spiritual witness, we offer them hope in God as an alternative to facing the evil that they continually have to face.

How do we do that? We can overcome evil with the goodness of being a friend in a time of need. We can be the prayer partner that lifts others to the Lord to give them a spiritual lifeline. We produce goodness by glorifying God in all of our actions, our words, and our attitudes. We defeat the evil influences by replacing them with holy interactions with God and our fellow man.

We must remember that Paul has been focusing on how we are to treat our enemies. With that in mind, what better way for our enemies to be encountered than to bombard them with love so that they will not only be surprised but convicted in their spirits as they realize that God has done something is us that they haven't experienced. The goal is that they will come to know God's grace in the same manner.

God is not about dishing out vengeance; He is continually dispensing grace. By our overcoming evil, He gets the credit and others are blessed.

DAY 233

Romans 13:1 *Everyone must submit himself to the governing authorities, for there is no authority except that which God has established. The authorities that exist are established by God.*

Ok, now Paul has apparently left preaching and gone to meddling. Well, that's the way a lot of people see it anyway. What about separation of church and state? What do governing authorities have to do with spiritual matters?

We need to remember that for the first eleven chapters of this book, Paul was laying out his theology, or how our Christian belief system works. When he reached chapter twelve, he began to take the belief system to the practical areas of our lives, and here he brings home something that impacts us all.

There are some key words in this verse. The first one is "Everyone." There are no exceptions here. What he has to say concerns the rich and poor as well as the connected and the disconnected. The second key word is "submit." Everyone must submit. Everyone needs to be humble for everyone has a boss that they need to respect and heed. The third thought involves "governing authorities." There are some people who have the full-time responsibility of leading the rest of us. Most Christians don't have too hard a time acknowledging Paul's emphasis here.

What catches us off guard is when Paul states that God has established all the governing authorities that exist. It's even more telling and confirming for us because Paul repeats this declaration twice. He claims that God is responsible for all the governing entities that exist.

How can this be, we say! What about Hitler and Nazi Germany, Communism and the Iron Curtain, and the human rights violations of the various evil empires? Or what about the Roman Empire of Paul's day? They were certainly no Boy Scouts.

Here's the answer. God can use whomever or whatever He wants for His glory. Examples are the Egyptian Pharaoh, Nebuchadnezzar, the Assyrians, and numerous other evil empires of the ages. He can raise them up to do His bidding, and He can close them down when He is done with them. We will say more about this in days to come, but for now, let's realize that God is God and He can do whatever, with whomever He wants.

DAY 234

Romans 13:2 *Consequently, he who rebels against the authority is rebelling against what God has instituted, and those who do so will bring judgment on themselves.*

We see it in the news all the time: rioters, arsonists, rebel-rousers, and protestors who take their issues to the streets and cause chaos for the people who live by the law. Of course, there are many more crimes that go on behind the scenes, whether that be of the white-collar variety that steals millions, or the butcher who has his thumb on the scale, we see people who think that the law is for someone else rather than for them.

Paul is making a drastic charge with his practical application of Christian living. He is not speaking in theological arguments now, but in the literal and tangible ways that Christians abide in their communities. He is clear that there is no special privilege allowed in society just because one claims to be a person of faith. In the neighborhood as well as the church, the Christian is to be person who abides under the dictates of the law of the land.

As we walk with the Lord, we have to remember that we are citizens of two worlds and two kingdoms. Though the heavenly realm must always take priority in our lives, we also are human and live now in a world that often doesn't even consider spiritual matters, or anything that cannot be proven by science, or perceived through one of the five senses.

What becomes primary for us here is the witness that we leave with others. Going to church on Sunday may put us into a category that is in the minority, but that brand of Christianity alone will not win others for Christ. Our neighbors may see us leave our homes in our cars each Sunday morning, but what really impresses them is how we live the other six days of the week.

God has put us where we are for a purpose, and that purpose is to glorify Him, or make Him look good to the world around us. He has allowed the powers that rule our lands to take their places, and whether they do right or wrong, He will ultimately judge. In the meantime, we are to live peacefully and orderly so that our good deeds may win the respect of those around us in such a way that they will be hungry for what we have in Christ. Judgment will eventually fall on those who need judgment. Today, we are to live for the Lord so that people who watch us will see the difference Christ has made.

DAY 235

Romans 13:3 *For rulers hold no terror for those who do right, but for those who do wrong. Do you want to be free from fear of the one in authority? Then do what is right and he will commend you.*

O f course, Paul is speaking in general terms here, for there are down through history rulers who sometimes used their power to terrorize the righteous. Over the vast span of the ages though, these are the exceptions rather than the rule. Most leaders, even dictators, want order and peaceful co-existence with those over whom they rule in order to secure their position from rebellion and removal.

The principle given here by the apostle involves the Christian doing his or her part to live peaceably before God and man, so that our mission to build the eternal kingdom will not be compromised.

I remember walking to school when I was a small boy in first grade. Because we lived in a small town and because it was a different age, there were many times I walked the two blocks to school unescorted, though usually my brother, who was thirteen months older was with me. The only barrier between us and the school was the crossing of North 8th Street with its daily hum of traffic. On the corner next to the school each day was a policeman we only knew as Officer Fred. Some kids called him "Fred Goliath" because he seemed so big. Anyway, he had rules about how we were to cross the street, and we violated them at our own peril.

Once, I looked both ways and started across the street before Officer Fred gave the word that it was clear. In no uncertain terms he let me know that I was in the wrong, and he ushered me back to the curb until he announced it was okay to cross. Apparently, his authority made quite an impression on me because I still remember it these many decades later.

God puts leaders into their places so that they can guide us for our good. When they don't do as He wishes, He knows how to change the situation, but we need to always remember that His plan is long-term. For the short game, we need to obey the laws of the land, and do so as unto the Lord. The rules may cause us to chaff at times, but when we remember Romans 8:28 says that "in all things God works for the good of those who have been called according to his purpose," the law is doubly for our good.

DAY 236

Romans 13:4 *For he is God's servant to do you good. But if you do wrong, be afraid, for he does not bear the sword for nothing. He is God's servant, an agent of wrath to bring punishment on the wrongdoer.*

I don't know if you have ever thought about those who have authority over us as being God's servants, but Paul apparently thought about it. He also thought that they were in place for our benefit. They were able to control the circumstances that went on in the Roman empire to a certain extent because they had the force and power of the Roman army to back up what they ordered. Few dared to take on the wrath of rulers with that kind of power.

However, Paul doesn't speak here about the ruling authorities in a bad light. He genuinely sees those in leadership as instruments that God uses to bring about His purposes. Even those who "bear the sword" are His mercenaries, used by His unseen hand to create stability in the world.

In our day, we often see the worst that leadership has to offer. One must wonder whether politics and authority have always been strange bedfellows of corruption, or if it is just the few that get the headlines. Regardless of who is in office or what power he or she leverages, the real authority lies with God, and He is always looking out for us.

The police departments of the world get a bad rap these days. They are accused of racial injustice, bias profiling, and operating in bad faith toward the public they are sworn to protect and serve. I am sure that there are several within their ranks that deserve the criticism, but it is certainly unfair to paint any group of people with the same brush of evaluation. There is not a profession anywhere that has one hundred percent honest people in its leadership one hundred percent of the time.

We need to remember that our task is to represent Christ. Obeying those in authority is one way to do it, but also it is important that we show them some grace for the tough, split-second, life-or-death decisions they have to make regularly. We have been instructed to pray for our leaders and I believe that includes our law enforcers. I have met and fellowshipped with many really good ones over the years. Maybe they would be in greater number and be more effective if the people of God lifted them in prayer. It's certainly something to think about.

DAY 237

Romans 13:5 *Therefore, it is necessary to submit to the authorities, not only because of possible punishment but also because of conscience.*

The laws of the land are in place to bring about conformity to a pattern of life that is mutually beneficial for everyone. Of course, that is the ideal. We all know that some laws are impractical, unfair to some, and some are just dumb. However, to the best of our ability, if they don't violate God's laws, we are to live under their scrutiny so that the greatest amount of people will benefit from them.

I have long felt that the reason behind any law or rule is because people in their natural state can't be trusted. Speed limits are posted on our highways because we know that if they weren't, some folks would drive far too recklessly for the highways to be safe for the rest of us. There are laws against libel and slander because if there were none, smear tactics would be employed continually by the people with the loudest voices and the most money. Even in the church there are rules because people need guidance to keep them from doing things that are not in their best interests spiritually. Standards are set, penalties for violations are put into place, and then enforcement officials respond to make corrections when people are not in compliance with the rules and laws.

The people of God are called to a higher standard than to just obey the law so that they won't be punished. We have a responsibility to raise the bar high so that we will lead others by our examples. When Paul speaks about the violation of our conscience, it has to do with the harm we do to others when we don't make following the Lord appear as a good thing for everyone. We don't want to disappoint the Lord by giving people the impression that we are above the laws they are required to live under.

I used to have a license plate frame on my car that just read, "Pastor." Another pastor once told me, "I could never have that on my car. I drive too fast to set a good example for others." To me, that seemed inconsistent with the message of obedience that we need to portray before others. If we don't set the example for good behavior, who will? I am convinced that God always expects the best from us because we are a reflection on Him. If Christians don't represent Christ to our world, again, who will?

DAY 238

Romans 13:6–7 *This is why you pay taxes, for the authorities are God's servants, who give their full time to governing. Give everyone what you owe him: If you owe taxes, pay taxes; if revenue, then revenue; if respect, then respect; if honor, then honor.*

Don't you just love to pay taxes? Doesn't it give you such a warm feeling inside when you pull out the W-2 forms, the 1099's, and Schedule A's and Schedule C's, and grab the calculator so you can get to work? I know that around the world, and even in each state in the USA, the formats are somewhat different, but taxes are taxes, and it looks like they will be around longer than we will.

Just as the government assignments feel heavy upon us today, they did to the people of Paul's time too. Certainly, the people of the Roman empire had a different scale of calculation than we do, but people always chaff under the load of taxation that is assigned to them. When Paul wrote these words, he was well aware of the temptation to cheat and find ways around paying what was assigned to the populous. As long as there have been taxes, there have been people who have tried to get out of paying them, but such actions always come at a cost.

One cost that has to be considered for the Christian, far beyond the government penalties, is the witness that is left before the world. The bar for Christians is, and should be, very high. We don't have the luxury of living like the rest of the world because we represent the King of kings and should do everything within our power to keep from causing shame to come to His name. This is why every decision we make, every action we take, every word that we speak or write, should be done with the greatest of care. It's not so that we will stay out of trouble, though that is a nice perk, but so that in all things God will be glorified through the followers of His Son, Jesus.

Notice that Paul didn't just leave his admonition with taxes. We are to give everyone what they are owed, whether revenue, or respect, or honor. We could spread this over a much wider field. It includes our marriages, our children, our money, and our interactions with our neighbors and our enemies. In everything we are to make God look good. That's why we are here; to live for the glory of God.

DAY 239

Romans 13:8 *Let no debt remain outstanding,*
except the continuing debt to love one another, for
he who loves his fellowman has fulfilled the law.

This is a touchy point for modern and post-modern era Christians as well as for the first century that Paul occupied. Live lives free of debt; it sounds almost like an impossibility, but here is the deal. If you buy a $100,000 house with a thirty-year mortgage at 2.85 percent interest, you are going to pay $85,500 in interest payments alone before the debt is satisfied. By going into debt, a person pays almost twice as much for a purchase than if they paid the asking price in cash. The same is true for any purchase we make when there is an interest charge attached. As Proverbs 22:7 says, "The rich rule over the poor, and the borrower is slave to the lender."

But as we keep this section of scripture in context, we must remember that Paul was not speaking primarily about money. In relation to our paying taxes, paying revenue, paying respect, or paying honor, we should not be in debt and found wanting. Being miserly in such areas casts a shadow over our Christian witness and brings shame to God. What Paul is really trying to get the Romans to grasp is that they should be free from whatever puts them in a bad light so that God will always look good to those who watch.

The debt that we are instructed to focus on is the debt of love. Jesus said it most clearly, "Love the Lord your God with all your heart and with all your soul and with all your strength and with all your mind'; and 'Love your neighbor as yourself" (Luke 10:27). Love is to be the essence that exudes from our lives and love should be the aroma that people smell when they spend time around us. We should be so deeply in debt to God that we can never get out of the depths of mercy in which we find ourselves. Because God has so loved us, we in turn owe it to love Him back, and to love those around us as a debt that can never be paid. It is this kind of debt that concerned Paul for the Roman Christians the most.

As we look over our lives, what do we see? When our family member, our friends, our co-workers, our neighbors, and even other members of the church describe us, do they do so in terms that show our depth of love? Do they want to be around us because we are so much like Jesus that they want some of Him to rub off from us? That's the debt Paul wanted us to have.

DAY 240

Romans 13:9 *The commandments, "Do not commit adultery,"*
"Do not murder," "Do not steal," "Do not covet," and
whatever other commandments there may be, are summed
up in this one rule: "Love your neighbor as yourself."

The Ten Commandments give a lot of people concern. In this age of liberality, many consider them to be old fashioned, out of step with the times, or just irrelevant—even for Christians. After all, they were written thousands of years ago for a people far, far away, and established the old covenant of God with His people. The question often asked by many sincere Christians is, "Since they were written for the Jews of the Old Testament and we now live in the age of the Spirit, are we bound by them today?" It's a good question that deserves an answer.

We first must acknowledge that Jesus thought the commandments were important. In fact, He said, "Do not think that I have come to abolish the Law or the Prophets; I have not come to abolish them but to fulfill them" (Matthew 5:17). Of course, Jesus was a Jew also, so we may need to look deeper. Paul would proclaim in Galatians 5:1 "It is for freedom that Christ has set us free. Stand firm, then, and do not let yourselves be burdened again by a yoke of slavery." It almost sounds like He was on a different page than Jesus.

In my opinion, this is the best way to understand the requirements of the Law. We are not saved by adhering to the Law, but because we are saved, we naturally live out the tenets of the Law. God hasn't changed and He never will. What He designed and desires for His people of all races hasn't changed. The rules are for the benefit of mankind, but they are for the people of God to live as examples of the Spirit-changed life. Where once the Law caused people to be in bondage in order to try and fulfill every jot and tittle of its requirements, now because of the fullness of the Spirit in the believer's life, the following of the Law is no longer a burden, but a privilege. God has changed us so that we can follow Him with joy.

The key to it all is found in Paul's focus on love. Loving our neighbor as ourselves is a chore if it is done from a human perspective. But when Jesus transformed our hearts, He replaced the desire for self-preservation with an urgency to be a blessing to others. As God loves, we love also.

DAY 241

Romans 13:10 *Love does no harm to its neighbor.
Therefore love is the fulfillment of the law.*

P eople say that love makes the world go round. We have slogans and songs which state, "Love is all you need," "We found love," "Burning love," "What the world needs now is love, sweet love," and even "Love the one you're with." The concept of love pervades our airwaves, our conversations, our relationships, and our commitments.

However, what is often meant by love in our present culture could easily be better defined as carnal lust. We want love for what we can get out of it, how it makes us feel, and in the words of another oldie, to "Help us make it through the night." Let's be clear, this is not love, it is lust, plain and simple.

When Paul uses the word "love" here, he is using the Greek word, "agape." Agape love is God's love. It is not based on our emotions; it doesn't regard self as a high priority, and it always seeks the best for others. In my book, *The Fifteen Flavors of Love: A New Look at an Old Word* (Outskirts Press, 2014), I walk through Chapter thirteen, verses four through seven of Paul's first letter to the Corinthians. Those few verses paint a completely different picture of love as compared to the lust of the ages, as it relates love to be patient, kind, not envious, not boastful, not proud, not rude, not self-promoting, not easily angered, not a record keeper of wrongs, doesn't delight in evil, rejoices with the truth, always protecting, always hoping, and always persevering. This is the kind of love that flows from the throne of God.

This love does more than not harm our neighbor, it betters our neighbor. It prays for his well-being, his concerns, and his family. It is the kind of love that is able to win people to Christ because it comes directly from Jesus through us.

That's why love is the fulfillment of the law. God gave His law for the benefit of mankind and the world He created for man to live in. Love puts God first and then our neighbor in the next slot of importance. We can't do that on our own; we need the fulness of the Holy Spirit in our lives for this to happen. Trying to figure out what is best for our own life can be confusing and difficult, so surely, we don't know what's best for our neighbor. But we do know they need love, and they need God, for love plus God is fulfillment for all people.

DAY 242

Romans 13:11 *And do this, understanding the present time. The hour has come for you to wake up from your slumber, because our salvation is nearer now than when we first believed.*

One has to wonder how Paul viewed the times in which he lived. He was no doubt as limited in perspective as any of us, but I have to think he would have been amazed to think that 2000 years would roll by before Jesus would bring the age to a close. I guess every generation thinks that theirs is going to be the last, and then time will be no more.

He is so right about one thing though. Our ultimate salvation is closer now than it was during his day. Every minute that ticks by puts us one step nearer to eternity and to the end of the age. When it comes to determining just how long it will take for us to reach that point though, I am as clueless as was the Apostle Paul.

There is something for us to consider here concerning slumbering, however. Sleep is a sweet gift for those who can attain it easily and keep it going for an entire night. I've rarely had that experience in recent years. My pattern is to go to sleep quickly, but then wake up after three or four hours, stay awake for two to three hours, and then go back to bed for a brief nap to finish out my night. I'd like it to be different, but that pattern seems to be my lot in life.

Because of my strange sleep schedule, I sometimes get tired in the afternoon, and am usually ready for bed fairly early. When I am working, I have to sometimes force myself to keep at what I am doing because of drowsiness. I stay at it though because I believe that what I am doing is important.

Paul tells us that living in the Spirit and building the Kingdom of God here on earth is as important as things get, so we can't doze off whenever we get the urge. We are to be frontline workers, living daily as representatives of the King, and not forsaking our duties regardless of how tired we might get along the way. There's too much at stake concerning the eternal destiny of mankind for us to be sleepy and complacent about it all. While it is still light, we have work to do for Jesus, for the night is coming when no one can work, so I want to get in all the time I can for the Master while I can.

DAY 243

Romans 13:12 *The night is nearly over; the day is almost here. So let us put aside the deeds of darkness and put on the armor of light.*

It should be obvious to anyone who has an ounce of discernment, that we as Christians are in a war against the powers of darkness. It seems like that with each new day and with the development of each new avenue of technology, the potential for temptation and corruption is increased in like measure. Relativism battles against holiness and sin raises its ugly head at every opportunity.

Paul reminds us that in the midst of this battle we need to recognize that the struggle itself has a time limit. If Jesus should delay His return for another two thousand years, as humans we are more limited our time left to work. Our time of three score and ten years pass very quickly and even when we get more time added to our personal calendar of life, it is limited at best.

Therefore, we are to dress appropriately in the armor of light while we can. There is no time for Christians to dabble in areas of darkness when the whole world is desperately needing us to show them the true and living Light. It is only through Jesus, the Light of the world, that any person can ever be saved from their sins and enter into eternity as a victor, so it is important that we don't lose the urgency of that message.

The deeds of darkness are everywhere, but they are powerless against the light of holiness. When the two collide, there will be an impact and a battle, for our foe doesn't go down without a fight, but righteousness will win at the end of the day. Our task is to remain faithful to the fight as if our eternal destiny, and the eternal destiny of our family, neighbors, and friends depend on it, because it does. Time is rolling by, and we have much to do for Jesus.

This is why there is no retirement date set on our labors for Christ. We may get enough years on the clock to be eligible for a pension and a monthly social security check, but that doesn't end our days of service for our King. Jesus calls us to take up our cross and follow Him, and we are not finished with that task until He calls us to our eternal home with Him. Soldiers of the Light are not dismissed from duty until we close our eyes for the last time and breathe our last breath. If we stay faithful, we will be rewarded in due time. Until then, we have Kingdom business that calls us into action.

DAY 244

Romans 13:13 *Let us behave decently, as in the daytime, not in orgies and drunkenness, not in sexual immorality and debauchery, not in dissension and jealousy.*

Paul gets very specific here when he mentions the actions of the dark. The analogy he uses is very dramatic as he contrasts how Christians and non-Christians are to live. I find it interesting how he names specific areas of sin that are exhibited as a contrast to living in light.

Sexual sin, alcoholism, division, and coveting what belongs to others, are vices that run to the core of our world's societies. It may seem like a broad generalization, but when one comes right down to it, these are the sins that have been affecting mankind since Adam and Eve left the Garden of Eden. These things are addictive and the virus of their impact on the world spreads more quickly and is more deadly than Covid-19 ever hoped to be.

The reason that these areas of the night are so powerful and so pervasive in our world, is because they are the tools that the enemy of our souls finds so effective in his attacks against us. The draw to sexual activity is so strong because the continuation of our species depends on it being that way. It is only when this appetite is abused and distorted that it becomes the sin that destroys. Sex, when it is used within the boundaries of marriage that God established between men and women, is a wonderful and holy thing, but when it is misused for our own selfish desires, it becomes a weapon of Satan that can cost us our souls.

Likewise, drunkenness has a strong attraction. Our societies of the world revel in the keg parties, the bar scenes, and the humor of seeing how people act when they have had too much to drink. While it is true that the Bible never speaks against drinking alcohol, it does condemn drunkenness continually. The problem is that too many people can't set limits for themselves, and that becomes a problem for the rest of us. On April 10, 2017, I was almost killed by a drunk driver. Many others before and since that date actually have died as a result of someone else's excess and lack of control in their personal habit. Jealousy also is a deadly sin. It causes us to crave what others have. These things are tools of Satan. For us to behave decently, we must be people of the day, not of the night.

DAY 245

Romans 13:14 *Rather clothe yourselves with the Lord Jesus Christ, and do not think about how to gratify the desires of the sinful nature.*

People spend a lot of money on clothes. I can't imagine what our national sales in apparel amounts to, but when I go through the stores and the malls, I see seemingly endless amounts of merchandise that are offered to the public. I guess somebody is buying a lot of new stuff.

A lot less emphasis goes into our Christian garments. I'm not talking about what we wear to church on Sunday, but what we wear every day of the week. Paul speaks of clothing ourselves with Jesus, and I don't think he was implying that we need to wear a robe and sandals like He did. No, I believe he was referring to the likeness of His presence covering our lives in all our actions, our words, and our connections with our world.

Around the church we used to refer to other members as "brother" or "sister." There was such a strong awareness of the family of God that we even verbalized it in how we addressed each other. This not only made for a close communion, but it also helped us to hold each other accountable for our actions. If we saw a brother or sister acting in such a way that the image of Christ was marred before the world, it was expected that we would call them on it. The fear of the Lord was stronger than the fear of pushback.

Though at times this was overdone and perhaps needed to be refined in how we approached each other, today we have too often neglected our responsibility to hold each other to a high standard in Christ. In other words, we have thrown the baby out with the bathwater. We are more afraid of causing offense, or being embarrassed, than we are with others discarding purity of heart and life.

The strong tendency of our world is to disregard the admonitions of Paul concerning focusing on gratifying the sinful nature. In fact, much of the world is continually focused on how to satisfy the desires of the sinful nature. This is why we are urged as Christians to live to a higher standard to glorify God, but also to give a witness to what He has done and is doing in our lives.

My dog focuses continually on satisfying his basic desires. We as humans, and especially as Christians, are called to be better than that.

DAY 246

Romans 14:1 *Accept him whose faith is weak, without passing judgment on disputable matters.*

One thing that we always need to keep in mind when it comes to dealing with our brothers and sisters in Christ, is that all of us are at different stages of our journey with the Lord. Some have been a part of the church family since birth, some have just recently come out of a life of sin, and many are somewhere in between those two extremes.

As a result of the different levels of understanding in our faith walk, we have a great need to show grace to people on every step of the journey. Regardless of the insights we have accumulated along our way, we must remember that it took time for us to reach the level of understanding and training we possess, and it will take others different timeframes to reach where they need to be.

This is why the wise heed Paul's words here and do not pass judgment on things that don't matter. We all have our preferences—even in the church—when it comes to styles of music, length of services, acceptable dress, version of Bibles, and a host of other things. While these things may seem highly important to us personally, in reality they are just that—preferences. They are like the kinds of food we eat. Some things we like; some things we don't. But they are not things that should divide the body of Christ, for we all have freedom in the Spirit.

Of course, this is different when it comes to concerns of doctrine and clear biblical teaching. In these matters we should hold our ground, with grace and in love, even unto death, but it's usually not the doctrinal things that divide a church on the local level. Usually, our judgment comes to life when we see people doing something that is out of line with local traditions and preferences.

The key words here are "disputable matters." If they are matters that can be disputed, then the law is not set in concrete. If they are fluid, then grace must certainly be the path we should take.

Leaders wiser than me once said, "In essentials unity, in non-essentials liberty, and in all things charity." That's good advice for us all.

DAY 247

Romans 14:2–3 *One man's faith allows him to eat everything, but another man, whose faith is weak, eats only vegetables. The man who eats everything must not look down on him who does not, and the man who does not eat everything must not condemn the man who does, for God has accepted him.*

We who like to congregate also like to nitpick. The more of us there are, the more we find things over which we can differ. This is true in society on the general level, but in the church, it becomes more noticeable because our relationships go so much deeper.

This closeness that we experience causes us sometimes to begin to think about things that pertain to what we see as essential to the faith we share. Paul spoke to the Roman church with words that serve as a warning to keep brothers and sisters from exercising undo pressure on the family concerning what Christians view as essential in serving the Lord.

The matter of eating meat involves meat that had been offered to idols in the pagan temples. After the offering was made, the meat was sold in the common markets and was purchased by whoever wished to buy it. Because Christians did not approve of the sacrifice to an idol, to many the idea of eating the meat promoted idolatry and a worldly way of thinking. Because of this connotation, they would just eat vegetables mainly in their diets. Those who realized that idols were just false gods with no real value, saw no problem in eating whatever they received with grateful hearts. Such differing opinions had the potential of causing great conflict in the church and posed a danger for the fellowship of believers in general.

This message is good for the first century and still good for the twenty-first century. We are not to look down on our brothers and sisters in Christ when they don't see issues the same way we do. Our degree of faith and our grasp of what God teaches in His Word, is different from person to person and from church to church. Love must be the key in every situation if we are to represent Christ in the way we have been instructed. Whatever promotes unity in the Spirit, love for the Christian family, and a lost world hearing the words of life, is good. If our opinions take away from that, it becomes a bad thing. Jesus prayed that we would be one. Let's not let our eating divide us.

DAY 248

Romans 14:4 *Who are you to judge someone else's servant? To his own master he stands or falls. And he will stand, for the Lord is able to make him stand.*

There is a dark part of my family's history that I discovered while researching my family tree. Our branch of the James family came from Wales to the American colonies in 1673 to begin a new life. They settled in Virginia, and in 1674 Thomas James was the first of my ancestors to be born in what was to be the new homeland of the clan.

Because Virginia was at that time a land where slavery was a way of life, and by 1778, when John, the grandson of Thomas passed away, he left in his will to his children, two slaves named Moses and David. Slaves were considered someone's property, and just as other items of the household passed from one generation to the next, so did their slaves.

I bring this up not out of pride, but of shame. For people to be able to own other people as possessions is a sin that has been highlighted by the events of the history and the conscience of man. However, when Paul made reference to people being someone else's servant, he fully understood that the owner's control over the property was complete. No one had the right to interfere with a person's control of his property.

This is why he emphasized that we who are in Christ belong to someone else. This is not a bad thing, but a very good thing. We have made the choice of our own volition to be a love slave to Jesus. But since we belong to him now, no one has the right to direct our path or judge our actions but Christ alone, since He is our owner. And because our Christian brothers and sisters are also under voluntary servanthood to Jesus, He alone has the authority of judgment over them. They will rise or fall according to how Jesus directs them, and we need to keep our hands and opinions on the matter to ourselves.

Paul brings this to light in the midst of his discussion about judgment in the church. We don't belong to ourselves, but to the Lord. We can advise from personal experience and pray for an individual's guidance, but judgment belongs to the owner. This is a lesson the church needs to remember because our owner is always watching.

DAY 249

Romans 14:5–6 *One man considers one day more sacred than another; another man considers every day alike. Each one should be fully convinced in his own mind. He who regards one day as special, does so to the Lord. He who eats meat, eats to the Lord, for he gives thanks to God; and he who abstains, does so to the Lord and gives thanks to God.*

Because I was raised in a very conservative branch of the Christian family, Sunday was unlike any other day. Our local church joined with many other Christian groups of the time and blue laws governing Sunday behavior were strictly observed. I was taught that because Sunday was the Lord's Day and we belonged to the Lord, Sundays were for worship and rest, leaving all other activities to other days of the week. We didn't eat out on Sundays, shop on Sundays, work on Sundays, and some didn't even read newspapers or secular books on Sundays. The Lord's Day was sacred and desecrating it meant that a person's soul was in eternal jeopardy.

I was in my first year of college, when in a time of venturing into the ways of the world, I went out to eat with a date in a restaurant after a Sunday worship service. To my utter amazement, across the restaurant from me sat my pastor and his family, enjoying a noon meal. My conservative training and instruction had an awakening I hadn't expected to experience.

Paul gives us insight here. We in the church are all raised differently and have different understandings about how best to serve the Lord. He reminds the Romans that whether one follows the Jewish habit of Sabbath or has a more liberal view, such ideas are between that servant and his or her Master, Jesus Christ. We do not have the right to interfere with how the Master instructs His servants.

What matters here is faith. We are to do what we do, whether considering all days the same or differently comes down to a matter of conscience before the Lord. If we are thankful to God for what we eat, when we eat it, or where we eat it, we do it unto the Lord. If conscience permits us liberty, then we should rejoice and give thanks for that liberty. If conscience restricts us, then we should be equally thankful. All things are done or not done for Jesus's sake, but He is the Judge, and we will answer to Him alone. We have no right to judge another person's property, for it belongs to the Lord!

DAY 250

Romans 14:7–8 *For none of us lives to himself alone and none of us dies to himself alone. If we live, we live to the Lord; and if we die, we die to the Lord. So whether we live or die, we belong to the Lord.*

It was John Donne of the late sixteenth and early seventeenth centuries, who penned the words that echo Paul's sentiment here. "No man is an island, entire of itself. Each is a piece of the continent, a part of the main." It was his poetic way of saying that all of our lives are interconnected, and every life is important to each other life.

Paul makes this clear regarding Christians as a part of the Church of Jesus Christ. Our lives in the faith are connected to each other and to the Lord. If the Lord grants us time on this planet, we are here for Him. If he chooses to take away the life we enjoy here, we go to reside with Him. Either way, we are all wrapped up in the Lord, His purposes for us, and His plan for our world.

Some people worry continually about the issues of life and death. During the days of the Covid-19 pandemic, many people live almost in terror that they might catch the virus and lose their lives. For the same reason some refuse to fly in an airplane, to ride a motorcycle, or do anything that is the least bit risky. They are often just too afraid of dying to enjoy living.

Paul was not a fatalist. He did not advocate the attitude of "whatever will be will be." He did, however, put his faith in the Lord Jesus and understood that our lives and times are in His hands, and as His vessel for service He controls the events that surround His followers. We can rest in the fact that we will live, then we will die, then we will live again. Death is an enemy to be sure, but it's an enemy that was conquered and defeated when Jesus was raised from the grave. It no longer has any power over Christ or over those who trust in Him. That doesn't mean that we won't die, for surely, we eventually will, but it does mean that death is not to be feared because our Savior will walk through that dark valley with us and be waiting to give us life everlasting on the other side of it.

We are to live boldly, victoriously, and unafraid of what may come. In the meantime, we are to build up our Christian family until Jesus comes. If we do that, then we are truly our brother's keeper and servant of Christ.

DAY 251

Romans 14:9 *For this very reason, Christ died and returned to life so that he might be the Lord of both the dead and the living.*

The story of the resurrection of Jesus Christ is unlike any other story in the Bible, or even in the secular world. It's the story of how God became man, lived among His creation, suffered at its hands, was killed, but then was raised to life on the third day. There is nothing anywhere else that has had the impact on our world like the story of our living Savior.

In this story we see that the cross was not an accident, or the fact of a mob of people thwarting God's purpose for mankind. Instead, the mob, the Pharisees, the Sadducees, the Romans, and all the rest are just a part of the divine drama that the Father has orchestrated to bring about the redemption of His creation.

We can now understand that Jesus has been on both sides of the eternal barrier. He lived, He died, and now He lives again, but this time forevermore. As the conqueror of life, death, and the grave, He reigns victoriously over both sides of the tombstone and provides us with the path for our lives.

It is so very true that because He lives, we can live also. We, who believe in Jesus as our personal Lord and Savior, will someday follow in His footsteps and be resurrected to a new level of life. We will have new bodies after the resurrection, and those bodies will be like the body of Jesus, never to deteriorate again, and never to die again. We shall be as Jesus is.

Christians sometimes get confused and think that heaven is the end of everything. That's not what the Bible says. Yes, we will have a time after this life to rest in a place we call heaven, or paradise, but there is more to come. There will be a resurrection of our bodies to live in the eternal Kingdom God is preparing. Jesus didn't leave His body in the grave and ours won't remain there either. It's from Plato that we get the idea of the body and spirit being separate entities, but from the Bible that we gain the knowledge of a full bodily resurrection. Do a careful reading of Revelation chapters 21–22 and you will get a better picture than just "pie in the sky by and by."

Christ is Lord of those who died and are now in heaven, with us who live here, and those who will yet live, but the resurrection is yet to come.

DAY 252

Romans 14:10 *You, then, why do you judge your brother? Or why do you look down on your brother? For we will all stand before God's judgment seat.*

I don't know about you, but I don't enjoy playing the part of being a judge. Even Jesus didn't seem to enjoy it when He walked this earth in the flesh. In Luke 12:14 there were two brothers who wanted Jesus to be the judge over who should receive their parts of the family inheritance, and Jesus refused to do so. I think we should learn something from that.

When Paul brought up this issue, he was referring to the matter of judging our neighbor as to their religious commitment and style of observance. Some chose to eat meat and be thankful and some chose to eat only vegetables and avoid the cholesterol. Some considered certain days as more holy than others, and some considered every day holy and given by God.

In our present styles of serving the Lord, some love to have loud contemporary music, and some prefer the old hymns. Some love the King James Version of the Bible, while others desire a more readable translation. Some baptize by immersion, some by pouring, and some by sprinkling. Some baptize only testifying adults, and other baptize infants. The point is, there are many different ways of doing church, and for us to judge someone else is really above our pay grade. We should do what feels the most comfortable to us, as best we understand the Bible, and then let the others find their own path with those who think as they do. As long as we all look to Jesus as Lord, and do not violate the essentials of the gospel, I really don't think it matters all that much to the Lord. In fact, He may smile with approval at the many ways we strive to approach Him and worship Him.

Our faith is all about Jesus. If my brother believes that Jesus is Lord, that He died for our sins, that He sent His Spirit to abide with us still to teach and guide us, and that we will all stand before God at the last day, then he is truly my brother indeed. I don't have to agree with him on the non-essentials or judge him because he doesn't see things like I do.

I still wear a suit on Sundays, but if my brother chooses to worship in shorts and a tee-shirt, I can let God and him work that out. I will keep my focus on Jesus and let Him be the Judge of all that matters.

DAY 253

Romans 14:11 *It is written: "As surely as I live,' says the Lord, 'every knee will bow before me; every tongue will confess to God.'"*

Any student of the Bible will recognize these words as being very similar to Philippians 2:10–11, where it says, "that at the name of Jesus every knee should bow, in heaven and on earth and under the earth, and every tongue confess that Jesus Christ is Lord, to the glory of God the Father." This is an adaptation of an Old Testament quote from Isaiah 54:23 that states, "By myself I have sworn, my mouth has uttered in all integrity a word that will not be revoked: Before me every knee will bow; by me every tongue will swear."

Most likely, this was part of a ritual saying that was used by Christians in early days of worship that preceded Paul but was used widely. In any case, it has certainly become a part of the modern Christian's creed and the hope by which we establish our worldview.

Christians believe that the wheels of injustice will not turn forever, for there is coming a day when the trumpet of God shall sound and time as we know it will come to an end. Just as there was a beginning of the age of mankind, there will be an end, and it is all in the hands of Almighty God as to when and how it will be.

The one significant difference from Isaiah's words to Paul's is the emphasis that he places on Jesus. He doesn't see Jesus and God the Father as two different tracks of power, but as one entity whose purpose and plan are totally in sync. As the Father has authority, so does the Son. In fact, Jesus made it very clear when He gave His disciples their Great Commission, as He said, "All authority in heaven and on earth has been given to me" (Matthew 28:18). John 3:35 reminds us, "The Father loves the Son and has given all things over into his hands." The honor and authority that is owed to and claimed by the Father is to be given to the Son as well.

These are words of hope for a world that is often blinded by the fog of war, hatred, injustice, crimes of all sorts, lies, and sin. There will be a day of reckoning and the scales of right and wrong will be balanced. Those who do not acknowledge the Father and the Son now, will bow before the majesty of the eternal throne then. What a joy, an honor, and a privilege to have a head start on others as we submit ourselves to the King right now.

DAY 254

Romans 14:12 *So then, each of us will give an account of himself to God.*

These words are powerful words. They leave us standing completely bare and naked before God. It reminds us of Luke 8:17, where Jesus says, "There is nothing hidden that will not be disclosed and nothing concealed that will not be brought out into the open." On the day when every knee will bow and every tongue will confess the name of Jesus to the glory of God the Father, the books will be opened, and we will give a full account of what we have done with the years of our life that were allotted to us.

Normally, this would strike terror into the heart of any person. When we think of all the things we have done that were sinful, all the words that were spoken in anger, all the attitudes that did not bring glory to God, and all the times we have been so selfish, how could anyone face God with that on our record. It appears that we have all earned a devil's hell and that there is no hope for any of us.

But along with that accounting, because we have put our trust in Jesus to be the Savior of our soul, because we have cast all our cares on Him, and because we trust by faith in His promised words of forgiveness, we have hope. We have hope for eternal life and fellowship with the Divine Trinity and the saints of all the ages, not because we deserve it or have earned it, but because Jesus promised it to us, and He never breaks His word. "Jesus Christ is the same yesterday, today, and forever" (Hebrews 13:8).

I am not an especially brave person, but I can walk with confidence in the relationship I have with Jesus. I will always be totally amazed that He would take time for me, but I know that He is with me constantly and even though I am so far from the perfection He deserves, He has mercy on me, and allows me to fellowship with Him.

So, the preacher in me has to ask, "How is your account before the Father going?" Are you making a list and checking it twice to see if you are good enough for God's favor? If so, I can tell you that such a thing is a waste of time, because you are not. I can tell you though, that if you cast your cares on Jesus, forsake the ways of sin, and trust Him for your salvation, your account will be clean. That, my friend, is what gives us hope. For there is no hope in this world or beyond, found anywhere else.

DAY 255

Romans 14:13 *Therefore let us stop passing judgment on one another. Instead, make up your mind not to put any stumbling block or obstacle in your brother's way.*

In the previous verses Paul has built a pretty good case as to why we are not to be judging our brothers and sisters in Christ. Here he turns his focus to a new idea, the thing we should be doing instead of being judges over our church family. We ought to be committed to not doing anything that would cause a brother or sister to trip as they pursue a walk with the Lord.

Now that sounds well and good, but it's not as easy as it may seem at first glance. It's a good start to make sure that our words and actions are free of anything that would cause someone else to lose confidence in our Christian testimony. But beyond that there is a fine line to walk if we would do our best to ensure the continued progress of the family of God.

There are two areas for concern here. First, we want to help believers to avoid all the things that might cause them harm. This is why so many churches have put rules in place—often to the extreme—and have tried to regulate a person's lifestyle. Rules like no drinking alcohol, no smoking, no dancing, no going to movies, no missing church services, etc. These are often well meaning, but they fall into what Paul says elsewhere. "Since you died to the basic principles of this world, why, as though you still belonged to it, do you submit to its rules: Do not handle! Do not taste! Do not touch! These are all destined to perish with use, because they are based on human commands and regulations" (Colossians 2:20–23). We can trap people into a rule-based religion if we are not careful, and it becomes a stumbling block.

The second area of concern is to be too lenient with our lifestyle. Having no standards is called antinomianism, and it makes grace just a cheap syrup that we pour over everything we decide to do, thinking God will just wink at our actions then. This too is a stumbling block.

This is why Christianity is a religion that is about a personal relationship with a living God. We depend on His guidance daily to help us walk the highway of holiness without veering to the right or the left. Communication is everything and Jesus is always available for us to talk to. We best avoid being a stumbling block by asking Him how best to do it.

DAY 256

Romans 14:14 *As one who is in the Lord Jesus, I am fully convinced that no food is unclean in itself. But if anyone regards something as unclean, then for him it is unclean.*

We used to hear a lot of people in the church talk about their personal convictions. One person would have a personal conviction about which translation of the Bible they should use. Another had a personal conviction about eating in the church. Some even would testify to having a personal conviction about not kissing on the first date.

These things may sound very spiritual, just like the people that argued with Paul about whether or not they should eat meat that had been sacrificed to idols. If it had been offered to an idol, then it must be contaminated, and some Christians felt they should stay away from it. Others would say that since idols were just imaginary gods anyway, there was no harm in eating it so long as one gave the one true God thanks for the nourishment it provided.

We need to be careful with our words because some things that are listed as personal convictions are really just personal preferences. Unless a person has had a heart-to-heart conversation with Jesus about such matters and has come away from that conversation with a strong opinion that is more than just emotion, we shouldn't call it a conviction. Our traditions and training run deep, but they are not always led by the Spirit.

The main point that Paul is making here is that we are to be considerate of how others view things, even if their opinion is different from ours. For example, I wear a suit when I go to church. It's not a requirement, it's not a conviction, and it's not a mandate from God. It's just a personal preference for me and I have my own reasons for doing so. Other people who don't have my church background and heritage see things differently, so they come to worship in shorts or blue jeans and a tee-shirt. I choose not to dress that way and they choose not to dress my way. True Christianity is about our concern for how to help other people best grow in the Lord, rather than about how we can get everyone to think like us.

In Christ we have liberty, we have freedom, and we have grace. Let's extend that which we have received from the Lord personally to others who are in the family of God. Let's respect and love each other rather than judge.

DAY 257

Romans 14:15 *If your brother is distressed because of what you eat, you are no longer acting in love. Do not destroy your brother for whom Christ died.*

One of the slogans we hear shouted from the streets of our land is "I've got my rights!" We are taught that no one should ever take advantage of us because we are free individuals, and no one can require our allegiance. However, that's the worldview of people who consider that this present world is all that there is. For Christians, there is something much bigger to consider.

With every decision we make in life as Christians, we have to ask the question, "How does this make God look to others?" and a good follow up question is, "How does this affect the people that are around me?" If everything we do is based on those two questions it will greatly impact how we are perceived by God and man. We dare not take this lightly.

The basis of all Christian action should be the foundation of love. Claiming our rights at the expense of someone else's rights doesn't smell of divine direction. Paul's words to the church in Philippi come to mind here, as he says, "Your attitude should be the same as that of Christ Jesus. Who, being in very nature God, did not consider equality with God something to be grasped, but made himself nothing, taking the very nature of a servant, being made in human likeness" (Philippians 2:5–7). That doesn't sound like someone who is clamoring to get his own way.

Whether it is a matter of what we eat or drink, as it is in the passage in Romans, or in the matter of how we treat waitresses, co-workers, check-out clerks, or bosses, we are always in the business of representing Christ. Getting our way but destroying a relationship or causing someone else to be hurt, especially spiritually, should never be the model for the servant of Jesus. We need to go out of our way, go the second mile to keep from causing distress and spiritual confusion for those who are watching. Our very witness for God and reputation for our own lives depend on it.

We may not think we are destroying someone else's faith by how we act, but we should think about it. Every soul is one for whom Christ died, and we shouldn't be satisfied until all of them we meet sees Christ at work in us.

DAY 258

Sometimes it's really hard to tell what is right from what is wrong. The messages that comet from the world seem to change with every new wind that blows across the land. What used to be confirmed as completely wrong is now considered by much of society as completely right, and to think otherwise is completely wrong. Situation ethics, post-modern thinking, and mass hysteria all seem to blend together into a hodge-podge of muddled uncertainty.

But for the child of God, we have a foundation that does not change. We know that Jesus never changes (Hebrews 13:8), and we know that the Word of God never changes (Matthew 5:18). With this strong underpinning we can carefully work our way through the untruths of society and find what pleases God. That, in part, is the job of the church.

Once we have found truth, we need to hold on to it, propagate it, and be convinced of it always. For example, society now says that it is wrong for the church to condemn abortion, saying it takes away a woman's right to choose. Of course, it does take away a woman's right to choose murder, but that involves the breaking of another commandment. Science itself tells us that the baby in the womb has a DNA different from the mother and often a different blood type. The child is attached to the woman's body but is not a part of the woman's body. The world says that it is wrong to limit marriage to only a man and a woman. They say that men should be able to marry men and women should be able to marry women, and that the church should celebrate these things, even though the Bible completely condemns such actions as abhorrent to a holy God.

We are told by Paul in Romans 12:18 that as much as possible, we should live at peace with all men. However, we cannot as Christians accept evil as good and wrong as right. We cannot take what is holy and allow others to disregard and trash it without us speaking up. We are people of peace and violence is not a part of who we are, but we are also a people of truth and God's truth must never be silenced, watered down, or diminished.

We have been raised up for such a time as this. Let's be good for Jesus' sake, and for the sake of the gospel to our world.

DAY 259

Romans 14:17–18 *For the kingdom of God is not a matter of eating and drinking, but of righteousness, peace and joy in the Holy Spirit, because anyone who serves Christ in this way is pleasing to God and approved by men.*

As much as people love to eat, what we eat and where it comes from, should not be the main focus of our lives. In the previous verses Paul has been trying to convince the Romans about the freedom we enjoy in the Spirit and the love that we should impart to one another in that freedom. He urges them, and us, to focus on something else—the Kingdom of God.

It is this Kingdom that we as Christians are working to attain. Our labors for the Lord are for the sake of bringing that Kingdom to pass, and the method Jesus has chosen to be the main instrument in that effort is His church. It may sometimes seem like a big and impossible undertaking, but God doesn't make mistakes, and this is how He is bringing it to pass.

Notice the attributes of the eternal Kingdom: "righteousness, peace, and joy in the Holy Spirit." These are the weapons of war we use to fight our spiritual battles. Others may tell us to take up arms, to win at the ballot box, or even take to the streets in protest of wrongdoing in the world. Jesus did none of that. He showed us the way of love, the way of compassion, and the way of living in the presence of the Father. It is in this way that kingdoms of the world are toppled, and the Kingdom of God will make its entrance.

Also notice the results of living out these attributes. It makes us "pleasing to God and approved by man." There should be nothing higher on our priority list than to live in such a way that would be pleasing to God. Having His smile on our life is the greatest blessing anyone could ever experience, as saints for 2000 years could easily testify. Being approved by man is a lessor priority, because God's approval is what we strive for, but when we live a life of love, then even our foes can't conquer what exudes from our witness.

It comes down to focusing on what matters most. We can bicker over church rules, and how they are to be or not to be obeyed, or we can throw ourselves into the "righteousness, peace, and joy" of Jesus Christ. One will lead to continual frustration, but the second will lead to peace, and bring others along in that way as well. Which will you choose?

DAY 260

Romans 14:19 *Let us therefore make every effort to do what leads to peace and to mutual edification.*

Some may read this verse on its own and think that Paul is talking about bringing tranquility to our fight-ravaged world and ushering in an age of love. Well, that would be nice, of course, but he is really aiming at a different target. As we keep this chapter in context, we must remember that Paul is speaking about the relationships people have with each other in the church. The world outside the church will always struggle to get along, usually without much success. But within the church family, things are supposed to be different, and if Christ is truly at the helm of the Gospel Ship, they will be.

All through this chapter Paul has been focusing on the importance of caring for our brothers in the faith. Specifically, it involves what we eat or don't eat, because our eating or not eating could be the cause of our brother's spiritual demise, or his spiritual fortitude.

But since we usually don't have this debate within our modern/post-modern church, let's look at it from another angle. Verse seventeen ties the concept of eating with drinking, and that's something with which we can identify. To drink, or not to drink, is the question that troubles many churches in the twenty-first century. Of course, we are talking about drinking alcohol here.

Many Christians who choose to imbibe state correctly that the Bible never says that we shouldn't drink, but only that we shouldn't get drunk. But the issue here is to do what brings about peace and builds up our brothers and sisters in the faith, not about drinking per se. Didn't Paul say over in I Corinthians 8:13, that if eating meat would cause his brother to fall into sin, he would never eat meat again? Wouldn't he have said the same thing about drinking beer or wine? I think he would have.

Again, the issue is not about eating or drinking, it is about what is best for our Christian witness to our brothers and sisters. It's about doing what leads to peace, and what builds others up in the faith. If my wearing a tie causes others to fall, or my actions at a football game cause others to be weakened, how could I do anything but avoid such things for their sakes. Christianity is not about pleasing ourselves, for we have died to ourselves, but we are alive unto God. Let's live like it for the sake of those who are watching.

DAY 261

Romans 14:20 *Do not destroy the work of God for the sake of food. All food is clean, but it is wrong for a man to eat anything that causes someone else to stumble.*

It is so easy for us to get all worked up about things that really don't matter in the long run. It's not that some things are not more important than others, because they are. However, we can't die on every hill, and some things should be considered more personal in value than universal.

It is amazing how much time the Apostle Paul spends on this matter of eating and drinking. The importance of the topic though doesn't come from the matter of eating and drinking, because here he declares all things clean. As a matter of fact, in the Gospel of Mark 7:19, we are reminded by Jesus also that all food should be considered clean. That should settle the issue, but the focus of the matter goes much deeper.

The question at hand is, "How much do I care for my brother?" Jesus cared enough to enter this world as a man, lived a humble life, and died a death on a horrible Roman cross. That's how serious He is about how valuable our brothers and sisters are, and if He holds their value to be so high, how can we let our personal preferences destroy those whom He died to save?

There are some things that are essential, and those things shouldn't be sacrificed for anything. The faith that we have in God is essential, our love for all people is essential, and the desire to see the Kingdom of God come to pass on earth as it is in heaven should be essential. Besides those things, everything else pales in comparison. We must not let those things that really don't matter in the scheme of the salvation of the world take center stage.

So, let's understand what we are dealing with here. No type of food or drink has a bearing on ours or anyone else's salvation, for all of us are equal at the foot of the cross. For that reason, we need to consider the needs of others more valuable than our own because that is what Jesus did. When we focus on keeping others from stumbling, we are accomplishing our due diligence as Christians, and walking in the way that Jesus demonstrated and taught others to act. We may never face the issue of eating and drinking exactly as Paul did, but if we keep the welfare of others first and foremost, we are on the right path.

DAY 262

Romans 14:21 *It is better not to eat meat or drink wine or to do anything else that will cause your brother to fall.*

I only had one brother. He was born thirteen months before me, but in those early years we were very close. Mom would often dress us alike and people would ask if we were twins. Because we moved a lot (mom said eighteen times before I stared school), we were often each other's only playmate, so there were times when we were little angels together and there were times we fought like dogs. I guess that's what brothers often do.

As we grew older, we grew apart in our interests. My brother had his eyes on girls, making money, and auto mechanics. I also focused on girls (different ones of course) but turned my interest more to sports and things connected with the church. We were raised alike, but we saw the world with a different worldview over time.

When I was twenty-two and he was twenty-three, I received the terrible news while I was away at college, that he had been killed in a construction accident while running a jackhammer. The underground powerline carried thousands of volts, and when he hit it, he was gone instantly.

Over the many decades since then I have thought about him often and wished I could have been there to stop him before he crossed that underground line. I would have done anything to keep him safe. I would have argued with him, fought with him, tampered with his car, or anything else I could think of to cause him not to be where he was on that fateful day.

It is this feeling of desperate concern that Paul relates to the Romans. If he could have, I believe he would have screamed though his pen in this letter, "Don't do anything that will cause your brother to fall!" "Protect him, pray for him, run interference for him, and do whatever it takes to make sure that he doesn't get tripped up on things that don't really matter. Our brothers are too few and too precious.

I pray to God that we could catch that kind of spirit in the church as we consider the value of those around us. Let's go out of our way, let's be inconvenienced, let's even be put upon, if it means keeping our Christian family walking in the right way. Anything else is just not being Christian; anything else is too great a price to pay.

DAY 263

Romans 14:22 *So whatever you believe about these things keep between yourself and God. Blessed is the man who does not condemn himself by what he approves.*

Here's a good thought to remember. Personal convictions are personal. What you feel in the depths of your being does not require others to feel the same way. I know there are certain subjects, especially when they are tied to the religious world or your church, that seem like matters of life and death. However, if the scripture is not crystal clear, and if the authority of the church universal, which has a two-thousand-year history, is not dogmatic on the issue, it's probably best not to be too rooted in concrete ourselves.

We are people that have been created to a great extent by our culture. That culture may or may not involve the church, but it certainly involves the experiences we have had in our lives, and who we are is the end result of these years of pressure and molding. If one comes from an abusive alcoholic home, then his or her focus and view concerning social drinking may be completely opposite the person whose family were tea-totalers. People who were raised in a cash-strapped, single parent home probably see life through a completely different lens than those who were raised with two parents and comfortable incomes.

Add to this mix the different cultures of church life. Some churches have congregations that dress up for worship and others are very casual. Some sing hymns primarily and others sing only contemporary worship choruses. Some are very liberal, and others are very conservative, but in all these church families we have people who are a part of the body of Christ.

Realizing that we can be different, and realizing the difference between conviction and culture, can be huge in the building or breaking of relationships. Paul's advice to the church of his day is that they are to agree on the things for which Christ died but have charity and allow privilege in those areas that are not essential. Everyone has a right to his or her own personal views, and if they are convictions that God has placed on them, they must remember that God placed those convictions on them—not on others, because they are personal. Live free in the Spirit and allow others to do the same. You will be happier, and God will bless others for it too.

DAY 264

Romans 14:23 *But the man who has doubts is condemned if he eats, because his eating is not from faith; and everything that does not come from faith is sin.*

This is an interesting verse, especially the last part of it. "Everything that does not come from faith is sin." That phrase deserves a deeper look.

Eating from faith and not from faith has nothing to do with the content of what one is eating. As we have noted earlier, even Jesus declared that all foods were clean (Mark 7:19). Eating from faith or not eating from faith involves the level of freedom we enjoy in our relationship with Christ, and the importance what we consider concerning our relationships with others. If my eating or my drinking something causes spiritual loss in my fellow man, then that would not be eating and drinking from faith. If the spiritual walk of others is not affected by what I do, then I am free to eat and drink whatever I choose so long as my own conscience doesn't bother me. That is eating and drinking from faith.

What becomes the fly in the ointment here is the fact that we don't always know who is watching us or why. Could it be the new Christian that doesn't understand yet the faith relationship they have just entered? Could it be the children of our household who may not have the same maturity level we enjoy in our free walk with the Lord? Could it be the co-worker or schoolmate that holds our opinion on spiritual things in high regard, and we are not even aware that they are noticing? These are all important questions that could have eternal consequences for someone.

How much do I care for others? How much do I value my Christian freedom? The balance between those two questions will determine how we are to live our lives before the Lord, and before the world. If we are conscious of being watched as a role model for the people of faith, then our obligation is great, for we are our brother's keeper. Though we value our Christian freedom, our actions are still subject to how our freedom will influence others.

Being Christian is not for the weak, for walking with Jesus brings huge and immense responsibilities into our lives. No longer are things just about what affects me, but what affects the image of Christ in the eyes of other believers, and before the world. We always must consider the big picture.

DAY 265

Romans 15:1 *We who are strong ought to bear with the failings of the weak and not to please ourselves.*

This book of Romans is a really good guide for people who like to post on social media sites. We read something that we know is suspicious at best and possibly lies at the worst, and we feel the need to take it upon ourselves to let the world know who really has the honest truth.

First, few people ever change their minds due to Twitter or Facebook arguments, but more importantly we show our level of restraint by how we respond to the endless cycle of posts on everything from diets to politics. If we can't control our fingers at that point, then we find out just how weak we really are.

It is the Christian way to be strong and composed when the rest of the world is losing its minds. Allowing people the freedom to make mistakes, and hopefully learn from them, often requires the greater amount of strength as compared with our setting things straight, even if we are right. Our witness for Christ often depends on whether we can show the self-discipline that is needed when faced with societal issues. Being right is one thing but forcing others to accept that fact is entirely something else.

Paul taught that a brother with spiritual insight concerning personal behavior, has to yield to the brother who doesn't, so long as it doesn't diminish the gospel or hinder one's Christian witness. This doesn't mean that we should tolerate and accept sin, for that is never the right thing to do. It does mean, however, that we should let others make their own choices when it comes to things that have no eternal ramifications. Freedom to make choices, freedom to fail, and freedom to learn from those failures is a hard rule to live by, but one that pays big dividends in the long run as immature disciples become mature and are strengthened from the journey of life.

Perhaps today will be the day that we can take that first step of allowing others to make choices without judging them about those choices. We are talking about other Christians who may see things from a different perspective of time and experience from us. Our quiet observations and availability for continuing the relationship may be what wins the day. Be strong and let the weak lead sometimes. It may be the best gift you can give.

DAY 266

Romans 15:2 *Each of us should please his neighbor for his good, to build him up.*

This verse sounds like the mark of being a good citizen in whatever society we find ourselves. Doing what pleases our neighbor, acting for good on his behalf, and working to build him up seems like a wonderful way to live.

So why don't we do it naturally? Because many of us don't even know the names of our neighbors, where they work, what they like, the names of their children—or if they even have children. Usually there is a lot more that we don't know about our neighbors than what we do know.

But can you imagine what a difference it would make in our witness for Christ if our neighbors actually felt that we were interested in their well-being, their activities, and their eternal souls. Would if matter if they saw us cutting their grass on occasion, shoveling their snow in the winter, offering to baby-sit, or just gifting them with a plate of warm cookies, or a freshly baked pie? What if we actually invited them into our home, our interests, and into our lives? Maybe that would be awkward, at least at first, but I believe it could produce some really big dividends over the long haul.

Couldn't we at least pray for them? Maybe our neighbors wouldn't know about those prayers for a while, but I have the feeling that eventually our prayers for them would spur us to be more proactive toward them—and they would notice that.

What the Word advocates here is that we take our faces away from our televisions and our noses out of our electronic devices, as we open the curtains of our lives to let the sunlight of God's love within us shine through on those who live right next door. There aren't many neighbors out there who don't need a little extra light shone in their path from time to time. If we truly are to rejoice with those who rejoice and weep with those who weep (Romans 12:15), then it is important for us to know our neighbors well enough to know what we are to rejoice or weep about. Here's an idea. Try it for thirty days. Choose a neighbor to bombard with prayer, asking God to open a door for you to connect with them. After that, try to build a bridge for interaction. As you continue to bathe the relationship with prayer, I believe God will do some amazing things. Why not give it a try and find out?

DAY 267

Romans 15:3 *For even Christ did not please himself but, as it is written: "The insults of those who insult you have fallen on me."*

Isn't the first part of this verse amazing! "Christ did not please himself..." That's too powerful to fully grasp in its bare essence. Christ the King of Glory, the Creator of the universe, the Name above all names, left it all behind to not only not please Himself, but to suffer the insults of His creation, and suffer pain and anguish on our behalf. Talk about amazing grace! There are really no words to describe the wonder.

Paul uses the Savior as an example of how we should treat one another. Just as Jesus did not put Himself and His own needs above the needs of even those who hated Him most, we certainly should go the extra mile to be the image of goodness to our neighbor. Remember, "For God so loved the world, He gave..."

As I understand the historical record, there were approximately 400-420 million people alive on this planet when Jesus walked over the hills of Galilee as a man. In January of 2020 the population surpassed 7.8 billion people on our big blue marble. If it is true that God loves people more than anything, then we have been given a whole lot bigger stage upon which to show that love than the Christians of the first century had. We have more resources, more technology, more medical breakthroughs, and more transportation opportunities to bring us together, and help us to have longer lives as we learn how to better care for each other.

Our responsibility as Christians continues to grow as the population continues to increase. People need to hear about Jesus and see the love of His family in action so that they too can find the joy, the blessing, and the hope that we share. It's not just someone else's duty, or the duty of preachers. It is what every disciple of Christ has been called to do for as many people as possible, as often as possible.

No doubt Paul saw the great opportunity we have to build Christ's Kingdom through acts of kindness and genuine love. Imitations and scam artists are always out to take advantage of the unsuspecting, but we can show the real thing. We have a love poured out on us that we need to slosh around onto someone else. That's task number one for us all today.

DAY 268

Romans 15:4 *For everything that was written in the past was written to teach us, so that through the endurance and the encouragement of the Scriptures we might have hope.*

Ecclesiastes 1:19 tells us that there is nothing new under the sun. However, we who are in church work sometimes forget that bit of information as we try to recreate the wheel in the area of scriptural information and spiritual insight. For example, I know that there have been a countless number of writers and scholars who have studied these verses in the book of Romans—and I do learn from them—but though I don't have a lot to add, I want to update our understanding of them for this generation.

We truly do stand on the shoulders of those who came before us. Others have labored in the Gospel vineyard, and we are recipients of those efforts. When we use the massive information systems that are available to us today, we are finding ways to communicate old truths to people that have not yet been exposed to them, and that's a good thing.

Paul saw the historical writings of his generation as schoolmasters that taught him and the early church members the value of having a firm foundation. The scriptures provide a measuring tool for determining right from wrong, yet it also speaks concerning how to build a relationship with our God and with our fellow man. We are greatly indebted to those of the past who penned the words of life that we enjoy.

Not only do the scriptures show us the way to live, but they provide hope for the journey of life to us. We see how the saints of old lived before God and how they sometimes succeeded, and sometimes failed in their efforts to bring Him glory. We can learn from these things, and continue to pass along the hope of life, life abundant, and eternal life to others.

This is why it is so important that we study the Bible to learn what it has to say, as well as how to properly interpret the words for our generation today. In every age there is a need for men and women to be able to apply biblical truth to the challenges that more time brings to light. Bible teachers will never be obsolete or out of a job. We may not be paid for it, but we will always have a job to do. We are obligated to pass on what we know from the Word of God to the next generation in a way they will understand it. That is our main task.

DAY 269

Romans 15:5–6 *May the God who gives endurance and encouragement give you a spirit of unity among yourselves as you follow Christ Jesus, so that with one heart and mouth you may glorify the God and Father of our Lord Jesus Christ.*

Did you pick up on the first thought of this verse? *It is God who gives.* Whatever we have comes from His hand, and in this instance, He is giving out a three-fold blessing for His people. We are told that He is the one who provides endurance and encouragement, so when we are in short supply of either of those commodities, our heavenly Father is the source we go to.

The prayer specifically here though, is for God to give to the Romans a spirit of unity in the Christian body. This gift—and it does come from God—is vital to any church anywhere if they are to be effective in carrying out the mission of the cross and the Kingdom. When people try to do their own thing without uniting in fellowship and energy within the church, they always end up doing less than they could have or messing things up to the point where someone else has to come along and fix what they started.

There are some other key ideas in these verses. First, there is a condition for receiving endurance, encouragement, and unity, and that is that we follow Christ Jesus as Lord and King of the church. We cannot say it enough that it is His church, not ours, and we are only instruments in the church that He wants to use to accomplish His purposes.

Also, it is to be noted that the unity asked for here involves the heart and the mouth. Of course, Paul is not thinking about biology here, but spirituality. Being united by one purpose and speaking with one voice makes the church more effective as a unit than any individual could ever be on his or her own.

Finally, it should be acknowledged that the prayer made for endurance, encouragement, and unity, is so that God the Father would be glorified as the end result. We don't need strength for our own sakes, or a pat on the back so we will feel better, or even a oneness of purpose and effort to accomplish what we want. Our blessings from God are for the sole purpose of bringing glory to God. We are His creation, we are His church, we are the witnesses of Him to the world, and He deserves all the credit and glory for it all. Let us never forget that fact.

DAY 270

Romans 15:7 *Accept one another, then, just as Christ accepted you, in order to bring praise to God.*

Every once in a while, I wish I had a time machine so I could go back to biblical events and see them with my own eyes instead of just reading about them. It would be so interesting to see how the first century church looked, worshipped, and treated each other as they tried to wrap their heads around the new life they were experiencing in Christ.

The instruction Paul gives here concerning the acceptance of one another almost seems like a no-brainer. Certainly, we should accept everyone. Of course, we should treat everyone just as Christ treats us. Why would that be so hard to understand?

But then I stop and think about the class differences in the Roman culture. I think about those who were slaves and those who were free. I remember that men and women were on different levels of social recognition, and that the military and government had tremendous power over the common people. Maybe it wouldn't have been so natural to accept one another as equals after all.

The sad truth is that things haven't changed all that much in the last two thousand years. There are still barriers that divide us much more than they should. We are too often divided by race, by economic status, by social acceptance, and age differences. We sometimes let our politics get in the way of who we are willing to associate with, and who we even want to be around.

Behind all the relationship challenges we must never overlook the prime directive for every Christian. We do what we do with others, as Christ does with us, so that we will *bring praise to God.* Everything we as Christians do in life must be filtered through the prism of whether it will bring praise to God. This includes my actions in and out of the church. It includes what I post online. It includes who I am willing to share a meal with, and who I am willing to let into my family for fellowship.

We might excuse the first generation of Christians for having not learned these lessons, but we of the twenty-first century should know better.

DAY 271

Romans 15:8–9a *For I tell you that Christ has become a servant of the Jews on behalf of God's truth, to confirm the promises made to the patriarchs so that the Gentiles may glorify God for his mercy…*

It's a pretty big thought to grasp that Christ became a servant of the Jews. The Creator of all things, who first chose Abraham out of all the people of the earth and allowed him to be revered as the father of the faithful, became the servant of what He created and chose.

All this was done to bring out God's truth and prove that He never changes. The promises He made to Abraham, Isaac, and Jacob held true throughout the generations after them right up to the cross of Calvary. The story of our salvation through Jesus Christ not only changed Israel forever, but certainly impacted the rest of the world as the word got out concerning what God has done on our behalf.

This takes us back to the point Paul has made repeatedly. All that Jesus did, and all that the church does is to glorify God. We have no higher purpose. Here we see that we are to glorify Him for His mercy because out of that mercy we were able to hear the words of life and be saved from our sins. We are being remade into His image as a result of His mercy. We too become servants of others so that God will be glorified by those to whom we show mercy.

The promises made to the patriarchs were true and we are seeing them fulfilled to this very day. We know that all nations of the earth are being blessed because Abraham was faithful to God (Genesis 22:18). We know that the descendants of Abraham, because we who are in Christ are also included, have become as many as the sands of grain on the seashore and as many as the stars in the sky (Genesis 15:5; 28:14). We know that God has raised up a leader after His own heart, Jesus the Christ, who brings glory to the Father in every way (Genesis 35:11).

Not only are the promises confirmed, but also Jesus, the servant of the Jews, has set the example for us to be servants of all men as well. Putting the needs of others before our own is one more way we can make God look good to those who see our actions. That remains our highest goal, to glorify God and show His mercy to our world. It's the best and toughest job ever!

DAY 272

Romans 15:8–9 *For I tell you that Christ has become a servant of the Jews on behalf of God's truth, to confirm the promises made to the patriarchs so that the Gentiles may glorify God for his mercy, as it is written: "Therefore I will praise you among the Gentiles; I will sing hymns to your name."*

In the simplest understanding of the "Gentile" concept, it included and includes everyone that is not a Jew. That's a pretty large majority of people that are not listed as being a part of the original group of "God's chosen people." For the purposes of the Christian faith and understanding that all who are in Christ are a part of the "New Israel," and are "True Jews," then we take these words to mean that Gentiles are those who are outside of the family of Christian fellowship.

When Paul quotes the psalmist here and speaks of bearing witness to the Gentiles through the avenue of praise and singing to the Lord, he is giving reference to the importance of people in the faith proclaiming the Good News to people outside the faith. We sing to the Lord and give praise to the Lord not only because He is worthy of our adoration and praise, but because doing so points unbelievers in the way of life everlasting.

While it may seem that the world is a wacky and dangerous place, and in many ways, it is, behind the scenes like a growing plant, the Kingdom of God is being established day by day. We have such a long way to go before we see it fulfilled and Jesus set up on the throne as its King, but we have come so far from the days when Jesus had only twelve followers in whom He poured out His life and His Spirit. The church is ushering in the Kingdom, and we are called to do all we can to advance Christ's church so that more and more people can be added to the Lamb's book of life.

So where do we begin. Well, Paul gives us two very good places to start. We begin by living lives of praise to the Lord and singing hymns that glorify Him. While not all are singers, especially singers that others want to hear, those who are need to do it as unto the Lord, being aware that others are listening to what they sing. For the non-singers, we are to live in such a way that those around us notice that something is different, something is holy, so that we will remind them of God and want what we have. By doing so, the "Gentiles" in our lives will be attracted to the King of kings for God's glory.

DAY 273

Romans 15:10 *Again, it says, "Rejoice, O Gentiles with his people."*

It really isn't such a big word, just seven letters long, but even uttering the sound produces a response within the heart of every person who is a child of God. "Rejoice!" "Rejoice!" "Rejoice!" It's the expression of something that comes from deep within our souls because of the new life Christ has placed within us by His Holy Spirit.

It reminds us of the angels who announced the birth of Jesus over the countryside outside of Bethlehem. It's the word that Hannah used when she found out she was pregnant with Samuel. It's the sound that was made when the rebuilt wall of Jerusalem was dedicated in the days of Nehemiah. It's the same word that the Apostle Paul would use again and again throughout his letters. Rejoicing is the language of the redeemed.

In this particular passage Paul is quoting from Deuteronomy 32:43 where Moses is calling for rejoicing because God was going to balance the scales of justice before the enemies of His people. Whether Jew or Gentile, the people of God are continually called to rejoice.

Why is this so important? It's because one of the things that happens when the Holy Spirit of Christ comes to reside within us is that we receive a sense of joy from on high. It's not dependent on the circumstances of our lives, because they can be anything but joyful at times. In fact, the worse things get, the more we are to rejoice because we know that in the end we win, as we trust in Jesus.

As Gentiles, we can rejoice that we who were once on the outside looking in at the workings of God with mankind, can now be included in the family to whom all the promises of God belong. The grafting that God makes into His holy vine is a blessing that should bring a smile to the dourest of believers. God's mercy is everlasting, and we have been included in all who receive that mercy by faith.

Today is a good day to rejoice. It's a good day to sing praises to the One who has made us and commissioned us to serve Him. It's a good day to be thankful for His many blessings and to express that thankfulness in audible words. We have been called to rejoice—and that's reason enough to do it.

DAY 274

Romans 15:11 *And again, "Praise the Lord, all you Gentiles, and sing praises to him, all you peoples."*

Throughout most of my early years until I went off to college, I was raised either on a farm or near a farm. My dad was raised as a farmer and I guess it was something he wanted to pass along to the rest of us. Anyway, I spent many hours of my teenage years walking through the rolling woodland of our eighty acres. It was a place where I hunted, hiked, picked up rocks, farmed the land, and sang. Maybe singing was the most important thing I did there.

You see, it was in those times of being alone that I sang through the songs that I had learned in Sunday School and church. I sang the old hymns along with the modern choruses of the day, and I did so in isolation with only the tractor and the fields to hear me. Some of my fondest memories are wrapped up in those long hours where my voice was my only musical entertainment.

It was in that place and through those times that I really learned the value of praise to the Lord. Because I was a church kid and was there in nearly every service on Sunday mornings, Sunday evenings, Wednesday nights, revival meetings, Vacation Bible Schools, and every other special event the church offered, I learned the songs of faith. I memorized them to the point that I rarely would need a hymnbook today to sing them (if churches still used hymnbooks). Praise comes naturally to my quiet times to this day, even more than when I am in church. In solitude I do my best singing.

I believe it is so important that the people of God learn how to praise Him. We don't all have singing voices, but that's why I do most of mine in private. I have learned to praise Him by quoting the scriptures I have memorized over the years and talking to Him as I talk to a friend. I rarely ever listen to the radio in my car because those hours of traveling are my quiet times when I can feel like I am back on the tractor again, and I can sing the old songs. Praise is something I do, but I am so far behind in how I need to praise that I will never be able to catch up.

How are you doing in your praise to our Lord? Maybe you do it through modern music, and listening to the songs is what sets your heart to joyful adoration. Maybe you have other ways to make it happen, but please, give the Lord the praise He deserves. He is worthy of it all and more!

DAY 275

Romans 15:12 *And again, Isaiah says, "The Root of Jesse will spring up, one who will arise to rule over the nations; the Gentiles will hope in him."*

The Prophet Isaiah lived approximately three hundred years after the time of King David, but people of his generation were still talking about him. By that time, the nation of Judah had witnessed many kings from David's linage who had occupied his throne, but David was then, and remains to this day, not just a king, but *the king*! He was the youngest son of Jesse who became the second king over Israel, following Saul, and preceding Solomon. David was the king that really pulled the twelve individual tribes together and made them a force to be reckoned with in the ancient world. People of his time adored him, and people after him revered him. He remains one of the most fascinating people ever to come out of the descendants of Abraham.

This verse, however, focuses on the heir to David's throne that would exceed his greatness in a big way. David may have been the one who conquered Goliath, but Jesus, the eternal King, conquered the grave. He is the root of Jesse that has brought, does bring, and will bring hope to countless numbers of people that travel through the pages of time.

We are told that He will arise to rule over the nations. Really? How is this to be? Well, even though there are many who push for national borders to be eliminated, in the eternal Kingdom to come there will be nations. The big difference in the everlasting Kingdom of God though, is that there will be no wars or conflicts over boundaries, riches, or territories, for the Lord will judge fairly over them all, and every nation will live in peace.

It's hard to imagine such a place and such an experience as that when we look around at the way the world is now. This is where our hope lies though. Just as Jesus destroyed the power of the grave and death for us, He gives us our hope for a world to come. We may not see the aligning of nations in our earthly days, but it will happen according to the timetable the Father has put into place.

When Jesus does take His place to rule, every eye will see it, and every knee will bow before Him. It is because His Spirit lives in our hearts now that we can see such things with eyes of hope. The King lives and reigns forever! Blessed be the risen Lamb, the Almighty Son of God!

DAY 276

Romans 15:13 *May the God of hope fill you with all joy and peace as you trust in him, so that you may overflow with hope by the power of the Holy Spirit.*

This one verse describes the big difference between living a life in the Spirit or living it by our own power. Paul's desire for the Roman church was that they would intimately know the *God of hope*, who would be able to do wondrous things in their lives. A life in the Spirit connects us to the source of hope that never diminishes in power, possibility, or potential. He is the person who gets us up in the morning and the reason that we want to get up. Our God is the essence of hope.

Contrast that with the spirit of the present age. All we have to do is open a conversation, read a newspaper, turn on a television, or look at social media for even a few minutes and we will find an abundance of doom, gloom, anger, frustration, and pain. All of these things lead us to pessimism on a level that causes many to have to start taking medications, hire counselors, and live in disfunction. Hope is the cure for all these things, but we can't have real hope without going to the real source to find it.

The God of hope is not selfish. He is not hopeful because He is above the fray and can look upon His world like a gambler at a racetrack, waiting to see how it will all turn out. He is hopeful because He is the source of all things, including hope, and He loves to pour it into the hearts of those who will seek Him. Whether the problems we face are mammoth in size or whether they are the run of the mill daily inconveniences, we can have hope when our Father pours it into our very being through the abiding power of His presence in us.

This is the God that Paul wanted the Romans to know. He is the God that we need to know today. He is the answer to our weary world that is always looking for solutions and who run after the latest guru with his or her latest magic bullet to make life more tolerable. We can have life more abundant through the Maker of all things. We only need to put our trust in the work Jesus has done for us on the cross to redeem us, and then allow the Spirit of the Father and Son to direct us in our life's journey. When that happens, we are filled with hope, for we are filled with Him, the ultimate source of hope.

DAY 277

Romans 15:13 *May the God of hope fill you with all joy and peace as you trust in him, so that you may overflow with hope by the power of the Holy Spirit.*

There are too many perks to count when one enters into a personal relationship with the God of hope, but two of them are listed by Paul here in the form of joy and peace. These commodities are sought by people in every generation the world over and would top the stock market every day of every year if someone could put a price on them and sell them to the masses. The reality of the matter though, is that both are absolutely free.

Joy is the inner fountain that springs from God's fullness within the deep places of one's being. You can't find it with an x-ray or an MRI, but it is as real as any organ of our bodies. It can't be produced by any other source on a permanent level other than by the power of the Holy Spirit in our life. His presence emits joy within us like a blessed radioactive isotope.

Peace is the calmness and tranquility that is present no matter what storm of life may come our way. The world can literally shake to its foundations and society can come apart at the seams, but the peace that Christ provides is not dependent on anything but our relationship with Him. It's sad that when so many people are deprived of sleep by worry, and frustrated by the events of world affairs, that they often overlook the source of all inner serenity and security. Peace is not the absence of conflict and strife, but a quiet confidence that all things are under the control of our Creator, and that He will work things out for our ultimate good.

Joy and peace are often confused with happiness, but they are not the same. Happiness is fleeting and determined by events that may or may not be under our control. These precious gifts are God given and no warranty for them is ever needed, for they never lose their effectiveness as long as we remain in Christ.

It's not uncommon to hear of the woes that beset our families and our friends. We don't have to be in a large group, and we don't have to have conversations very long before hearing of tragic events that stagger lives and leave ruins in their wake. Joy and peace are the buffers that get us through those days, but they are only found in a faith walk with God.

DAY 278

Romans 15:13 *May the God of hope fill you with all joy and peace as you trust in him, so that you may overflow with hope by the power of the Holy Spirit.*

The old song says, "Tis so sweet to trust in Jesus, just to take Him at His word..." It seems like such an easy concept, and it seems like it's something that everyone should do, but I'm certain that we will find that this is not always the case.

We are told over and over throughout the Bible that we are not to be people of fear. In fact, every time there is an encounter between a divine being and man in the Bible, the first words from the divine is to not be afraid. Actually, just doing a quick internet search of the words, "Don't be afraid," produces seventy-one listings in the Bible with those words of instruction. It is pretty clear that the Lord doesn't want us to live in fear, but to trust Him.

In this age of Covid-19 we are trying to find a new normal. Learning to live without fear without being reckless is a bit like walking a tightrope. We don't want to ignore the advice of professional medical people, but we also don't want to quit living and wither away. I sometimes think there is more damage being done in many homes by isolating from the world rather than facing the unseen enemy and proceeding with our lives cautiously. Of course, each person and family have to make the call on this matter based on their own level of wellness, age, and circumstances. But the key issue here is that even in these times of uncertainty, we are not to be afraid. That's not how Christians are to live. We are people of faith, not people of fear.

The result of living fearlessly, with our faith in the Lord and not in ourselves, is that then we can experience the God of hope who produces joy and peace in us. In fact, we are told in this verse that we can *overflow with hope* rather than to cower in fear. This is not because we are exceptionally brave or because bad things can't happen to us, because we probably aren't all that brave, and we know that rough times come to us all. Our trust though is in the Lord, knowing that He has promised to be with us, and that He will provide for our needs according to His huge storehouse. If the flowers of the fields and the birds of the air don't have to worry, and don't have to be afraid, then we who are the children of God can also walk without fear in faith.

DAY 279

Romans 15:13 *May the God of hope fill you with all joy and peace as you trust in him, so that you may overflow with hope by the power of the Holy Spirit.*

This is such a wonderful verse. Just knowing that the God of hope continually provides joy and peace in us as we trust in Him, even to the point of overflowing is good news indeed. Everyone who struggles to keep their hopes up or finds it hard to be joyful during such trying days, should find great comfort in these words.

However, there is one last thing to consider before we leave this verse. All these gifts from the Father are made possible only through the power of the Holy Spirit. These blessings of joy and peace are not made possible by our own doing, but by the Holy Spirit who comes to dwell within us.

Jesus gave us this promise, "I will not leave you as orphans; I will come to you" (John 14:18). In the two verses just before this one in the Gospel of John He said, "And I will ask the Father, and he will give you another Comforter to be with you forever—the Spirit of truth. The world cannot accept him because it neither sees him nor knows him. But you know him, for he lives with you and will be in you" (John 14:16-17). We are not alone in this journey of life as we put our trust in Christ for our salvation, for His Holy Spirit lives within us continually.

I'm sure that some people will scoff that this idea as just being the wishful thinking of old people or people in crisis, but we who have come to experience this divine presence know better. Jesus warned us that the world would not recognize the Comforter that has come, but we who have received Him, know Him to be the source of all that is good in our lives.

The power of the Holy Spirit gives us our boldness, "For God did not give us a spirit of timidity, but a spirit of power, of love and of self-discipline" (II Timothy 1:7). He is the presence of the divine Godhead that accompanies us always and makes possible the joy and peace that Christians have, but that the world without Christ knows nothing about.

Thanks be to God for giving us such a gift! Thanks be to God for providing us with such a resource to give us hope! Glory to God in the highest!

DAY 280

Romans 15:14 *I myself am convinced, my brothers, that you yourselves are full of goodness, complete in knowledge and competent to instruct one another.*

It's a wonderful thing to have confidence in people. I'm talking about when you can give someone a responsibility and know that you don't have to worry about it anymore, because you know that they will do the job you have asked them to do. That's what every employer is looking for, and what leaders in the church are constantly after as well.

Perhaps the secret to what Paul is saying here, and the reason for his confidence, is in the fact that he is convinced that the Romans are genuinely good people, and that they are mentally and educationally fit to be teachers. Blessed is the pastor of a local church who can say that all his or her teachers within the church, the Sunday School, or the small group ministries, are "complete in knowledge and competent to instruct one another." Too often, this is not the case, but when it is, it is a beautiful thing.

The foundation to Christian education is in the attribute of goodness. Goodness is a fruit of the Spirit and is so much more than just a person that does good things. Evil people can at times do good things in order to achieve their own personal agenda, but goodness goes so much deeper because it is the source of one's actions, the reason for doing what a good person does.

Since goodness is a fruit of the Spirit, and these Romans are proclaimed to be full of goodness, I take it to mean that they are full of the Spirit as well. This definitely keeps with the context of the previous verse and explains why Paul had such confidence in the people there.

This takes us back to the goal of Christian ministry. We are to proclaim the possibility, the hope of, and the reality of being filled with the Spirit of God. Everything we do as Christians should come from the realization that we are not able in ourselves to do the work God has called us to do but are enabled by the Spirit as we allow Him full control over our lives. The sanctified life is not an idyllic dream, but a reality for all who will surrender themselves fully into the hands of God. The result of such an action is displayed by goodness, knowledge, and competency in what really matters in life, namely our service to God Most High, as found through Jesus Christ.

DAY 281

Romans 15:15–16 *I have written you quite boldly on some points, as if to remind you of them again, because of the grace God gave me to be a minister of Christ Jesus to the Gentiles with the priestly duty of proclaiming the gospel of God, so that the Gentiles might become an offering acceptable to God, sanctified by the Holy Spirit.*

If there are two things we can count on when it comes to our study of the Apostle Paul, it is in the facts that he can be very bold sometimes, and it is also true that he has a tendency to repeat himself for clarity. Some of his sentences run on as paragraphs. However, what he has to say is usually worth focusing on because God has used those words to guide the church down through the centuries.

As he so often did in other letters, he reiterated the fact that he is a minister of Christ Jesus to the Gentiles. He never wavered on this. Whether people believed him or not, or whether they thought it was proper or not, he was convinced that God had set him apart to spend his life serving as an ambassador of love to the Gentiles. He was faithful in that calling to the end.

He saw his assigned task as something more than just an appointed job to do, however. The ministry in which he poured out his life was to be a spokesman for Jesus. He saw it as a priestly duty, just as important as those who handled the sacrifices in Jerusalem's temple, and perhaps even more so. Telling the story of God's plan of salvation for all mankind was a thankless job during his years, but one that literally changed the world for all generations to come.

I am convinced that we each have a priestly duty before the Lord, as Paul did. It may or may not be preaching, but it certainly requires our best at doing what God has assigned us to do in life. It could be in the medical field, in the classroom, in the mechanic's garage, in the woodworker's shop, or in the automobile assembly line, but just as Paul was called, we also are called.

Can you imagine what a difference we would make if we turned our love of baking bread and cookies into avenues for connection to the people of our neighborhood to build relationships to win people to Christ? Can we think of other ways that God could use us as His priests for His glory? Paul was called and we are too. The question is, will we answer the call?

DAY 282

Romans 15:15–16 *I have written you quite boldly on some points, as if to remind you of them again, because of the grace God gave me to be a minister of Christ Jesus to the Gentiles with the priestly duty of proclaiming the gospel of God, so that the Gentiles might become an offering acceptable to God, sanctified by the Holy Spirit.*

In this passage Paul echoes a sentiment that he used back in chapter twelve, when he urged the Romans to offer their bodies to God as living sacrifices. In his thought, this would make them holy and pleasing to God. Here he moves the needle a bit from instructing the church as to what it should be doing, to focusing on himself and his work of preaching. It is through the ministry of preaching that it would be possible for the Gentiles to be pleasing to God.

Preaching goes in cycles it seems. The style of preaching, the length of sermons, and that quality of the craft changes from church setting to church setting. Once, and still in some parts of the world, anything less than an hour in length would be considered a waste of the hearer's time. This would especially be true if the worshiper had walked hours or miles to get to the place of meeting. In most western cultural settings, the time is much shorter. A half-hour is like an eternity to some people because our attention span is geared to the television programs, and we are used to sporadic interludes of commercial advertisement in the midst of it all. Time is so precious for our busy families and individuals.

However, Paul saw preaching as the tool that changed sinners into saints. It wasn't the sermon per se, but the message of the cross and Jesus lifted up that changed lives. It was, and I believe still is, the avenue God has chosen to bring awareness of sin, conviction for that sin, and redemption from sin to the individuals who hear. Through preaching, God changes Gentiles and Jews alike from self-focused sinners to Jesus-focused saints. It is the life of being a saint that causes God to be pleased with us.

Of course, this proclamation that has such a profound effect is not from man's doing. It is the sanctifying power of the Holy Spirit that changes the preacher and the hearer alike. A sermon without the Holy Spirit's influence is merely another speech. God is pleased when lives are truly changed.

DAY 283

Romans 15:17 *Therefore I glory in Christ Jesus in my service to God.*

I love this verse! It does something to me just to read it. "I glory in Christ Jesus in my service to God." There is something very profound in that simple statement that puts everything I stand for in life in the proper perspective.

I don't think that anyone who knows me has any doubt about the fact that I love what I do. Preaching, teaching, writing, and traveling are right at the top of the vocational loves in my life and as long as I can do any one of them, I will pretty much be a happy camper. Because as a pastor, as an evangelist, or as a missionary I get to do all of them, my job puts me in a happy place most of the time.

One thing that is always before me though, is that my calling is always under the direction and scrutiny of my Master, Jesus Christ. My service to God is just that, service to Him. This calling and this service is not something I dreamed up but came as a result of my being commissioned by the Almighty. Anything good that ever comes of this ministry comes about as the result of His work and blessing, not because of my talent, education, or skill level. All that I have and am comes from Him, so I have no right to take credit for anything good that happens, though I will be the first to acknowledge my failures are mine. It's when I don't listen carefully enough to His voice, or if I am not obedient to His desire for my life and work, that I usually make a mess of things. His way is perfect, my way, not so much.

That's why, along with Paul, I can say, "I glory in Christ Jesus in my service to God". I take joy from what I do when I am pleasing to Him. I see success in what I attempt when I follow His direction. The Lord is my strength, my hope, my comforter, my guide, and my great blessing in life. As the old gospel song says, that I used to sing in days gone by, "It is glory just to walk with Him!"

I feel so sorry for people who don't have this experience. I know that there are so many people who don't have any kind of relationship with God, and their lives prove the loss of what could be theirs. Jesus makes everything good possible and without Him, all that we do comes to nothing eventually. Being in service to the King is by far the best way to live, and our job is to let as many others know that fact as possible.

DAY 284

Romans 15:18–19a *I will not venture to speak of anything except what Christ has accomplished through me in the leading the Gentiles to obey God by what I have said and done—by the power of signs and miracles, through the power of the Spirit.*

Sometimes I tend to beat myself up over what I perceive to be the wins versus the losses of life. We pastors are all about building up congregations, encouraging believers, and reaching out to new acquaintances with the words of life. When I have good days and see some of my goals achieved, then it's a very satisfying feeling. But when I don't see some of my objectives reached, it's very easy to be hard on myself and play the blame game, bringing about a degree of depression.

The words of Paul here are encouraging to me in such times, for he helps me to realize that whatever is accomplished in my ministry is not really me that is bringing it to pass, and even in areas where I am not successful, well, that part is still the Lord's work too. My own version of success and failure is not the last word on the matter, for our Lord is the one who succeeds and will succeed ultimately, regardless of what I do or don't do.

This takes the pressure off me as I labor. Though I never want to shirk my duty or take my assignments lightly, I can rest in the fact that what has been accomplished through any of us has been accomplished by Christ. Since He is the power source and the guide for our lives, we know that He never fails—even when we feel like we haven't contributed as much as we would like to the task. He is always victorious and since I am on His team, I can speak of success for His glory in whatever happens.

The signs and wonders Paul spoke of are always done by the power of the Holy Spirit who is continually at work. His power is unending and unlimited. We can brag about something like that. We really don't ever have any reason to pat ourselves on the back, but we can give credit where credit is due when it comes to our Lord. We just need to be reminded of what is ahead as spelled out in Revelation 11:15, "The kingdom of the world has become the kingdom of our Lord and of his Christ, and he will reign for ever and ever." Every good work done in His church now will bring glory to Him, because it is an eternal Kingdom He is building, and we get to be a part of it.

DAY 285

Romans 15:19b *So from Jerusalem all the way around to Illyricum, I have fully proclaimed the gospel of Christ.*

Illyricum is the country that today is known as Albania. It's on the northwest side of Greece, so that means it is approximately 6830 miles that Paul had traveled in order to do the work that Jesus had called him to do. That's a long way regardless of your means of travel, but for Paul in the first century, it meant that he had to cover the miles on foot, horseback, or by sailing vessel. It also means that what he was doing was no game. He was fully invested in carrying out the calling God had placed on him.

It's only when one takes in the big picture that we see just how desperate the early leaders of our faith were to present the message of the crucified and risen Savior to their world. They didn't get paid. They didn't have a denominational backing. They didn't have a parsonage or a retirement plan. They didn't even have a congregation to start with. Paul, and people like him, set out to change the world one person at a time, and didn't quit on their job until they were called out of this life.

As I ruminate on these words, I am convinced that we of the twenty-first century have gotten pretty spoiled and perhaps a bit careless as we have carried on the work that has been passed down to us. I have to wonder if we are as invested in the success or failure of the divine mission as was the Apostle Paul and the masses of unknown Christians that first launched the evangelism campaigns in the early days of the faith.

Perhaps we should consider just how serious we are with the task of carrying out the Great Commission. What will we do if churches lose their tax-exempt status in our nations? What will we do if only bi-vocational ministries would be able to continue? What will we do if Christianity becomes an outlawed religion, and we are sent to jail or brutalized for sharing the Good News?

This is the world the Apostle lived in. He drew his support from God and from people who had mercy on him. He didn't have it easy, but he never gave up. He didn't stop sharing about Jesus until he literally lost his head for doing so. Can we say the same? Is our dedication complete? Are we fully proclaiming the Gospel of God? Surely, our Lord knows.

DAY 286

Paul was a unique individual to say the least. He had not only a God-driven call on his life, but it was mixed with an entrepreneurial spirit as well. He wasn't bound by denominational directives, by clerical peer pressure, or even by precedent. His work for the Lord broke new territory for all of us who would follow him down through the centuries.

Some people are content to manage and shepherd the flock of God, for that is where they are gifted. For people like Paul though, that could never be enough. He saw too many areas of the world where people had not yet heard the good news about the resurrection to come, and he wanted to fix that.

As years roll by, we who are involved in preaching, teaching, and discipling, can become a little bit satisfied with our work, and after a life of serving it's easy to make plans to wind down and take it easy for our last few years on this earth. Though this is certainly every person's choice, Paul would have none of it. He wanted to keep building, keep preaching, and keep spreading the news of salvation through Jesus Christ, and he would do so until his death.

Building in new territory is not easy, especially when opposition to what you are building is strong. Paul saw the challenges as part of the job though, and regardless of how many people urged him from time to time to take an easier route, he pressed on with all the strength within him, and with all the urgency that the times required.

Maybe today we need more of that drive. Even though there may be a church on every street and every corner, there are still a lot of people in every community who have not heard the words of life in a way that truly impacts them. Maybe they need to hear those words from us. Maybe they would respond favorably to the Christian way if only they had someone who would share the way and walk it with them. Today is the day of salvation. It will never come again for some people, so time is of the essence. Would you pray about planting where no one else has, as Paul did? If not, why not?

DAY 287

Romans 15:21 *Rather, as it is written: "Those who were not told about him will see, and those who have not heard will understand."*

This quotation comes from Isaiah 52:15 where it is making reference to the suffering servant of God. It's hard, when reading the whole Isaiah chapter in context, not to see the parallel of the prophet's writing with the sacrifice and suffering of Jesus. Without eyes to see the Messiah Himself, Isaiah, inspired by the Holy Spirit, put the work of the cross in perfect perspective.

All of this goes back to the fact that God has been in the redemption business for His creation since it went astray back in the Garden of Eden. Without hope, mankind has struggled in the mess he has made down through the ages, but the divine Suffering Servant paid the price that would provide a way out of the mire.

The work that Jesus did on the cross made possible the story of life to go out to people who didn't ask for it, didn't believe it, and didn't deserve it. The Jewish nation that didn't recognize Him when He came, still benefited from His act of sacrifice that provided for their salvation. The many tongues and nations of the world that had never heard of Him would eventually receive the message that would change their lives for eternity.

This is why it is so important that we who know the story keep on sharing it with as many people as possible. Paul's quotation of Isaiah here is both a prophecy in the process of being fulfilled, and a call to all who have found faith to help others find that way as well.

Who do you know who has not heard the news, seen the way, or understood the truth that has been found in Christ? We sometimes think that only those who live on a faraway island somewhere are the only ones who still walk in the darkness of ignorance about the redeeming work of Christ. Sadly, though, it's the people that you meet in Walmart, those you connect with on social media, and those who pass you in cars on the highway. We don't have to look very far to find people who may have heard the words but have not reached a level of understanding that has had an impact on them. Isaiah also said that the people who walked in darkness have seen a great light (Isaiah 9:1), but it's up to us to reflect the light of the Son of God to all the Father puts in our path. That's the Great Commission still before us.

DAY 288

Romans 15:22 *This is why I have often been
hindered from coming to you.*

T he Apostle Paul's point is that he had been hindered from coming to
the church in Rome because he felt he was called to focus his ministry
on places that had not yet heard the Good News about Jesus, and obviously
since there was already a church in Rome, this was not a new place to work.

Everyone has different talents and different gifts from the Spirit of God that
equip us for different roles in the body of Christ. Paul was a church planter. He
had to be the first one in to break the ground and establish the direction for
people to follow in a walk with Jesus. I have often wished I had such a gift, but
though I believe anything is possible with God, to this date I have not been such
a pioneer. I feel my gifts are more in the areas of administration, preaching, and
teaching rather than digging out a new work from scratch.

The reason I think it's important to focus on this though is because I
wonder how many people have been distracted from their primary calling in
the Lord to follow some other avenue that may be good, but not the best thing
that Jesus has for them to do.

Paul definitely felt that he had the responsibility given to him by Jesus to
minister the words of life to the Gentiles. Since there were not yet churches
among the Gentiles, someone was going to have to start them and begin on the
ground floor with the making of disciples for Christ. He didn't stay long at most
places, for his longest tenure was in Ephesus where he stayed for three years. In
Thessalonica he was only there for three weeks. He stayed long enough to get
a church established and then he moved on to do the same thing someplace
else. He had a job to do and wouldn't let anything hinder him from doing it.

Have you let things hinder you from being and doing all that God
wants you to do? Has the influence of family, friends, co-workers, peers, or
circumstances caused you to make excuses and take a different path from
where the Lord wants you to be? What would it take to get you back on track
again? I believe that this short sentence provides us with some powerful food
for thought. To the Galatians Paul asked, "Who has bewitched you?" To us
he might ask, "What has hindered you?" Maybe it's time to get back on track
with the Lord's plan for our life.

DAY 289

Romans 15:23–24a *But now that there is no more place for me to work in these regions, and since I have been longing for many years to see you, I plan to do so when I go to Spain.*

In some ways, I am a kindred spirit with the Apostle Paul. Though I could never hope to compete with him on any other level, I too have been bitten by the wanderlust bug and I continually long to see what is over the next horizon and in what new area I can minister. I have had the privilege to date of working in eight countries, getting to preach or teach in six of them, and I really do hope to add to that number greatly before my time here on this planet is finished. Something inside keeps me moving, and I wouldn't have it any other way.

Paul seemed to be like that. His traveling conditions were not nearly as plush as mine have been, and he had to face many more dangers than I will ever think about, but that didn't diminish his desire to keep telling the story of Jesus everywhere that people would listen. Here we find that he is connecting with Rome, a place he has never been, and making plans to go there, and then on to Spain. All of this was part of his mission for the King of kings who had redeemed him. While there was still time to work, he couldn't be still, and couldn't stop writing, traveling, preaching, and teaching. That's what the calling on his life had produced in him.

We don't know for sure whether he ever made it to Spain because church legends and traditions split on this matter, but we do know that he made it to Rome. It was in Rome that he finally died a martyr's death, but whether he made it to Spain before that happened, we really can't be positive. We do know that his impact was eventually felt in Spain, whether or not he actually got there in person. There is a strong Christian history in that country, so in some way Paul's mission to reach the people there with the gospel was fulfilled.

We know that Paul most likely spoke Hebrew, Aramaic, Latin, and Greek, but Spanish, well, we can't be sure. He did speak the words of love and life eternal though, and that translates to everyone everywhere. In that regard, we can imitate his efforts. Hopefully, today will provide such an opportunity for many Christians around the globe.

DAY 290

Romans 15:24b I hope to visit you while passing through and to have you assist me on my journey there, after I have enjoyed your company for a while.

I f nothing else, the Apostle Paul shows here the value of the family of God in action. There are three thoughts that stand out to me as I focus on this short sentence at the end of this verse.

First, there is the blessing of visiting one another in the name of Jesus. I am thankful that I grew up in the generation where pastors still made calls on individuals and families in their homes. I always tried to imitate that effort as a pastor myself, because as one of my professors once told me, "A home going pastor makes a church going people." It's also true that my ministry was enriched by seeing how the people of my congregation live, where they live, and the blessing they received as they invited me into their residence. Having the opportunity to pray with people in their natural surroundings was and is a treasure that I hope many others get to experience. Pastors who do not do home visits truly don't know what they or their people are missing.

It's also important to note here how Paul requested help from those he would visit for the sake of the gospel. I don't ever remember asking for personal help from people when I would go to visit them, but on several occasions, I received help, either for me or for the church I served before I left. After all, we are in this Kingdom work together and helping one another along our journey on the Highway of Holiness is a very good thing.

Finally, I am intrigued by Paul's expectation of joy that would come from being together with God's people as they would labor together. I confess that there have been some calls I have made over the years that I don't wish to repeat because the reason that took me to certain homes were over points of contention, or a need of spiritual correction. Though needed at times, those aren't the fun visits. However, there were many more places where we drank coffee together, shared a meal together, watched ball games together, laughed together, and sometimes even cried together. Getting to enter into a part of people's lives is a rare privilege that should never be taken for granted. Paul looked forward to meeting and mixing with people he didn't know. Thankfully, we too can gain much from ministry and mixing with people we need to know better. I hope you will give it a try.

DAY 291

Romans 15:25 *Now, however, I am on my way to Jerusalem in the service of the saints there.*

Paul traveled many a mile over a period of several years in his service of King Jesus. Along the way he brought the words of eternal life to the many cities and provinces of the Roman Empire through which he passed. He never took his eyes off the heavenly calling to which Jesus had called him.

However, while focusing on the eternal, he didn't lose sight of the present and the physical world. He realized that compassionate ministry, doing good to the bodies of men and women, went hand in hand with the words of eternal life, for he wanted the best for all people now and forever.

The church in Jerusalem had fallen on hard times and Paul wanted to alleviate their suffering, so he took up collections as he traveled in order to be able to present the Jerusalem church with a love gift that would help sustain them through their current crisis. Paul mentions in various places in his writings that those who have received spiritually have an obligation to give back in material ways to those who have made the spiritual enlightenment possible. In other words, it is important to share physical provisions with those who provide spiritual insights.

Centuries later, John Wesley, the founder of the Methodist movement, would say that he knew of no gospel but the social gospel. He wasn't pushing for a socialistic society, but pushing the idea that it is a legitimate ministry for a church, and for Christians, to care for the bodies of mankind as well as their spiritual needs. We are our brother's keepers in many aspects.

While I too recognize the value of social programs through the church, I have also witnessed too many times how the social tail sometimes begins to wag the gospel dog. Churches can get so involved with being good neighbors, feeding the hungry, clothing the naked, caring for the sick, and comforting the prisoners, that they sometimes forget to bring the gospel along with their actions. When that happens, the enemy of our souls has won, for he has gotten us to focus on the material present to the exclusion of the eternal future. Let's be careful to not neglect either area. There is no reason why we can't follow Paul's example to care for the physical needs around us, while still sharing the gospel via the highway of holiness.

DAY 292

Romans 15:26 *For Macedonia and Achaia were pleased to make a contribution for the poor among the saints in Jerusalem.*

Macedonia and Achaia were Greek provinces within the Roman Empire during the time in which Paul was traveling and telling the good news about the resurrection of Jesus Christ. The churches of Philippi, Berea, Thessalonica, Corinth, and Athens are within the boundaries of these provinces, and have become famous among those who study the Bible.

Because Paul spent a considerable time and energy in his work throughout these provinces, he was able to establish a rapport with these new believers, as he helped them to understand the spiritual impact that the gospel message was having on their lives, and how they had a responsibility help provide physical support to others who were in need.

I like Paul's choice of words here, as they were "pleased to make a contribution." Not all giving is done with joyful spirits and not all asking is framed in such a way that causes the giver to be able to be joyful with their gifts. Paul apparently had the spiritual gift of giving because he first had the spiritual gift of getting. He knew how to convince people that giving was the right thing for Christians to do.

It's easy to get "giving fatigue" in the present day however, for the needs never seem to stop, and all of us have a limited amount of resources available for us to give. Every organization, from the local charities to churches to mission groups to homeless shelters, are constantly after our gifts, and such enormous pressure from so many places can easily cause us to be more like Ebenezer Scrooge than St. Paul. At some point the natural tendency within us all is to just say, "enough is enough!"

Here is where we need to remember the words of Jesus as He admonished us to be "wise as serpents, but harmless as doves," (Matthew 10:16) and also to "not give dogs what is sacred; do not throw your pearls to pigs" (Matthew 7:6). This means we must be discerning with our gifts because we can't give to everything. It falls upon us to prayerfully research where the best place for our money should be, and then give joyfully to that cause or causes. Though I believe the ten percent tithe belongs to the local church, the other ninety percent will be judged by the Lord too. Let's use it all wisely.

DAY 293

Romans 15:27 *They were pleased to do it, and indeed they owe it to them. For if the Gentiles have shared in the Jews' spiritual blessings, they owe it to the Jews to share with them their material blessings.*

Paul hits the giving focus one more time before leaving the subject. The point is simple. If you have received, then you also have an obligation to give. It is better to be cautioned about being too generous rather than being criticized for being too miserly. God truly does love a cheerful giver (II Corinthians 9:7).

Twice in this short verse Paul makes the statement that the Christians of Macedonia and Achaia "owed it" to the Jerusalem Jews to be liberal givers. They had found their spiritual life because of what came out of Jerusalem, so in turn, they needed to share in the responsibility of helping their benefactors physically when the need arose.

What does this say to us? Who do we owe our thanks for the spiritual life that we enjoy today? I can think of pastors, Sunday School teachers, professors, co-workers, and predecessors where I have served in ministry, but I'm sure the number I owe is much greater and deeper. Because I am of an age where many of those who provided spiritual help for me in my formative years have gone on to their reward, what should I be doing to pay my fair share in today's world?

Perhaps we should look around us and ask the Lord to open our eyes to see those who are in need who are near where we live, as well as those who are far away. Does my pastor need help financially? Many clergy families are struggling today, as they always have. Is there a person in whom I can invest my time? The retired, the sick, and the lonely often feel like no one cares. Perhaps they have been front line workers for the King of kings when they had better days, but life's circumstances have changed things and now they are in need? Who in my family, my church family, or those who are in training to be leaders in our churches need a boost along the way? Perhaps we can help if we really try. I am convinced that God gives to us so that we can give to others. All the tangible things we possess we are going to lose eventually. Why not give them with joy while we can? Thank you, Macedonia and Achaia for showing us the way!

DAY 294

Paul had a job to complete when he wrote these words. He had to take the all the money he had collected from the various churches he had planted, to give an offering to the church in Jerusalem. Raising financial support for others has always been a big part of the mission of the church since its foundation. Paul sets a good example for the rest of us. The fact that he tells us that his mission to the church there wasn't done until he had made sure that the money got to where it had been intended, also provides a good leadership practice for us. Making sure of our stewardship before the Lord is making sure that the causes to which we donate are legitimate and honest. Providing funds for others requires us to investigate to make sure the money we give goes where we intend for it to go.

But when having fulfilled that obligation to the Jerusalem leadership, Paul had every intention of visiting the church in Rome, and gaining their help to open the gospel message to the people of Spain. We don't know for sure whether that mission ever took place because when Paul got to Rome he was in chains as a prisoner. The book of Acts records his last missionary journey as one who was a captive, and one who suffered real hardship. No doubt, when he finally did get to meet the people who were receiving this letter, they saw him in a different situation than he had expected to be in.

The trip to Spain may have happened. It's possible that Paul was freed while he was in Rome, was able to go to Spain and present Jesus to the people there, before returning to Rome again, and being arrested on other charges. We just don't know for sure, but long church tradition tells us that he eventually died a martyr's death in Rome under the hands of the Emperor Nero. I guess at this point we will have to just wait and see until we can ask him about it.

There are two quick observations here. First, I love the way Paul is always on a mission. Even while writing to the Romans, a church he has never met in person, he is already planning a campaign in Spain. His fervor for Jesus never wanes. He is also big on fellowship. He wants to spend time in Rome. His love for ministry and for the church family should be an example for us.

DAY 295

Romans 15:29 *I know that when I come to you, I will come in the full measure of the blessing of Christ.*

This verse intrigues me. Let's read it through again. "I know that when I come to you, I will come in the full measure of the blessing of Christ." I am fascinated by a couple of thoughts that it brings to my mind.

First, I love Paul's optimism. He fully assumes that he will eventually get to meet the Romans face to face, and that nothing is going to hinder it happening. Of course, he has no idea what actually is going to happen over the next few years, as he will eventually be taken prisoner, beaten, lost at sea, shipwrecked, bitten by a deadly poisonous snake, and continue his ministry in ways beyond his dreams. He just knows that he will come to the Romans. He's not a prophet here; he's just an extreme optimist.

Also, I love the picture that he paints concerning what his visit to the Romans will be like. He is going to be the source of Christ's blessing that will fall upon the church because of his arrival there. If we didn't know Paul so well, it would almost seem like he is a bit egotistical. Being a blessing, the full measure of blessing in Christ, mind you, is what he claims he will be to the church. That's a lot to live up to. We aren't told exactly how it turned out, but I have great confidence that he was what he claimed he would be.

What would we have to do or be to bring about the full blessing of Christ to our church? Would it mean that we would preach eloquent sermons that take people right into the presence of God? Would it be that we could sing songs, or play an instrument in such a way that the Divine would seem to truly be in our midst? Would it be that we would have such a winsome personality that everyone would consider us to be the life of the party, and just be glad that we were there?

Any of those things might be true, but I really don't see Paul in that picture. I see him bringing the fullness of God's love that has been poured upon his life through the continual presence of Christ, that would flow from him to the people whom he met. Experiencing the blessing of Christ is experiencing Christ himself. Being so full of the abiding presence of the Master to the point where Jesus just splashes over on others is what I see. It is life in the Spirit that becomes contagious to others. That's the blessing of Christ!

DAY 296

Romans 15:30 *I urge you, brothers, by our Lord Jesus Christ and by the love of the Spirit, to join me in my struggle by praying to God for me.*

If there is any one thing of which the Apostle Paul was aware, it was that he was in a battle. He didn't see people as his enemies though, he was in conflict with the powers of darkness that though they were defeated by Christ on the cross, still hold sway over the population of this world. As we are freed from the dark power of sin through faith in the work of Christ in our lives, we live without its bondage personally, but still have to deal with its effects on society.

This is what concerned the Apostle at this point in his life. He knew that the enemy of his soul was doing everything possible to end Paul's effectiveness, but had not been successful at this point of his ministry. The Apostle's only defense and source of strength for this battle, however, was found in his relationship with Christ. By himself, he was totally vulnerable, but in Christ his armor was more than sufficient.

This is why he continually strove to stay in close connection with Jesus. He knew that he would succumb as prey to the enemy should he try to win the battle on his own. This is also why he pleads for those in Rome to join in the battle on his side by praying to God for him. He would always remain weak in his own abilities, but through Christ he would be strong.

There are some things for us to remember here. One, is that we really do need each other. When someone asks us to pray for them, it is not something we should take lightly, or forget to do. Prayer to God is where our source of power lies and where the victory is won. Without that divine connection we are helpless as we face each new day.

How do we win victory for others in prayer? Through "the love of the Spirit." "For God so loved the world..." (John 3:16), he gave us His Holy Spirit to help us in our time of need. In John 14 Jesus promised the continued presence of the Spirit to aid the disciples in their mission, and we can count on the same power from God for us. The Spirit never leaves any believer alone. He is always there to strengthen us regardless of the circumstances.

Praying is power. Power is from God. We are conquerors only with Christ.

DAY 297

Romans 15:31–32 *Pray that I may be rescued from the unbelievers in Judea and that my service in Jerusalem may be acceptable to the saints there, so that by God's will I may come to you with joy and together with you be refreshed.*

Paul seemed especially concerned about two things as he continues with his letter to the Roman church. First, he fully understood that there would be many people who thought as he once did, that this Jesus talk had to be stopped, once and for all. Because he mentions that his adversaries were in Judea, it is pretty obvious that he saw a much bigger threat from inside the Jewish community than from the Gentiles outside of it.

The second thing that particularly concerned him is that his coming trip to Jerusalem would be fruitful and that the saints in Christ would see his coming to them as a blessing more than as a hardship. He wanted to be of service for the glory of God more than anything else he did.

In his thinking, these two prayer requests being answered would produce an effect that would affect the Romans also. If he was rescued from the unbelievers in Judea, and if his service was pleasing to the Jerusalem church, then he would be free to come to Rome and enter into a joyful and healing relationship with the Christian family there.

In the twenty-first chapter of the book of Acts we find out what happened though. Though Paul did get to give his monetary gift to the church leaders in Jerusalem, and though they were no doubt grateful and pleased to receive it, the unbelievers of Judea attacked him, beat him, had him arrested, and tried repeatedly to kill him. Through the rest of the book of Acts we have the account of his imprisonment and his eventual journey to meet the church in Rome, while in chains.

Life doesn't always turn out as we plan. Like Paul, we have hopes for good things and good relationships, but sometimes situations just go in a totally different direction from what we had envisioned. However, like Paul, we can count on the presence of the Lord to be with us, to continually guide us, and to provide for us until He calls us home. Paul did get to meet these people to whom he was writing, but as a prisoner. God used even that situation though, and He will use the path we take for His glory as well.

DAY 298

Romans 15:33 *The God of peace be with you all. Amen.*

Peace is an interesting concept. We talk about it all the time, wish for it at Christmas, and think about it being the ultimate goal for all the world. Yet, it always seems to be the elusive dream, just out of the reach for most individuals and nations of the world.

There is a reason for this. People desire peace without connecting it to the source of peace, the person of God Himself. The idea of peace is considered by most people to be the absence of conflict, and if we can just get all the problems out of the way then we can have peace. Unfortunately, that is a fool's mission, for peace will never be found if all the circumstances of life have to be in perfect order.

Peace is a gift of God. It is one of the fruits that comes from the Holy Spirit to the life of a believer and follower of Jesus Christ. One can no more have peace without Jesus than grow a banana without the peel. The ingredients that bring about peace are bound together by a presence that makes holiness the central point of attention, and there can be no substitutions in the formula. If there is no God, there is no peace. Where God is, peace is possible. It's just that simple.

When Paul pronounced his blessing of peace, it was to the church at Rome he was speaking. He blessed them with an attribute from the God of peace, not some ethereal desire or wishful hope. He knew what we know, that God alone could give the Christians of this young church the inner awareness of a divine presence who would calm all the storms that could rage within.

Though Paul didn't know it at the time of his writing, he would in the coming days be put to the test concerning his faith in Jesus like few others would know. Beatings, betrayals, imprisonment, trials, shipwrecks, and long journeys lay before him. But the thing that would sustain him through it all would be the peace of God through the personal relationship he had with Jesus Christ. His example helped others grow in their own awareness of peace. In our own troubled times, the circumstances may be different, but the truth has not changed. When we need peace, we need God. With Him we have it and without Him, we never will. To that thought, we can join with the apostle and say a big, "amen."

DAY 299

Romans 16:1 *I commend to you our sister Phoebe, a servant of the church in Cenchrea.*

In this chapter and verse the apostle begins a long litany of greetings and thank you messages to various people connected to the Roman church congregation. Though he has never been there to meet them in person, his various travels have allowed him to cross paths with several individuals.

The description that Paul has for Phoebe is one that should inspire every child of God to emulate, for being a servant is the highest-ranking order in the Kingdom of God's list of important people. Jesus made this very clear when He said, "You know that the rulers of the Gentiles lord it over them, and their high officials exercise authority over them. Not so with you. Instead, whoever wants to become great among you must be your servant, and whoever wants to be first must be your slave..." (Matthew 20:25–27). There should be no question as to what position is most important in God's eyes when it comes to ranking among the body of Christ.

Something else to notice here is that Phoebe was a "servant of the church." She apparently made it her business to be in a place of submission and support when it came to the work of God as connected to the local body of believers.

Cenchrea, the place where Phoebe served, was a port in the city of Corinth, in Greece. Corinth was a city known widely for its immorality and disgusting behavioral habits, but it is where the church was—and where the church should be. In the midst of where the world is most like hell, the church's role is to be light for God, shining as a beacon for all those around to see. It was in such a place that Phoebe worked as servant to Paul and others of the holy fellowship.

Her life should be an example for people everywhere. In the places where sin is rampant, the church should be there also. As the church ministers in such a place, people like Phoebe, real servants are needed in order to make the gospel available to everyone. We are not told what she did; only that she served. Our talents will vary, as will our spiritual gifts, but wherever God needs us to be, that's where we will find our work. May the church of the 21st century rise up and imitate Phoebe and her service for the Kingdom of God.

DAY 300

Romans 16:2 *I ask you to receive her in the Lord in a way worthy of the saints and to give her any help she may need from you, for she has been a great help to many people, including me.*

Phoebe had apparently made quite an impression on Paul, for he considers her worthy of the hospitality of the Roman church, and even the status of sainthood before the people—although it is important to remember that Paul considered everyone who abides in Christ as saints. Sometimes we call people saints because a branch of the church says so, but in his varied letters, Paul declared that all who are in Christ deserve that title.

I love the fact that Paul doesn't have to list Phoebe's attributes, talents, or skills. He just said that she has been a great help to many people. That's a wonderful reputation to have.

I have been blessed to have had so many people who have been of great help to me over my years in the ministry. Some have helped financially, some have helped me with physical labors such as property repairs, shoveling snow, or church cleaning. I have always been grateful for the many cooks that have provided meals at the church and in their homes for us and others, and those who took it upon themselves to take the pastor's family out to eat, or give us gifts on special occasions. Many have been encouraging to me in spiritual ways as they have taught the saints, carried the load for others in prayer, and wept under the burden God gave them for people locally and around the world. I have been blessed with those who gave their time to me personally to counsel me, fellowship with me, and hold me and my ministry up before the Lord. The reason Phoebe is so important to the Christian story and Paul's reference to her is because she had the gift of helps. The church always needs people like that.

Here is where we can learn and grow in our own ministry development. How can we serve others and be a helper like Phoebe? What talents and gifts has the Lord provided to us that we could use to be such a blessing to the body of Christ. The church, regardless of the size of each congregation, always needs willing workers to pray, plan, dream, implement, and review. The church always needs counselors, teachers, and tithers. Being Phoebe's replacement in your setting could be the best gift you could ever give.

DAY 301

Romans 16:3-4 *Greet Priscilla and Aquila, my fellow workers in Christ Jesus. They risked their lives for me. Not only I but all the churches of the Gentiles are grateful to them.*

I once had a college professor tell our class of ministerial students, "Every Paul needs a Timothy, and every Timothy needs a Paul." Over the several decades since that time I have found those words to be prophetic and true. None of us are an island unto ourselves because we all need people to help us along the way in our life's journey.

Priscilla and Aquilla would have fallen into the category of "Timothy" in this regard because Paul was able to explain the way of Christ more clearly and help them in their spiritual and ministerial growth (Acts 18). They would also take the role of being a "Paul" to others as they labored in Corinth to share the good news and later in Ephesus helped the young and powerful preacher, Apollos, understand the way of faith in Christ. Wherever this couple is mentioned they are presented in a positive light as people who truly shared in the mission of the Kingdom of God. We are told by Paul that they risked their lives for his sake and were blessings to the Gentile churches wherever they traveled.

Their example is one I wish all Christians, including myself, could continually emulate. I want to be a person who works for Christ, puts it all on the line for Christ, and ends up being a blessing to others for the sake of Christ. I believe I could happily stand before the Lord someday if such were my record of service.

We are not told anything about their background except for the fact they were tentmakers like Paul and that they worked together in their daily labors as well as in the work of the church. They had come through hardship because they were evicted from their home city because of their Jewish heritage. We don't know if they were rich or poor, but we do know that they were faithful. Apparently, they had found their way back to Rome because Paul gives them his greetings in this verse.

Wouldn't it be great to have people like them in our local church? Wouldn't it be great if we would pattern our lives from their examples? Wouldn't the Lord be pleased? Well, if that's the case, let do it, and continue their work.

DAY 302

Romans 16:5a *Greet also the church that meets at their house.*

Though there were places of worship where people gathered to bring praise to the Lord and hear the message of the gospel since the early days of the church, it wasn't until after A.D. 325, and the Roman emperor Constantine's proclamation, that Christianity would be the official religion of Rome, and the church building would begin to take on the look and size that we continue to enjoy today.

Churches, when Paul was ministering, were usually held in houses or in rented halls that were large enough to hold the number of people that would gather. As in other parts of the world even to this day, when the church had to go underground because of persecution, they would meet in small groups that could be easily dispersed quickly when they needed to do so. Church buildings may be the norm now, but it hasn't always been that way.

Paul is referencing Priscilla and Aquilla here as the hosts of the local congregation. It is most likely that there were several house churches in Rome as this letter was being written, and it was expected that Paul's words would be shared with each of them. Priscilla and Aquilla were just some of many people that were working to keep the gospel message moving throughout the Roman empire.

Though this may not be the focus of Paul's words, it is good to note here the value of doing church on a smaller scale rather than on a larger one. There is a place for both the big and small congregations, but when a church has less buildings and grounds, they have more fluidity for ministry and often a closer connection to their neighbors. We have said many times that the church is not the building, but it's the people, but we often build like the building is the identity of the gospel. Bigger is not better; bigger is just bigger. It's more important for the church people to be the church wherever they find themselves than for a building—which often sits empty most of time—be the image of church for a community. Property often becomes the tail that wags the gospel dog. I think it would be wise if we saw a need to change that.

Ahead of their time, Priscilla and Aquilla opened their home and made their lives the church. Maybe we need to rethink how we do church and see if their model would be effective where we are. It's something to think about.

DAY 303

Romans 16:5b *Greet my dear friend Epenetus, who was the first convert to Christ in the province of Asia.*

Can you imagine what it was like to be the first person to experience Christ in your whole part of the world. There were no church buildings, no pastors, no potluck dinners, no smoke machines, strobe lights, pulpits, or even altars. All that Epenetus had to lead him in the way of salvation was the one person who told him the story of Jesus. Imagine getting saved that way!

Seriously, this is a great example of how the gospel is spread. It moves from person to person, situation to situation, and crisis to crisis. Jesus stands ready to enter into fellowship with anyone who will receive him, but what is often needed is a person to share the opportunity of new life with the one who doesn't know about it.

You may be able to identify with Epenetus. You may not have been the first person from your part of the world to find Christ, but you may have been the first in your family, on your block, or among your group of friends. You may have been the one fortunate enough to have someone who loves you share the words of life with you and lead you into a new walk. If that is the case, then you can feel a little of what this believer did, but if so, there is another part of the story that you need to understand.

Just as it was noteworthy for Paul to mention this person from long ago, it is also vitally important that the gospel story didn't stop with him. Eventually, the Christian message spread throughout the whole province and beyond, and I like to think that perhaps Epenetus had a little bit to do with that. Good news begets good news, and Christians who really experience the transforming power of Jesus want to tell someone else about Him.

This is just a greeting that Paul requests, but in essence it tells us so much more. It speaks of a life that was forever changed. We aren't told whether Paul was the person who led him to Christ, but here is something to think about. You can be the person who leads someone else, like Epenetus, to Jesus. You can do for someone else what someone did for you; you can tell what Jesus has done in your life and offer that gift of salvation to someone else. We may not go down in our history books for doing so, but I guarantee that the effort, and the result of that effort, will go down in God's books.

DAY 304

Romans 16:6 *Greet Mary, who worked very hard for you.*

Mary is such a common name. It's the name of the mother of Jesus and it is the name of my wife. Down through the centuries countless women have been branded with this moniker and it has served them well. To be named after the mother of Jesus is quite an honor indeed.

Because we don't know who this particular Mary was, we would have to speculate and guess to come to any kind of conclusions about her. The only things that we know for certain—and perhaps this is why Paul included her in his letter—is that she worked very hard, and that she did that work on behalf of the Roman church.

My wife, who as I said, also bears that name, is a hard worker. She is a great housekeeper, but also a wonderful cook, a close confidant, wonderful in the garden, and can fix just about anything that ever gets broken. I like to brag on her when I can because I know that churches over the years have called me to serve them for a number of reasons, but they kept me because of her.

Being a hard worker is an admirable trait in this day and age of people always looking for someone else to take care of them. But this Mary, worked with a purpose in mind apparently, because what she did, she did for others. That is an even greater blessing and gift.

I have been blessed over my years of service in the church to see many, many people who were like this person Paul was referencing. Men and women both have worked diligently without pay for others. They have cleaned, cooked, repaired, trimmed, decorated, taught, offered personal care, and prayed. Many people of God I have been blessed to know have been giants in the area of service and have asked for little or nothing in return. They serve, they work, because others need them to, and because they believe that such labor is pleasing to our Lord.

I think they are right. Mary, and the many like her, have the spirit of being a Christ-like servant wherever they see a need. Without these people the church could not function and families would fall apart. We, who love them, should not only imitate their actions, but thank them for their service.

DAY 305

Romans 16:7 *Greet Andronicus and Junias, my relatives who have been in prison with me. They are outstanding among the apostles, and they were in Christ before I was.*

There is some speculation as to who these two people actually were. Even though Paul lists them as his relatives, we are still left with questions. Were they two men or were they husband and wife? Though Andronicus literally means, "Man of Victory," Junias in the Greek language (the language in which this book was originally written) is feminine, but that doesn't necessarily mean Junias was female. This was also a Roman family name surname that gives reference to the sun god, Juno, from which we today get our month of June. We can't be definite about their identities.

We do know that Paul considered them family. Whether this was a literal blood link, or perhaps he mentions this because they were also Jews as he was, could give us a clue. The names are Gentile names, however, so again we can't be sure as to a lot about their identity.

Paul did say they were in prison with him. He also tells us that they preceded him in the Jesus movement and they were worthy of great tribute among the apostles of Christ. Apparently, they came to the church at Rome with good credentials.

What can we take away from this verse? Well, these two should inspire us. They were willing to go to prison for the sake of Jesus. They had been in the faith for some long time, since Paul describes them as his seniors in Christ. They apparently were in it for the long haul due to the transforming power of the Holy Spirit.

Wouldn't you like to have people like this in your church? Well then, why not like as they lived. It doesn't mean necessarily that we have to go to prison in order to be noticed for Jesus, but it does mean that we have to stay in the faith long enough to make an impact on those around us. People don't become super-saints overnight. Walking with the Lord is a lifetime vocation and it is from the saints who have weathered that storms that life brings us that have the greatest influence on others. We may not know exactly who Andronicus and Junias were, but we know they were faithful. If we can follow them in that regard, we will surely be on the right track.

DAY 306

Romans 16:8 *Greet Ampliatus, whom I love in the Lord.*

N ow, this is a strange name to our modern ears. The Eastern Orthodox church considers Ampliatus as one of the seventy disciples sent out by Jesus in the Gospel of Luke 10:1. Some believe that he eventually became a bishop of the church in Bulgaria, but other than that we really don't know much about this person with a strange name.

What we do know, however, is that Paul loved him. Apparently, they had connected at some point along their life's journeys and by this time Ampliatus had some connection with the Roman church. The fact that Paul loved him in the Lord is not unusual, because God's love in us causes us to love everyone, but it is interesting that Paul singled him out.

Love is such an amazing attribute and such a tremendous life-changer. When Jesus places His Holy Spirit into our lives, we begin to see the world and the people in it with different eyes. Where once fear and hatred may have reigned, when God moves in—because He is pure love—love moves in as well. Who He is becomes a part of who we are.

There is quite a difference between merely loving and loving in the Lord though. The people of all walks, races, languages, and creeds speak of loving others. Romance reigns supreme in many minds. Certainly, erotic love dominates the airwaves. But the love that comes only from God is different. The Greek root of the word Paul uses here is *agape*, a love that only God can provide, and a love that only comes to those in whom He has placed His Spirit. It is more than a brotherly love or a family love, it is a strong declaration that we consider others more valuable than ourselves. It is a life-changing love that transforms and grows as we continue to grow in the Lord.

When Jesus spoke about us being perfect in Matthew 5:48, this is what He was talking about. Our love can be made perfect for God and man through the infilling of the presence of the divine. It is the answer to every relationship problem that has ever come along. Paul loved this man in the Lord. He was a dear family member in the eyes of the apostle. God had made that happen and He can make it happen in us as well when we allow God His way in us. Paul loved God and loving God caused him to love people, for God is love. That's the way He works in each of us still.

DAY 307

Romans 16:9 *Greet Urbanus, our fellow worker in Christ, and my dear friend Stachys.*

Urbanus was a common slave name during the days of Paul. His name is in direct contrast to Ampliatus, whom Paul had previously mentioned. Ampliatus was listed as an imperial freedman on an inscription in A.D. 115, so the implication here is that Paul has warm feelings toward both the slave and the free, for all are brothers in Christ.

There is a Stachys listed as on ancient inscription as a member of the imperial household. We can't be sure of the classification of three men's social status, but what a contrast they are! Regardless of one's place in life, all are family in the body of Christ.

This message is so important as we go through our routines in the twenty-first century. As the world becomes smaller through our many media connections and global traveling becomes more commonplace, it is vital that we see all people as our equals and especially those who belong to the family of God. There is no place for prejudice or bias in the church, for we all serve the same King, and regardless of our bank accounts, our skin color, our language, or our caste in society, we are all first class and A-listers in the Lord.

Some of the most memorable times of my life have been when I have been able to sit in meetings, or enjoy meals with people from various nations and backgrounds. I learn so much from the different customs and stories from places I have never been, as well as from the experiences I have never had. Whether a person has been raised in a palace or spent years in a prison, whether they are millionaires or live in poverty, when Jesus enters the picture, we all become family.

I am so thankful for the people of God. I am thankful for the love we share for each other and for the mission to which Christ has called us. This is true not only for different standings in life, but also for the different denominations of the church that have differences in practice but become one in Jesus.

Some people pass off these verses as just scribbles of farewell from Paul, but from them we learn much. May we emulate his love and his practice.

DAY 308

Romans 16:10 *Greet Apelles, tested and approved in Christ. Greet those who belong to the household of Aristobulus.*

Apelles is a typical Jewish name. Aristobulus is also Jewish, but the family connection takes one back to days of royalty among the Hasmonean ancestors who served in the position at times as both ruler and high priest. The names here have no significant meaning for this book in particular, but it does reflect on the wide array of connections that the Apostle Paul had.

Apelles has an especially interesting comment made about him. He had been tested and apparently had done well in this test, for he was approved in Christ. For a follower of Jesus, that's just about as good a recommendation that anyone can get.

He stands out as an example for us all, for anyone who walks with Jesus very long will find that he or she will definitely be tested. Of course, the degree of testing will be different for each person and each circumstance one finds oneself, but that there will be testing is a certainly.

The Lord Himself was tested by Satan, attacked publicly by those who would try to trick Him with His own words, and eventually He would face the testing of being betrayed by a friend, forsaken by His followers, and suffering under the scourge of Roman torture and a cross. If Jesus Himself faced such testing, why would any of us think that we should be exempt?

Our tests today may come from those who would belittle us and scoff at our faith. The tests may come from family members or even from other members of Christ's church who are not walking in the light of love that they should. Tests could come from anyone, anywhere, and they will be with us for as long as we live in this world.

The important part of this greeting is that Apelles passed the test and was approved in Christ. That's the goal that each of us should be aspiring to reach. To be tempted is not a shame, and to be tested is not unexpected, but when we come through such things standing firm for our Savior, that's the best we can do.

Today, as you face what the Lord allows in your path, be aware that you are being tested. Know that through Christ, you too can pass with honors.

DAY 309

Romans 16:11 *Greet Herodian, my relative. Greet those in the household of Narcissus who are in the Lord.*

Herodians were people connected to the reign of King Herod. Some say they were part of a political focus like the Pharisees or Sadducees, while others would claim that they were part of the royal family. Either way, it is apparent that Paul had contact, and perhaps even a family connection to a person identified by this name. We really don't know more than that.

Narcissus in Greek mythology was the son of the river god Cephissus and the nymph Liriope. He was said to be a hunter and known for his beauty and love of everything beautiful. Most likely though, this Narcissus was a Greek who had been named after this ancient fable.

As a Jew and a Greek, these people would come from two different worlds normally, but Paul sees them as family within the body of Christ. Throughout this sixteenth chapter of Romans, the apostle seems to be going out of his way to emphasize the fact that he loves people from all walks of life. It is most likely that the church in Rome was made up of these people, so it becomes evident that it was a very cosmopolitan worshiping community. How blessed they were to get a head start on what it means to be a Christian church.

Revelation 7:9 records what the revelator John saw from the heavenlies, "After this I looked and there before me was a great multitude that no one could count, from every nation, tribe, people and language, standing before the throne and in front of the Lamb." When we get to the next world, there will certainly be a mix of people from every walk of life.

How blessed we are to have this chapter from Paul to show us how Christianity is to be understood. The way of faith doesn't belong to Americans, Africans, or Asians. It doesn't prefer one language over another, or one culture as being "the right way." God's family is diverse, huge, and growing more and more each day. As Paul said back in Romans 1:14, "I am obligated both to Greeks and non-Greeks, both to the wise and the foolish." We have so much to learn from each other, and in Christ the family of God continues to grow and flourish. May we all have open arms and open hearts for all whom the Lord will bring into our path, for His glory!

DAY 310

Romans 16:12 *Greet Tryphena and Tryphosa, those women who work hard in the Lord. Greet my dear friend Persis, another woman who has worked very hard in the Lord.*

Women often get a bum rap when it comes to things concerning church life. Of course, this varies with different places and cultures, but traditionally the church has looked at the role of women almost as second-class citizens when it comes to ecclesiastical leadership. Thankfully, this is changing for many, but progress often moves at a snail's pace.

At different points in my ministry, I have asked laymen and clergy how they felt about having a woman as their pastor. Way above average is the response that they would prefer a man in that position. Old traditions die hard.

Paul didn't see things that way though. He clearly considered women as valuable laborers in kingdom work. I get the picture from his writings that he didn't just see them as babysitters and building cleaners, but vital participants in the active ministry of spreading the gospel of Christ. He lists no fewer than ten women in this chapter and he has glowing things to say about all of them. In Galatians 3:28 he says, "There is neither Jew nor Greek, slave nor free, male nor female, for you are all one in Christ Jesus." In four of the six times that Paul mentions Priscilla in his writings, she is mentioned before her husband Aquila. Paul apparently did not think that women were on a lower rung of the gospel ladder.

These three women, Tryphena, Tryphosa, and Persis were obviously women who knew how to work. Paul calls them out for special honor because of their labors. Their faithfulness to the cause of Christ puts them in a place of recognition for centuries after their death.

Throughout my years in the church, women have served in prominent place of leadership, and the kingdom would be much poorer without them. In fact, in many places the church would not even function if women didn't take a prominent role.

So, our hats are off to you ladies. Thank you for your tireless service and thank you for your dedication to the Lord. You bless us in a big way!

DAY 311

Romans 16:13 *Greet Rufus, chosen in the Lord, and his mother, who has been a mother to me, too.*

Rufus is only mentioned twice in the Bible, here and in Mark 15:21, where it says, "A certain man from Cyrene, Simon, the father of Alexander and *Rufus*, was passing by on his way in from the country, and they forced him to carry the cross." Cyrene was an ancient Greek and later a Roman city in Libya, in north Africa. It is most likely that Simon, Alexander, and Rufus were black in skin color, which could be why the Romans of the crucifixion could have thought Simon should be tasked with the menial job of carrying the cross of Jesus. Little did they know that this act would give him a legendary status in the eyes of the church.

We don't know for sure that this Rufus was the son of Simon, but since Paul's letters were written before the gospel accounts, the odds are pretty good. Why else would Alexander and Rufus be mentioned in Mark's gospel unless they had been people who would have been known by the readers.

Regardless of his identity, Rufus seems to have come from good stock. If, in fact, his father carried the cross, that would have been a pretty good introduction to the story of Jesus. The mother of Rufus apparently looked favorably on Paul and his ministry, treating him as if he were a son.

All this points to the fact that our households are vitally important to the work of the Kingdom. A parent's highest goal in life should not be to see that their children get into the best schools, get a prominent place on the local sports team, or even land a great job. Every parent's highest priority should be to make sure that their children know Jesus and know Him in such a way that their life is changed eternally by that knowledge.

I am long past the years of raising children and the parents who raised me are both gone from this world. However, I treasure the upbringing in the church that I was given, and my wife and I tried hard to make sure that our offspring understood that whether or not they served Jesus would be the most important decision they would ever make in their lives. Nothing else even comes close. What we should strive to pass on to the next generations is what we have found in Christ, for all this stuff around us is going to pass very quickly. Rufus found the truth. I pray all our kids will as well.

DAY 312

Romans 16:14–15 *Greet Asyncritus, Phlegon, Hermes, Patrobas, Hermas and the brothers with them. Greet Philologus, Julia, Nerseus and his sister, and Olympas and all the saints with them.*

I believe wholeheartedly in the power of the forgotten names. Not only are these names hard to pronounce, but what they did and who they were have been basically lost to the memories of our modern age. All we know about them for the most part is that they were people who were connected to the church at Rome that Paul wanted to greet in the closing words of his letter. Around these figures is historical silence, but actually their impact is not lost on us.

These people are wonderful examples of the multitudes of saints down through the centuries that have carried the banner of Jesus without fanfare, notoriety, or publicity. They have loved, worshiped, prayed, served, paid, and sacrificed so that the cause of Christ could go out to the far reaches of the earth to build the Kingdom of God. They are the parents, grandparents, and great-grandparents of people who would have an impact through the gospel message to the equally unknown masses and the prominent leaders of the world throughout the ages.

I was raised in a small church. At times in my years of ministry I have pastored small churches. I have fellowshipped and worshiped with wonderful people who will never be known by anyone outside their family circles and their hometown areas. These have been the ones who have carried the load for Jesus as they were His hands and feet when they fed the poor, visited the prisons, ministered to the sick, clothed the naked, and sent out funds to support mission work to people they would never know or hear from. These are the saints who will be rewarded, as the John the Revelator wrote in his book: "Now the dwelling of God is with men, and he will live with them. They will be his people, and God himself will be with them and be their God. He will wipe away every tear from their eyes. There will be no more death or mourning or crying or pain, for the old order of things has passed away."

Thank you, you often forgotten Christians. You are not forgotten by your Master, and you will be rewarded in due time. You are the church, indeed!

DAY 313

Romans 16:16 *Greet one another with a holy kiss.*
All the churches of Christ send greetings.

This is probably one of the more famous verses of all Paul's writings. Though it is often the source of smiles, smirks, and giggles, it actually has a pretty good foundation for our conduct. In many middle eastern countries this is a very common greeting, though it hasn't caught on in much of the western world, or in many Asian cultures. Paul emphasizes that it is to be a *holy* kiss, one showing the love of God from one person to another. At the end of his letters to the churches, he admonishes both the Romans and the Corinthians to do it.

In this age of civil unrest and public distrust, it is good for the church to be reminded of our obligation to love. It doesn't matter what political party to which we may or may not be affiliated, and it doesn't matter if the feeling is mutually felt or returned. We are people of love. Jesus gave us our marching orders concerning our conduct when He said, "A new command I give you: Love one another. As I have loved you, so you must love one another. By this all men will know that you are my disciples, if you love one another" (John 13:34–35).

We may not get back to the point of providing a holy kiss, a holy hug, or even a holy handshake for some time because of the effects of the Covid-19 virus, but that shouldn't stop Christians from loving our brothers and sisters in Christ, our families, and even our enemies. We were purchased with the price of love on a cross, and we cannot ever pay back such a debt.

I knew a pastor and wife who were very elderly and served in a very poor and dysfunctional community. It was their practice to greet everyone who came through the doors of their church for a service with a holy kiss on the mouth. I'm not sure how sanitary it was, but I saw that church grow from a handful of people to the point where there was barely room for me to stand on the platform as a guest speaker. Love wins, always! Love attracts. Love stands the test of time, and love changes lives. No wonder Jesus spoke so strongly about it.

When you face the world as it is, love it with the resource Christ provides. It will change more than the world. It will also change you.

DAY 314

Romans 16:17 *I urge you, brothers, to watch out for those who cause divisions and put obstacles in your way that are contrary to the teaching you have learned. Keep away from them.*

" Danger, Will Robinson! Danger" That's a line from the old 1960's sci-fi show, "Lost in Space." It's pretty funny to see the old reruns now, but as a child I was enthralled by the adventures of the Robinson family in space.

Paul is using almost the same urgency as he warns the people of the Roman church as to what they can expect in the coming days. He knows that the way of the cross is never going to be easy. Crosses are rough and have splinters, and carrying one is a task that takes every bit of one's strength and determination.

The reason the highway of holiness is so fraught with pitfalls is because of people. Without the influence of Jesus, people tend to want their own way, and will go to any length to achieve their demands. Throughout Paul's ministry he was continually harassed by the Jewish community, and even by his Christian brothers who were Jews, but felt that he had gone far too liberal for his own good. They wanted to maintain the Law while still embracing the gospel of faith. Paul got in trouble with them when he told them that they could choose one or the other but couldn't have it both ways.

As goes the teacher, so goes the student. If they persecuted Paul and made his life difficult as a servant of Christ, then he knew that this young church in Rome would suffer also. It's hard to endure pain, but when we see our offspring experience it, it's doubly hard. That's why he strenuously warns them to be careful.

To this very day we have people who want to stop the church at all costs. When the church holds the banner of holiness high and sticks to the authority of the Bible, it will always raise opposition, because as Jesus said, "This is the verdict: Light has come into the world, but men loved darkness instead of light because their deeds were evil" (John 3:19). It's the job of the church to expose and expel darkness, but when it does, there is usually a fight. We are to be smart, creative, and careful in our service to the King, while being brave. Let's stay bold, but wise in our labors of love for Jesus, for whether we die out, rust out, or burn out, we are still out. Let's stay in, for God's sake.

DAY 315

Romans 16:18 *For such people are not serving our Lord Christ, but their own appetites. By smooth talk and flattery they deceive the minds of naïve people.*

Here Paul continues with his warning against those who would put obstacles and stumbling blocks in the path of those who are trying to find their footing in the way of the Lord. In the previous verse he identified them, but here he deals with the motives behind such chicanery.

The core problem of such folks is that they have "their own appetites." They want what they want regardless of how it affects others, or compromises what the Lord has taught. Paul spent his lifetime after his Damascus Road conversion giving up his own rights, being fodder for Jewish plots, and being the servant rather than being the chief. People who want to please themselves above all other things abound in number in secular society, but even in the church they sometimes raise their ugly heads.

Selfishness is at the core of all sin, for it is the outgrowth of idolatry. We live in a day when self has become the god of all gods, and what we desire supersedes all other motivations. When we worship who we are, what we are, or what we believe, to the exclusion of the teachings of the Word of God, we are traveling a dangerous road that can only lead to destruction.

The method that such people use is flattery. Everyone loves to be adored. Everyone loves to be thought of highly and complemented. Such schemers use these basic feeling to distort truth and entrap the naïve.

These warnings from Paul are so appropriate to our times. I guess they are appropriate for all generations because the god of self is always trying to win victory in every society. It is only when we bow before the King of all kings and submit to the way of saving grace through Jesus Christ, that we can ever be free from the enemy of self.

It's hard to face ourselves in the mirror and admit that we are the source of our problem, or that we are the source of the problem for others, but when we use the Bible to show us our reflection, that's what we often see. Thankfully, Jesus has the power to cleanse us of self and make us into the servants that can benefit others. We can't do it, but God can, through Christ.

DAY 316

Romans 16:19 *Everyone has heard about your obedience, so I am full of joy over you; but I want you to be wise about what is good, and innocent about what is evil.*

News travels fast and good news should be proclaimed as loudly and often as possible. This church at Rome was getting a reputation in the surrounding areas, not for wrong-doing or tragedy, but for being obedient to the mission assigned by Jesus to them. The result of such good news is that it brought joy to every true believer who had the story relayed to them.

When we hear about other churches that are doing well, I hope we can be joyful with them. We are not in competition with each other but are teammates and co-workers for the common goal of the Kingdom of God. Whether within our worshiping community or the church down the street, we need to celebrate every God-blessed happening in our community.

But along with the joy that Paul expresses, he is faithful to warn the Romans that pursuing goodness is the proper and correct way to go as they develop their ministry. Too many times the churches of our modern and post-modern eras have been publicized for splits, scandals, infidelities, and other acts of unfaithfulness. We of the faith have been too easily drawn after what is popular, what is socially acceptable, and what attracts numbers. Goodness, that is mentioned here, is a fruit of the Spirit of God and we need to always make sure that it is His Spirit that we are following and obeying, and not some latest theological trend that has captivated the gullible.

This is why it is important that we stay innocent when it comes to evil. I don't think that Paul means we should be ignorant about evil in our world, for that would be dangerous. However, we should be free from the taint of sinful influences when it comes to how we govern our lives and our churches. If we don't remain the church Christ died to create, then we have fallen into the enemy's trap and our mission will suffer as a result.

I can almost see Paul's face as he reflects on what he is hearing about this Roman church. They are obedient to Jesus and he sees how He is leading them. It's a beautiful statement that should bring joy to all of us. So why don't we strive to be like them and bring joy to our Christian communities today. It's a great place to start our path to being all God wants us to be.

DAY 317

Romans 16:20 *The God of peace will soon crush Satan under your feet. The grace of our Lord Jesus be with you.*

I love how the apostle always had a picture of the end game. He had traveled for years preaching, teaching, discipling, and suffering the pains that came from such a ministry in that time and part of the world. He had come a long way since his Damascus Road experience of Acts 9, and his worldview and mission in life had been radically altered. Through all the challenges, pain, temptations, and trials he faced, there was one thing that kept him going. It was the fact that in the end, we win. Jesus and His coming Kingdom are going to be victorious.

It's so easy to take our eyes off the prize and forget that Satan is a defeated foe. The cross of Christ did Him in and broke the power that he had over the whole world. Because of the victory of Jesus through the resurrection from the grave, the way to victory for the rest of us may be long and sometimes difficult, but the ultimate triumph has been assured. In Christ, we too are achieving the complete defeat of the enemy.

It may not seem like we are winning sometimes as we look around. Sin is rampant, and even the definition of sin seems to be shifting in accordance with whoever has the loudest voice at the time. The Word of God doesn't change though, and those who leave its teachings to provide messages that itchy ears clamor to hear, will eventually pay for their error. Just as the God of peace will soon crush Satan under His feet, those who peddle the enemy's mixed messages will also have to answer for their deeds. It may not happen today, tomorrow, or perhaps even in our lifetimes, but make no mistake. God will have the last word concerning what is right and wrong.

In the meantime, we can join the Roman church that Paul blesses with words of grace. It's more than just a greeting or a hope for the people of God, but in fact, a prayer. God's grace is a wonderful gift that provides what we need for as long as we are in the world. As the old song says, it is not only amazing, but it is bountiful and liberally given from the Father to all who put their trust in Him. Paul knew that anyone who follows Jesus will need an ample supply of grace in order to stand firm for Him. We will never be in short supply though, for Jesus never runs out of it. His grace is sufficient.

DAY 318

Romans 16:21 *Timothy, my fellow worker, sends his greetings to you, as do Lucius, Jason and Sosipater, my relatives.*

It is at this point in Paul's letter to the Romans that he began to close out his message to the church, and he does so by acknowledging the team that worked with him. It's always nice and always proper to give credit where credit is due, for none of us can do the work of building Christ's church alone.

We recognize Timothy as Paul's young protégé in the faith. One of my early professors used to say that every Paul needs a Timothy, and every Timothy needs a Paul. Certainly, there is wisdom in training others to take our place as we work ourselves out of a job for the Kingdom of God. That's the way the church advances through the generations.

The others who are mentioned are not as familiar to us. Some think that Lucius could actually be Luke, the writer of the book of Acts, as well as the Gospel account known by his name. This is speculation, but certainly a possibility since Luke is recorded as traveling with Paul. There is also a Lucius of Cyrene listed in Acts 13:1, who was a teacher in Antioch, but we have no record of him traveling with Paul. In Acts 17:6–9, Jason is mentioned in connection with Paul, but again, we just don't know for sure if they are one and the same. In Acts 20:4, there is a man name Sopater, son of Pyrrhus from Berea, who was with Paul on his third missionary journey. This could possibly be the same man.

Though their identities are somewhat lost to history, these men had the privilege of working alongside one of the greatest laborers for Christ the world has ever known. Whether they were actual relatives or part of the Jewish family, or brothers in Christ, Paul considers them family. They were invaluable to Paul's work and the mission of reaching a pagan world for Jesus.

These men provide a good lesson for us. We may not be the headliner of any team, but if we can work alongside, or behind the scenes to support those God chooses to lead His work, then that is an honored position indeed. Not everyone can be chief, but every chief needs a tribe of people to lead if anything is going to get done. If that's you, then thank God for the privilege.

DAY 319

Romans 16:22 *I, Tertius, who wrote down
this letter, greet you in the Lord.*

We actually know very little about Tertius. Church tradition and this text has him listed as the scribe, who served as Paul's penman for this letter, and the Eastern Orthodox Church venerated him as one of the seventy disciples that Jesus sent out, as recorded in the Gospel of Luke 10:1–24. Some say that Tertius was another name for Silas, who was Paul's traveling partner after the split between Paul and Barnabas. Again, we don't know for sure because time has a way of erasing many details of history.

Still, it's another example of how the team Paul put together provided what not only served the purpose of his day but delivered to us this important book that has served billions of people down through time.

I like to reflect on how important it was for Tertius to write this down, and how important it is for us to record as written material what God is doing in our day as well. Though writing in cursive seems to be going the way of the dodo bird, at least we can with our computers and word processors, keep the written language of God's great deeds, alive and available for future generations to read.

I started writing a daily journal when I was in my first day of my first pastorate. I wish I had started sooner. I began using notebooks, then went eventually to a computer with records on the big floppy disks, then compact discs, and finally on thumb drives and SanDisks. Eventually, I would like to print them all out and put them into a book form that could be read when I am gone from this world. If that never happens then I will just leave my digital records for family to read if they wish.

Though it's not likely that any of us will ever write something with the impact of Romans, I do believe it is important for us to keep the continuing record of God's daily workings in our lives. We may not see them as important initially, but years later God can receive glory as we and others redeem the time through hindsight.

Tertius may never be a household name, but his signature on this very important book will outlive us all. Only God knows what kind of an impact something we write may have. Truly, only God knows.

DAY 320

Romans 16:23 *Gaius, whose hospitality I and the whole church here enjoy, sends you his greetings. Erastus, who is the city's director of public works, and our brother Quartus send you their greetings.*

Everyone loves Gaius—or someone like him, for he apparently knew how to make people feel at ease and provided hospitality to those who were around him. Paul certainly felt that way. There is a Gaius that Paul baptized in Corinth in I Corinthians 1:14, so it is possible that this is the same guy.

Erastus is thought to have been the treasurer of the city of Corinth. He is another example of how Paul reached the high and mighty, as well as the lowest of the low in slavery with the words of the gospel.

Quartus is venerated in the Coptic Orthodox Church. According to church tradition, he was born in the city of Athens and was a wealthy and noble man. He is said to have preached the gospel in many countries.

This trio of Greek men were traveling companions of Paul and co-laborers with him in his mission for Jesus. No doubt they prove a great comfort to their leader, who probably depended on them not only for moral support, but possibly in physical and financial ways too.

Christian leaders always need helpers. There is no way that the work of the Kingdom of God can be accomplished with only those up front doing all the work. It is imperative that laborers come alongside of church leaders to lend their skills and spiritual gifts to the task at hand. Without such companionship in the mission there would not only be a loss for labor, but also for fellowship and morale boosting, which helps the work to succeed.

I will always be grateful to the many, many people who have labored at my side in the work of ministry in the various congregations I have served. There are so many talents that I don't have, but those have so often been the ones that were supplied by my brothers and sisters in the faith. I have especially been blessed by other men who have shouldered the load with me and made my journey so much more enjoyable and profitable.

If we all do what we can with what we have where we are, we will do great things for God, for His blessings will follow our efforts. No task is too small or too large if it is assigned to us by Jesus.

DAY 321

Romans 16:24 *May the grace of our Lord Jesus Christ be with all of you, Amen.*

If you are trying to find this verse in your copy of the New International Version of the Bible, you are going to be disappointed. Though it looks strange, the reading jumps from verse twenty-three right to verse twenty-five, and it almost goes without noticing. The reason for this is because in the oldest manuscript copies that we have of this chapter, this verse is missing. It was added to some translations sometime in the fourth or fifth centuries.

This is merely a technical matter though because basically the same words are used in the closing to chapter fifteen, and is also used by Paul in II Thessalonians 3:16 and 3:18. It certainly is in keeping with Paul's writing and the focus that he had for all the churches. It's a matter for textual critics, but really doesn't have much of an impact on the apostle's overall message.

What does matter, however, is the thought that is being expressed. Regardless of where it is found in the Bible, the blessing of grace is always appropriate. It's a hope that the love of God will be poured out on the readers, and also an acknowledgement that Jesus Christ truly is Lord, and that His presence is continually among us.

I don't believe it's reading too much into this verse to say that Paul wished the best for the Romans, and the best he could think of was the presence of Jesus abiding with them in love. I could see myself praying that prayer for all of God's creation.

Formal greetings in letters today don't often include a religious flavor, but then this is no ordinary letter, nor ordinary book. This is God's book, and the fact that it remains after nearly two thousand years, and the fact that it has changed the lives of billions of people on this planet, puts it in a category all its own. God, working through the Spirit of His Son, lives among us, and we are so blessed that He does.

I hope that today you will give thanks for such a gift. It's not just good to remember at Christmas time that *Immanuel*, God with us, is a powerful truth. It is the message of our connection with the Divine that is good all year long. Wherever we are in our journey, grace is a wonderful gift.

DAY 322

Romans 16:25 *Now to him who is able to establish you by my gospel and the proclamation of Jesus Christ, according to the revelation of the mystery hidden for ages past, but now revealed and made known through the prophetic writings by the command of the eternal God, so that all nations might believe and obey him—to the only wise God be glory forever through Jesus Christ! Amen.*

This is the last verse of Paul's wonderful letter, but it is so packed with good things for us focus upon that it's going to take a few days to work through it.

This benediction opens with a wonderful thought: God is able to establish you. The word simply means to put something into place and help it to thrive there. That's what Paul says God is doing in the lives of true believers. He not only is our constant companion through the Spirit of Jesus Christ, but He is also the one who helps us put down our spiritual roots so that we won't be deceived or distracted by powers and people that would be stumbling blocks to us.

I believe it is the desire of every pastor that their flock would be strong enough in their faith and in their relationship with Jesus Christ, that they could stand firm, even if left alone, in the way of the cross. Though no one else go with them, they will follow Jesus. That's what matters most in life.

People who are like this are considered the pillars of the church community. They are the ones who teach the scriptures, love their neighbors, attend to the needs of the sick and aged, feed the hungry, cloth the naked, serve on the boards and committees, minister through music and technology, lift others in prayer, and represent Christ through their mouths and actions. They are the established ones. They are the ones who are building the Kingdom of God one person at a time.

Oh, how the church needs such established people! How it needs also to remember that it is Jesus alone who is able to make us established. Because of the Father's love, the sacrifice of Christ, and the continual nudging and checking of the Holy Spirit, we are able to make progress and go deeper in the things that matter. God is at work in us just as He was in the people of Rome in Paul's time. Let us pray that He will raise up a new generation of people who also will be established in Him.

DAY 323

Romans 16:25 *Now to him who is able to establish you by my gospel and the proclamation of Jesus Christ, according to the revelation of the mystery hidden for ages past, but now revealed and made known through the prophetic writings by the command of the eternal God, so that all nations might believe and obey him—to the only wise God be glory forever through Jesus Christ! Amen.*

Throughout this book, Paul has been presenting what he considers to be the true Gospel of Jesus Christ. He can refer to it as "my gospel," not because it belongs exclusively to him, but because it has become so much a part of his life that his mission for Jesus and his own existence have become continually intertwined. His life's being and purpose was wrapped up in the person and message of Jesus. What a wonderful way to live!

I wonder sometimes about how far we have come in our understanding of God's message for mankind from the days of the apostle. We have had twenty centuries to pour over his work and examine his claims about Jesus. The church that Jesus died to establish has gone from great lows to great heights in acceptance and scrutiny, and it has been responsible for some of the greatest blessings the world has ever known, as well as some of the most terrible tragedies. The gospel has truly had an impact on our planet.

Paul's gospel, the message of Jesus, has not changed, however. He shared what he experienced in the Lord throughout the middle part of the first century, but the remarkable thing about his life's labor is not only found in the message he proclaimed, but the way he went about it. Jesus and he had become one. They were so close that nothing else mattered in his life except that God would be glorified in the person of Jesus, through the power of the Holy Spirit. The mission Paul fulfilled was not just a part of his life; it was his life. It's hard to even imagine being able to separate Paul from the message he proclaimed. Preaching, teaching, traveling, and writing for Jesus were not just a part of his life, those things were his life.

How about us today? Can we say with Paul, "To live is Christ and to die is gain" (Philippians 1:22)? Are we committed to taking the gospel to the world in order to help establish the Kingdom of God? Our work is ever before us, and we must never back down on our commitment to it.

DAY 324

This part of the verse is especially important for all who are considered preachers of the Word of God. When Paul speaks of the proclamation of Jesus Christ, it is in reference to the fact that it is the tool God uses to establish His saints in the faith.

Those who would be preachers of the Gospel carry a tremendous responsibility upon their shoulders. They handle the precious words of life that can be used to transform or condemn individuals, and the masses of people who inhabit our planet. There is no other means to life everlasting except through the way of Jesus, so it behooves every preacher to always carry the words of life with fear and trembling.

Some people consider preaching just making a speech. By appearance the two may look a lot alike, but they are so different. Anyone who has the ability to speak can make a speech, but only those who are anointed by the Father can preach Jesus Christ as the Redeemer, Sanctifier, and hope of the world. It is the message that transforms people, but proclamation is the method God has chosen for human delivery of that message.

It seems like in every generation there are those who write obituaries for the case of preaching in the church. Some have tried different ways to reach different people—and though we should not discount anything God may choose to use—it has been through the ministry of preaching that generations have been saved. I don't believe it is going anywhere soon.

When we proclaim Jesus, we proclaim Him as Lord and coming King. We proclaim Him as the person with whom anyone can have a relationship and one that will never change in His love for us and His devotion to our needs. That Jesus saves, is the miracle of the ages, the blessing for all mankind, and the only hope of the world. No wonder it establishes the church and brings into focus the coming Kingdom of God.

DAY 325

These are interesting words, "the mystery hidden for ages past." A mystery requires something unseen or unknown that needs to be investigated, and in this case especially, the mystery unraveled shows that there has been a plan in place for a long, long time.

There are so many people in our world who are cynical fatalists, and they just believe that things happen because they happen, because the nefarious idea of fate will determine the outcome of all existence. Nothing could be farther from the truth, however. We serve a God who has had a plan for our world before He ever created it, and He has been actively involved in its day-to-day operations ever since. He is not a deistic being that pulled the universe together and then went off to see how it will all end up, for just as He planned the beginning, He also knows of its ending, and how everything will turn out along the way.

I don't believe in predestination to the point where God is the master puppeteer, and we have no choice but to do as He dictates along our life's journey. I don't believe the Bible teaches that, for we are given responsibilities upon which to function and a free will to do or not do as we decide. But even though God doesn't control our choices, He does know how things are going to turn out. Like all of creation, we have a specific beginning, and we have a definite end. Along the way, Immanuel, "God with us," guides us if we will allow Him to do so.

What happens in the meantime is the mystery being fulfilled in our lives. Just as the mystery of the revelation of the Gospel of Jesus Christ took time to unfold so that all could understand, our lives are similar. Abraham couldn't see how God's plan would work out to bring about salvation for the world, but the plan was there nonetheless, and we have life as a result. We too can't always understand the mystery, but God does and that's what matters.

DAY 326

Romans 16:25 *Now to him who is able to establish you by my gospel and the proclamation of Jesus Christ, according to the revelation of the mystery hidden for ages past, but now revealed and made known through the prophetic writings by the command of the eternal God, so that all nations might believe and obey him—to the only wise God be glory forever through Jesus Christ! Amen.*

I love the line from Amos 7:14 where he says, "I was neither a prophet nor a prophet's son…" When Amaziah the king of Israel told him to go back to Judah to do his preaching, that was his response. He didn't consider himself a professional prophet, but a shepherd and a fruit gardener, but God used him as a prophet, nonetheless.

We are blessed to have the record of the prophets. The major prophets usually are considered to be Isaiah, Jeremiah, Ezekiel, and Daniel, with the minor prophets of Hosea, Joel, Amos, Obadiah, Jonah, Micah, Nahum, Habakkuk, Zephaniah, Haggai, Zechariah, and Malachi comprising the rest of the Old Testament record. The major prophets are considered major because of the size of their books. The minor prophets are considered minor because their books are shorter. They are not classified by their importance or validity, but merely because of the number of words in each.

In this verse the Apostle Paul reminds his readers that the mystery of God's plan for mankind's salvation was laid out through the writings of the prophets so that they could bear record of God's plan to all people everywhere. The work God did through the sacrifice of His Son is not a secret, but one that was foretold centuries before it happened, and confirmed by the actual events. It proves that the message concerning Jesus is not a last-ditch effort by God to deal with mankind's rebellion, but something that He has had planned from the beginning.

It's also important to note that the prophets wrote "by the command of the eternal God…" The men who were called to write, were commissioned, and inspired by God to do the job He chose for them, and we are the beneficiaries of their labors.

How much the Father loves His creation, to go to such lengths to redeem it! May we always be grateful to the King who cares so much about us.

DAY 327

> **Romans 16:25** *Now to him who is able to establish you by my gospel and the proclamation of Jesus Christ, according to the revelation of the mystery hidden for ages past, but now revealed and made known through the prophetic writings by the command of the eternal God, so that all nations might believe and obey him—to the only wise God be glory forever through Jesus Christ! Amen.*

There are so many questions that surround the subject of God. They range from "Who is God?" to "Where is God?" to "Is there a God?" to "Where did God come from?" These and many like them are often too big for our finite minds, so sometimes we just have to say, "I don't know."

The fact that we don't know everything about God doesn't mean that we don't know anything about God though. By faith in Him and trust in His Word, all kinds of information is available. Hebrews 11:6 says, "And without faith it is impossible to please God, because anyone who comes to him must believe that he exists and that he rewards those who earnestly seek him." Just by believing in Him and seeking after Him, we find that He opens doors for our faith to increase and our knowledge about Him to grow.

All of this is possible because the eternal God wants to establish a relationship with His creation. As He walked with Adam in the cool of the day in the Garden of Eden, He longs to walk with us and provide us with a connection to eternity. Though the way may sometimes be difficult and our faith-walk a little cloudy because of life's circumstances, He is always there for us as we reach out to Him. Again, the writer to the Hebrews provides us with beneficial instructions, "Therefore, strengthen your feeble arms and weak knees. 'Make level paths for your feet,' so that the lame may not be disabled, but rather healed." As we make the effort to connect with the eternal God, we find that He is readily accessible.

Thankfully, God gave us guidance through His written Word when He commanded the prophets to put down the words of life for us to read. What once was a total mystery has now been made clearer by prophetic inspiration and instruction. The way of Jesus, though once misunderstood, has now been opened to us by divine revelation. We will never deserve all that God shows to us, but may we always be thankful for His unrivaled grace.

DAY 328

Romans 16:25 *Now to him who is able to establish you by my gospel and the proclamation of Jesus Christ, according to the revelation of the mystery hidden for ages past, but now revealed and made known through the prophetic writings by the command of the eternal God, so that all nations might believe and obey him—to the only wise God be glory forever through Jesus Christ! Amen.*

Is it possible that all nations could ever believe and obey God, live in harmony, and exist in peace? Paul certainly thought so, and John the Revelator felt the same way. In Revelation 21:24–26 we see a picture of what will eventually happen when heaven and earth become one. "The nations will walk by its light, and the kings of the earth will bring their splendor into it. On no day will its gates ever be shut, for there will be no night there. The glory and honor of the nations will be brought into it."

This is a picture of what it will be like when the Lord Almighty and the Lamb reign victorious and become the light of the New Jerusalem for eternity. It may seem impossible now, but as sure as the Bible is true, it will come to pass.

How then, will all "the nations believe and obey him?" To understand the process, we have to go back to Matthew 16:18–19, where Jesus was addressing Simon Peter and sharing His plan with the disciples. He said, "And I tell you that you are Peter, and on this rock I will build my church, and the gates of Hades will not overcome it. I give you the keys of the kingdom of heaven; whatever you bind on earth will be bound in heaven, and whatever you loose on earth will be loosed in heaven."

The process is a slow one, much like the parable of the yeast where Jesus taught that the Kingdom would be mixed in gradually and change the essence of the bread (Matthew 13:33). We present the way of salvation through Christ to one person at a time, and as they believe the Kingdom grows, and the will of God becomes more on earth as it is in heaven.

Oh, how we long for the day to come when "the nations will believe and obey him." We may or may not see it in this generation, but that day will come and then all the effort, all the waiting, and all the trials of life will be worth it. Someday all nations will bow at the feet of Jesus, amen.

DAY 329

We come now to the end of this verse and the end of this book. It is appropriate for Paul to end this letter the way that he does, and appropriate that we should echo his sentiments, "to the only wise God be glory forever through Jesus Christ." The faithfulness of the Lord cannot be over emphasized, for He has made possible the words from a quill and homemade ink to pass down through the centuries to encourage billions of Christians and provide hope and direction for those who are enquiring about the way of holiness.

We are way behind in our praise for our God! The way of the cross was such a tremendous burden for Jesus to bear on our behalf, but what a wonderful anointing of grace on mankind was made possible because of it. The foolishness of God (if there could be such a thing) truly is wiser than the greatest wisdom of man and we owe Him everything we have and everything we are.

Paul surely had no idea that his words would go so far. He, and his small band of fellow travelers and co-workers envisioned only mailing to a distance church in a bustling city, where hopefully it would be received with affirmation. But God took some things so small, like pen, ink, and parchment to make His way and His will known to the masses.

We are so blessed today to have these words from the apostle, and we are so blessed that they were inspired by the Holy Spirit of God. If we can take anything away from this particular verse it is that we need to be glorifying the Lord continually all the days of our lives. Giving God glory comes through our words, our actions, and our attitudes. It affects those around us, those who will hear about us, and also our own attitude. People of praise need to make their voices heard and we know that our Lord will hear and be pleased. Let's continue to lift up the name of Jesus for as long as we can!

Printed in the United States
by Baker & Taylor Publisher Services